THE HISTORY OF
THE ROYAL SUSSEX REGIMENT
DURING THE SECOND WORLD WAR

Compiled by Colonel Roderick Arnold
Late The Royal Sussex Regiment

The Royal Sussex Regimental Association Trust
Registered as a charity

The Naval & Military Press Ltd

Published by

The Naval & Military Press Ltd
Unit 5 Riverside, Brambleside
Bellbrook Industrial Estate
Uckfield, East Sussex
TN22 1QQ England

Tel: +44 (0)1825 749494

www.naval-military-press.com
www.nmarchive.com

Preface and Acknowledgements

The Royal Sussex Regiment was extremely fortunate when G. D. Martineau wrote its Regimental History in 1952. However, it has been felt for some time that, through no fault of his own, his development of the Regiment's historical record of the Second World War, particularly the detailed general and personal accounts of the numerous and exacting campaigns, was somewhat sketchy. It was therefore decided in 2011, that the historical record should be reviewed with a view to providing a more comprehensive account.

When he wrote the history, Martineau was unable to gain access to much of the detailed campaign material as the War Office, at the time had yet to release such documents as the War diaries of the 1st 2nd, 4th, 5th (Cinque Ports), 6th, 7th and 9th Battalions of the Regiment, nor those of each of the superior Headquarters of the respective seven Battalions. In addition, a number of individuals would later release their own personal accounts, which gave a more intimate appraisal of the actions and tribulations that occurred during the various campaigns. These later accounts range from individual jottings, through lengthy and detailed notes, to published books of varying style and content.

Having had access to these later documents, it has now been possible to update the Regiment's History of the Second World War, and the results are contained in this book. Notwithstanding this, The Martineau edition has been used as a base document for the updated history, with the later material being interwoven or used to amend, develop and expand the original account. The list of the Regiment's War Diaries that are lodged in the National Archives and which have been drawn upon are shown at Annex A. The principle books and documents, which have been consulted during the conduct of this review, are shown below, while other papers and documents are referred to in the footnotes of the History itself.

> *A History of The Royal Sussex Regiment.* G. D. Martineau, Moore & Tillyer Ltd, Chichester, 1953.
> *Cinque Ports Battalion.* Colonel E.A.C. Fazan, RHQ The Royal Sussex Regiment, 1971.
> Eritrea 1941. Arthur J. Baker, Faber, 1966.
> *The Desert and the Jungle.* Lieutenant-General Sir Geoffrey Evans KBE CB DSO, William Kimber, London, 1959.
> *The Shiny Ninth.* Murray Gillings, The Pinwe Club, 1986.
> *Not Forgetting the 9th.* The War Diary of Sgt. Cyril Grimes 1944-1945. Edited by Sylvia Fox, TimeBox Press, Poole, Dorset, 2013.
> *Green Shadows and Jungle Rain.* David Cash, 2003. Private account of the wartime service of Major J.M. Cash MC of the 9th Battalion The Royal Sussex Regiment.
> *Myitkyina to Mandalay- A Diary of the North Burma Campaign, 1944-45.* A record of A Company 9th Battalion The Royal Sussex Regiment. Captain Ian McArthur and Lieutenant Murray Gillings. Edited by the Company Commander, Major John Dickson MC.
> *The Royal Sussex Regiment Military Honours & Awards 1921-1966.* Richard Buckman, J&KH Publishing, Hailsham, 2004.
> *Age Shall not weary Them.* Major Roy Rees, Menin House, Eastbourne, 2011.
> *Fourth Indian Division.* Lieut-Colonel G.R. Stevens OBE, Naval & Military Press, Uckfield, Sussex.
> *The Battle of Cassino.* Notes made by Brigadier J.B.A. Glennie CBE DSO, RHQ The Royal Sussex Regiment.
> *Notes on Eritrea, Italy (Post-Cassino) and Greece.* Lieut-Colonel G.A. Phelps, RHQ The Royal Sussex Regiment.

Personal Memoirs Relating to Italy, Greece and Austria-1943 to 1945. Colonel J. Buckeridge.
Greece 1944-1945. Major J.D. Freer-Smith MBE, RHQ The Royal Sussex Regiment, 1987.
Greece-Austria 1944-45. Major H.G. Castle, RHQ The Royal Sussex Regiment.

All these accounts have been drawn upon and many aspects have been incorporated into the review, including some maps and diagrams, where appropriate. We are extremely grateful to have been given access to these books and papers, and for allowing the inclusion of the texts, maps and photographs in this updated history of the Regiment.

We owe a special debt of gratitude to Mr Alan Readman BA, the County Archivist of the West Sussex County Records Office at Chichester. For 34 years he devotedly ensured that every scrap of the Regimental records – documents, photographs, audio visual material, books and publications – had been catalogued, stored and made easily available for retrieval and research.. We have drawn fully on this knowledge and his efforts in the compilation of this history.

Contents

The Way to Dunkirk	1
Concept of War in France and the Low Countries	7
France and Belgium 1940	10
The 2nd Battalion in France and Belgium 1940	12
The 4th and 5th Battalions in France and Belgium 1940	21
The 6th and 7th Battalions in France 1940	33
Gallantry Awards for France and Belgium 1940	40
The Reformation of the 133rd (Royal Sussex) Brigade	43
Situation in North Africa from 1939 to 1941	44
The 1st Battalion in Egypt	44
Entry of Italy into the War	45
Preparation for Desert Warfare	46
Operations in Eritrea	49
Gallantry Awards for Eritrea 1941	57
The Western Desert in 1941	59
Battle of Omar Nuovo	63
Pursuit to Benghazi	69
Gallantry Awards for North Africa in 1941	71
Situation in North Africa in early-1942	73
Gallantry Awards for North Africa in early-1942	77
The Turn of the Tide in the Western Desert	79
Battle of Alam el Halfa	80
Battle of El Alamein	85
Gallantry Awards for North Africa in 1942	99
The Aftermath of El Alamein	100
The Beginning of the End in North Africa in late-1942	102
Advance to the Mareth Line	103
Operations in Tunisia	107
Gallantry Awards for North Africa in 1943	111
Persia and Iraq	112
The Italian Epic	115
The German Lines of Defence	115
The 4th Indian Division moves to the Italian Front	118
Battle of Cassino	121
The Advance through Italy - the Lower Adriatic Phase	142
The Advance through Italy - the Central Region Phase	146
The Advance through Italy – the Gothic Line Phase	148
Gallantry Awards for Italy in 1944	158
A Grecian Odyssey	160
Situation in Greece in 1944	160
Operations in Greece	161
Farewell to the 4th Indian Division	169
The Far East	171
The 9th Battalion is reformed	171
Conversion and Re-conversion	173
General Situation in Burma	175
Battle of Arakan	177
Northern Combat Area Command	181
Battles of Hill 60 and Thaikwagon	183

Battle of Pinwe	188
Battle of Shweli River	196
The Road to Mandalay	199
Gallantry Awards for Burma in 1944-45	204
North – Western Europe	206
General Service	206
Airborne Contingent	207
Higher Command	211
Concluding Stages of the Second World War	213
1st Battalion	213
2nd Battalion	214
4th/5th (Cinque Ports) Battalion	214
9th Battalion	215
Remembrance	219
Annex A – National Archives-Battalion War Diaries	220
Annex B – A German Perspective	221

List of Maps

France 1940

The German Advance out of the Ardennes in May 1940	8
The Allied Advance to the River Dyle in May 1940	9
Move forward to Vichte by 133rd (Royal Sussex Brigade	10
2nd Battalion's Initial Deployment in Anseghem Area	12
2nd Battalion's Withdrawal Rote to Bailleul	14
2nd Battalion's Deployment in Strazeele Area	15
British Expeditionary Force's Withdrawal to the Coast	17
4th Battalion's Initial Deployment in Anseghem Area	22
Deployment of 133rd (Royal Sussex) Brigade in Anseghem Area	23
4th Battalion's Withdrawal Route to Fletre	25
General Situation Around Caestre on 27/28 May 1940	26
5th Battalion's Withdrawal Route to the Strazeele Area	29
5th Battalion's Deployment in the Caestre and Rouge Croix Area	30
Jaws Tighten Around Regiment's Withdrawal route to Bray Dunes	31
German Advance to the Sea	35

Operations in Eritrea

The North West Africa Operational Areas	49
Area of Operations in the Sudan and Eritrea	50
The 'North Force' Advance Route	53
The Attack on Massawa	56

North Africa

The Sidi Barrani Operational Area in September 1940	46
Area of Operations in the Western Desert in 1941	60
Operation CRUSADER in November 1941	62
The Attack on the Omars – 22nd November 1941	64
The Pursuit to Benghazi	70
Escape Route from Benghazi in January 1942	74
Battle of Alam el Halfa	82
Battle of El Alamein	86
133rd (Royal Sussex) Brigade Attack on 27/28th October 1942	88
133rd (Royal Sussex) Brigade Final Attack	92
Operation TORCH – Task Force Landing Sites	102
4th Division Operations in Tunisia in 1943	104
Battle of Wadi Akarit	105
Closing Phase of the Tunisian Campaign	108

Persia and Iraq

Area of Persia and Iraq Command	113

The Italian Epic

The Main German Defence Lines in Italy	115

The Depth of the German 'Winter Line' Defences	116
Opening Moves Against the Winter-Gustav Line	116
Canadian and New Zealand Advance to Ortona and Orsogna	117
The Cassino Skyline	120
German Domination of Cassino Area	121
Main Features in the Cassino Area	125
D Company Raid on Le Piane	143
The Gothic Line Defences in Northern Italy	145
The Attack on San Maria di Tiberina	147
1st Royal Sussex Moves Round to Urbino	148
The Advance Through the Gothic Line	149
The Advance Beyond Urbino	151
The Attack on Pian di Castello and Cemetery Ridge	153
Final Operations in Italy	156

Greece 1944

Main Areas of Operations in Greece	161

The Far East

The Battle of Arakan	177
Burma Campaign Area	182
Battle of Thaikwagon	186
Pinwe – Action at Stourbridge Chaung	189
Pinwe – Withdrawal into the Battalion Box	190
Pinwe - Action at Bridge Chaung	193
The Battle at Shweli River	197
The Malay Peninsular	217

List of Photographs and Illustrations

Axis Prisoners taken at Omar Nuovo	68
German Prisoners Captured at El Alamein	96
General Von Arnim	109
General Von Arnim's Staff Car	110
The Battered Point 593 from Snakes Head Ridge	124
Sangars on Snakes Head Ridge	126
German Spandau Team in Action at Cassino	129
Stretcher Bearers Passing RAP at Cassino	135
The Meeting Point of the Jeep Track and the Mule Track	136
Advancing up the Mule Track at Cassino	137
Moving up through the Gothic Line	150
Attacking through the Gothic Line	151
The Attack on the 'Sausage' at Arakan	179
Bren Gun Team in Burma	191
Japanese Surrender in Malaya in 1945	218
Feldwebel Wilhelm Weier on Point 593 at Cassino	222

About the author:
The late Colonel Rod Arnold was a man who displayed a natural charm that made him a sought after companion in any company. A twinkle in the eye, an easy smile and a ready chuckle were recognised trademarks of his personality, but despite his bonhomie, he was a very private man who cherished his family life.

Born during the war at the end of 1941, Rod was brought up by his Great Aunt and Uncle, his father having been killed in action whilst flying with the RAF. Having always known that he wanted to be a soldier, he joined the family Regiment, The Royal Scots Greys as a potential officer straight after completing his education. After a quiet word from his CO, that his lack of educational provenance was unlikely to support a full career, Rod abruptly withdrew to try life in London. However he still hankered after a military life and after a Mons OCS commissioning course joined the 4th Battalion, The Queens Royal Surrey Regiment, an 'Ever Ready' TA unit in Kingston.

In 1965 Rod along with 122 other 'Ever Readies' from across the Home County Brigade, volunteered to stiffen 1 Royal Sussex who had been posted for an emergency tour of Aden. He did so well that the CO encouraged him to transfer from a TA to a Regular commission, which he did, with his commission being confirmed a year later in Lemgo in BAOR into the now amalgamated 3 Queen's.

Rod disproved his former RSG CO by attending staff college in 1973 and being selected as an instructor on the Junior Division of the Staff college in Warminster. On returning to the Battalion, Rod took B Company on tours of Belize, N.Ireland and on Green Goddesses during the fireman's strike. Life changed for him early in 1978 when he met Ruth and they were married a year later living in London whilst Rod was working in MOD.

Postings and promotion followed with tours as CO of 5 UDR and following the birth of their daughter Victoria and a further posting to MOD as GSO1 (Simulation) in Whitehall for a further five years and promotion to Colonel.

Leaving the Army in 1996 he took employment firstly with the Rail Regulator and then OFCOM, and for 9 months he became a NATO observer in Kosovo, before taking full retirement in 2006.

In 2009, he was invited to take over from Hugh Wyatt as President of The Royal Sussex Regimental Association. No one doubted his credentials; he was undoubtedly a Royal Sussex man through and through. He became a regimental historian of the highest order and his records of the Regiment, particularly during WW1 are peerless. Working tirelessly and enthusiastically in the Association's Cause, he promoted its interests around the County, supporting the branches and ensuring that the heritage of the Regiment remained intact.

Ultimately for 40 years he was a loving husband and proud father, sharing with Ruth the many joys and challenges of life, enlivened by his adored daughter Victoria.

THE HISTORY OF THE ROYAL SUSSEX REGIMENT DURING THE SECOND WORLD WAR

THE WAY TO DUNKIRK

Introduction

In the most authoritative memoirs written on the subject, Winston Churchill refers to the Second World War as "the unnecessary war". How far this description applies more to that conflict than to any other war provoked by a conspiracy to enslave free peoples may be judged from his volume entitled *The Gathering Storm,* which gives us a wide survey of the world situation. It is perhaps almost too wide to examine in these pages, and a professional soldier's impressions of events in Europe, immediately before and after the outbreak of the war, will serve our purpose more briefly. These may be found in *Operation Victory*[1], written by Major General Sir Francis de Guingand, who served as General Montgomery's Chief of Staff from North Africa to the Rhine.

De Guingand is really setting out to give his account of campaigns in the Middle East from 1941 to 1943, and these shall be referred to again, but he also provides a summary of the position and outlook in Britain, France and Germany during those critical days, which deserves the attention of a military student. As Brigade Major to the Commandant of the Small Arms Schools, he decided in 1937 to visit both France and Germany, with the object of gauging the strength of potential ally and enemy respectively. This he did out of his own pocket, since the War Office declined to finance such a project.

In France, at the Small Arms School at Mourmelon and elsewhere, he was received with kindness, frankness and consideration.

Everywhere, however, he found things being done on the cheap, with improvisation resorted to for lack of funds and equipment. He was taken to the devastated areas of the previous war, where guides emphasised constantly that the next conflict must not take place on French soil. France, he gathered, had a long way to go before she could be said to possess a really modern army, and there was an obvious lack of resolute spirit to combat an invader.

He then visited the German Infantry School at Dobrietz.

The experience was like that of entering a different world; it was not only more efficient, it was extremely vigilant; even the documents in his Berlin hotel room were examined by agents during his absence.

---

[1] *Operation Victory*, Francis de Guingand, Hodder & Stoughton, London, 1947.

The smartness and discipline of the German Army were balanced by an excellent relationship between officers and men. There was no sign of financial restriction, everything was being done on a lavish scale, and small-arms weapons and training methods were well in advance of the British. They had learnt much from the Spanish Civil War, particularly in the matter of the threat from low-flying aircraft, and were taking steps to deal with it.

At the same time, British guests were cordially received, speeches referred to the days when Britain and Prussia were allies, the enmity of 1914-1918 was described as foolishness, and France was frequently disparaged. The Hitler delirium was approaching its height, marching songs and the tramp of feet were heard everywhere, and the warning could have hardly been sounded more clearly.

De Guingand's next revealing experience was as Military Assistant to the Secretary of State for War in June 1939. In that capacity, he developed a considerable admiration for the much-maligned and ridiculed Leslie Hore-Belisha, who, in his opinion, showed considerable drive. In particular, he strove to popularise the Army, at whose expense the Royal Navy and the Royal Air Force had been gaining in their appeal to the public.

In 1939, more than a hundred members of Parliament voted against conscription, even after Hitler had already marched into Austria in April that year. Hore-Belisha had to go as far as threatening the Prime Minister, Neville Chamberlain, with his resignation if he would not agree to the Bill going before the House. Thus it was not until the middle of July that the first batch of Militiamen were being trained, so that six weeks later, the vast organisation had to yield place to mobilisation plans. Yet this transition worked with remarkable smoothness. None of these considerations saved Hore-Belisha from being blamed both for the delay in getting the Army into the field and for his decision to double the Territorial Army in 1939.

Though this decision might be considered unsatisfactory in that it denuded existing Regular and Territorial units of trained officers and men, and in some cases weapons, to strengthen the new, inexperienced, and untrained units, de Guingand considers that the following factors were in favour of the scheme: politically, at that time, it was a necessary step towards conscription; it meant financial approval for the extra money required for such needs as additional barracks and ranges; it gave the necessary authority for ordering weapons and equipment for the new units; and, as the readiness of units for war depended on weapons and war materiel, the plan interfered less with the production of trained formations than has generally been made out.

Meanwhile, on the Continent, an Anglo-French Mission was courting Russia. Molotov had wished for support in entering neighbouring states, particularly Poland, against what was termed 'indirect aggression', to which Britain could hardly agree at that stage. By the time military conversations had started,

Russian demands were increasing and, while matters were still in dispute, the German-Soviet Pact became known.

Two factors, in de Guingand's opinion, led to this decisive action on the part of Russia, which gave Germany a free hand to launch the Second World War. One was that Britain was unwilling to sign away another country's independence (although it has been argued that this was what Britain did to Czecho-Slovakia); the other was that Russia had gained little encouragement from information received regarding the support which could be expected from France and Britain in the West.

It is against this background, and against this conflict of ideas, that we have to see the British Army striving to make up for lost time in preparation for war. It is important to realise what a start the enemy were given, and under what handicaps the Regiment laboured, in common with others, for long after the struggle had been joined.

When the Germans began their attack on Poland, it seemed almost as though the pattern of the Great War might be repeated; the 1st Battalion was again overseas, this time at Moascar on the Suez Canal, and the 2nd Battalion was at home, stationed at Belfast. Though large Italian forces were available for action if Italy became involved, Mussolini was waiting to see how the situation developed before committing himself; and so the 2nd Battalion would be called upon, no doubt, to hold the road to Sussex, together with the expanding Territorial Battalions and any others that might be raised for the renewed conflict.

The Cinque Ports Gazette pictures for us the activity, which followed the expansion of the Territorial Army:

> *"Since then, a new army has been formed; new weapons, new tactics, new organisations. It is all very difficult but rather exciting, and we are rapidly getting used to all the changes – even to seeing the Battalion on parade in long trousers."*

Elsewhere we read *"individual officers have probably done more TA work than they ever dreamed was possible in times of alleged peace."* This expansion meant that the 4th and 5th Battalions had to recruit to twice their war strength and 'threw off' the 6th and 7th Battalions respectively. All these four battalions mobilised on 1st September 1939; the 4th at Horsham, the 5th at Hastings, the 6th at Worthing, and the 7th at Brighton. 'Vulnerable Points' had to be guarded by the 4th and 5th, both of which possessed weapons and transport, whereas their 'duplicates', the 6th and 7th, being less fortunately equipped, concentrated on recruiting and training, until they were in a position to take over guard-duties in turn.² 'Vulnerable Points' included such establishments as internment camps, around which the barbed wire had to be erected, as well as the normal points to be safe-guarded, varying from oil depôts to communication centres.

The 2nd Battalion, stationed at Victoria Barracks in Belfast, had also mobilised on 1st September and had received one hundred and sixty recruits on 6th September, although there was insufficient general service equipment to outfit all of them. The Battalion also received twenty-four reservists five days later. The next few weeks were committed to shooting and manoeuvre training, and with endless practice 'turnouts'.

There soon came a call from the British Expeditionary Force in France for reinforcements; and the 44th Division, to which the 4th and 5th Royal Sussex belonged, had to send troops overseas. These two battalions were not among those selected, and were feeling *'very jealous,'* as Captain Langham expressed it, when they then heard the good news that their Brigade, the 133rd, was to be strengthened by the addition of the 2nd Battalion from Belfast, where it had already mobilised. Thus there came into being a Royal Sussex Brigade, commanded by Brigadier J.I.B. Whitty DSO, and composed of a regular and two territorial battalions, which, though terrible tribulations lay ahead, would contribute greatly to the turning point of the conflict at a very crucial stage much later on.

Accordingly, the 2nd Battalion joined the 133rd Brigade at Maiden Newton in Dorset, soon after the two Territorial Battalions had moved to that part of the country for training early in December 1939.

The journey of the 2nd Royal Sussex from Belfast, just before Christmas, was attended by various quaint incidents, owing to the faulty marshalling of trains from Stranraer, so the majority ate the minority's rations. There was also an animated scene at the port, when the skipper, who had determined to treat Christmas turkeys and other livestock as 'first priority', was constrained by the Commanding Officer, Lieutenant Colonel M.A. James VC MC, to give precedence to the Battalion's baggage.

The 44th Division, considered one of the most advanced of the Territorial Army Divisions, was 'earmarked' for Finland at the time of the Russian attack on that country. Only the tragic but timely ending of the Russo-Finnish War prevented its going. Consequently, they became part of the IIIrd Corps, which was formed in Southern Command to join the British Expeditionary Force and become the reserve for the advance into Belgium – since for all their efforts to remain a neutral State, the Belgians would inevitably be involved as soon as the armies came to grips.

---

² In fact the 4th Battalion moved very early to Crowborough for training, handing over guards to the 6th Battalion and other troops.

When the time came for the 4th and 5th Battalions to go overseas, the 7th Battalion – belonging like the 6th, to the 37th Brigade of the 12th Division – took over 'Vulnerable Points' from the 5th Battalion. These were successively handed over to the 8th Battalion, formed out of the original 'Local Defence Volunteers'. Many an old Sussex soldier was to be found in this battalion, which was commanded by Lieutenant Colonel F.C. Temple CIE (brother of a late Archbishop of Canterbury). Subsequently, the 8th played a vital rôle during the Dunkirk and Battle of Britain crises, guarding threatened points and releasing younger men for more active duties; it eventually 'faded away' into a kind of limbo of the unfit. Other short-lived formations were the 50th (Holding) Battalion at Seaford, which sent Drafts to other Battalions, and the 10th Battalion, belonging to the 10th Independent Beach Brigade on the Sussex and Kent beaches. This was commanded by Lieutenant Colonel George Osborne MC, later the 16th Baronet, and who was also the garrison commander at Sleaford. His Military Cross had been gained with the old 7th Battalion in the Great War. A most popular character, as administrative officer at the Depôt when war broke out, he had helped greatly in the smooth accomplishment of mobilisation. Sir George Osborne, who is not to be confused with General Osborn (a Colonel of the Regiment), applied himself with the same thoroughness and determination as he had demonstrated during mobilisation, to defending the beaches with inadequate material (one of his grandsons would face similar restraints when he became Chancellor of the Exchequer in 2010).

Yet another fine battalion, formed in September 1940, was the 70th, and commanded by Lieutenant Colonel J.S. Magrath MC. Young men of 17½ were allowed to volunteer and, while defending vulnerable points in Sussex, Surrey and Kent, they had to stand up to bombing and machine-gun attacks from the air. They suffered a number of casualties, behaved gallantly on several occasions, passed later from defensive duties to providing trained Drafts to go overseas, and received the thanks and commendations of the GOC Eastern Command on their disbandment in July 1943.

Much of the fore-mentioned, however, was written in anticipation of events.

Before these events, however, there came a period, which was styled *'the phoney war'*. The term, coined by expectant neutral onlookers who desired slaughter on a large scale and who were evidently disappointed that it did not begin at once, was applied to the Western Front, where so many drastic events had followed in swift succession a quarter of a century before.

The important difference between 1914 and 1939 was that, in the latter case, Belgium was not immediately involved. Two years before the outbreak of Hitler's War, she had changed her policy from that of defensive alliance to one of strict neutrality. Moreover, when building fortifications around Brussels to resist a German attack, she also constructed defences against a possible invasion by the French. The effect of this was to put an end to all contact between the Belgian General Staff and that of the French and the British. Yet, when Britain accepted the fact of Belgian neutrality, it was stated that if Belgium were attacked she would expect immediate British aid!

No arguments that this assistance could hardly be effective, without the preliminary staff talks and the vital need for reconnaissance of the potential battle area, were sufficient to persuade the Belgians to abandon their attitude. General Gamelin considered that a move into Belgium at the beginning would shorten the Allied line and save about forty divisions. The denial of this advantage added heavily to the weakness of the Anglo-French front against the vast German strength.

Thus the Germans were able to finish off their Polish campaign without any danger of a serious offensive in the west, where Lord Gort was endeavouring to build up defences in depth with concrete pill-boxes, anti-tank obstacles, and every possible device for holding a long stretch of front with a thin line of troops. While some depressing political manoeuvres were driving Hore-Belisha from the War Office, the exultant enemy was building up forces opposite Holland, Belgium and France, ready for the decisive stroke. It was preceded by the invasion of Norway, which led to our ill-fated expedition in aid of that country and made further inroads upon an army already lamentably short of men and equipment.

CONCEPT OF WAR IN FRANCE AND THE LOW COUNTRIES

Before embarking on the 1940 campaign in France and Belgium, one should consider the Anglo-French philosophies on a likely Continental conflagration and, particularly, the French concept of the way that such a war should be conducted, as so much was influenced by their determination to wage a different type of war against the Germans. In 1939, as the Second World War loomed, the British and French had planned to fight an updated version of what happened during the Great War, but with some essential differences. In 1914, the French had suffered massive casualties in frontal attacks and thus were determined to maintain, initially, a defensive posture in Western Europe, while gaining the time to mobilise their military forces and industrial base in order to fight a total war subsequently; the French philosophy was not to take any offensive action until some two to three years after the start of hostilities.

This philosophy led to the concept and creation of the *Maginot Line*, replacing the crude trenches in which so much of the 1914-1918 War had been fought, and which now consisted of a sophisticated series of fortifications that were confidently expected to protect France's frontier with Germany, although crucially the *Maginot Line* did not cover the Franco-Belgian frontier. It was also apparent that the French military doctrine in the lead-up to the Second World War was heavily influenced by a national desire to avoid any type of war that might lead to a repeat of the high losses that were incurred in the relentless campaigns of the Great War.

When Adolf Hitler came to power in 1933, Winston Churchill remarked shortly afterwards, *"Thank God for the French Army"*. To Churchill at that time, France's army seemed a powerful bulwark against possible Nazi aggression towards other European nations. However, because of the change in France's war-fighting concept and its resolution, the defeat of this powerful army in a mere six weeks in 1940 stands as one of the most remarkable military campaigns in history.

Hitler was eager to follow up his victory over Poland in 1939 by attacking in the west but bad weather forced the planned offensive to be postponed. Then, in January 1940, a German plane crashed in neutral Belgium, with a copy of the western attack orders on board. Believing that his plan for the invasion France and the Low Countries had been compromised, he turned for advice to General Erich von Manstein, who proposed a more daring concept. In effect, Manstein recognised that the *Maginot Line* was too formidable for a direct attack from Germany, and proposed instead a subsidiary attack through neutral Holland and Belgium, but with the main blow against France to be launched a little later through the Ardennes. This was a hilly and heavily forested area on the German-Belgian-French border, where the Allies would be unlikely to expect an attack. The plan was to rely heavily on surprise *Blitzkrieg*[3]

---

[3] Blitzkrieg means *Lightning War* and was first used by the Germans in the Second World War. It was

techniques. For the British Expeditionary Force this meant that the main threat to its defensive positions would not necessarily always come from the east as

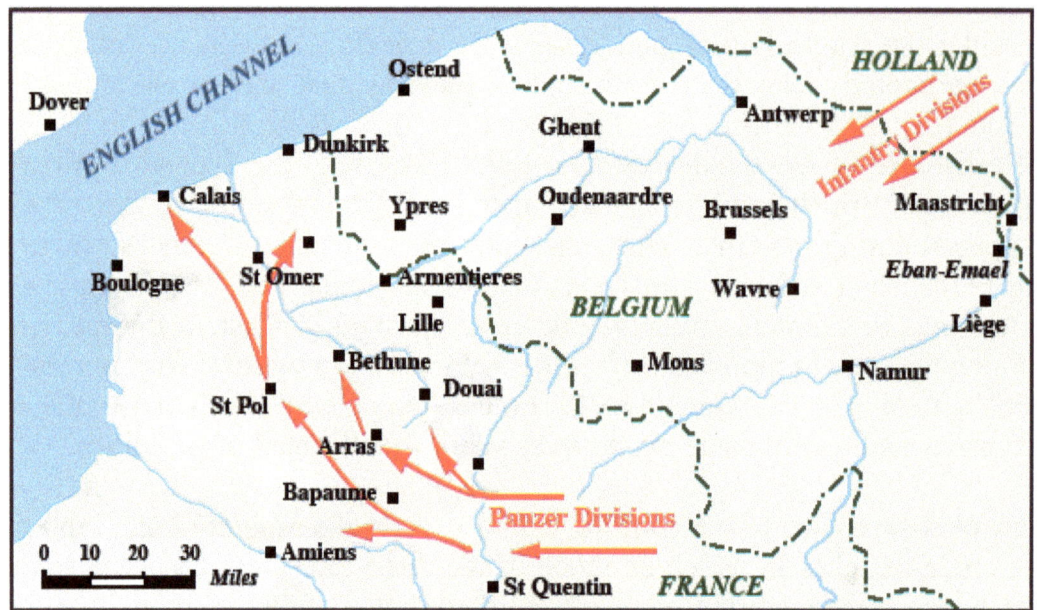

The German Advance out of the Ardennes in May 1940

expected, but would often manifest itself, unexpectedly, from the south or west, and would generally harass its right flank, at whatever level of command was engaged.

Contrary to a generally held belief, the Germans had, in fact, fewer tanks than the Allies (2,500 against 3,500) at the beginning of the war. However, their tanks were concentrated into Panzer (armoured) formations. The French had some equivalent formations that were of good quality, but they were dispersed rather than concentrated in the German fashion. Manstein's plan envisaged these Panzer divisions in a semi-independent role, striking ahead of the main body of the army, to disrupt and disorientate the Allies.

The attack began on 10th May 1940, with German air raids on Belgium and Holland, followed by parachute drops and attacks by ground forces. These two beleaguered nations were hastily added to the anti-German *ad-hoc* coalition that included France and Britain, but this only served to further complicate Allied command and control arrangements. The Germans seized the initiative, capturing the key Belgian fort of *Eben-Emael*[4] with a daring airborne operation. The speed of the German advance and the brutality of the air raids gave them a huge psychological advantage, and on 14th May the Dutch surrendered.

---

a tactic based on speed and surprise, and needed a military force based on tank units supported by aircraft and infantry.

[4] Fort d'Eben-Emael is located between Liège and Maastricht on the Dutch-Belgium border and was designed to defend Belgium from a German attack across the narrow belt of Dutch territory in the region.

The British and French had responded to the original attack by putting into operation a plan to advance to the River Dyle in Belgium. The Allies pushed their best forces, including the British, into Belgium. Although the initial stages went reasonably well, a French force advancing towards Breda, in

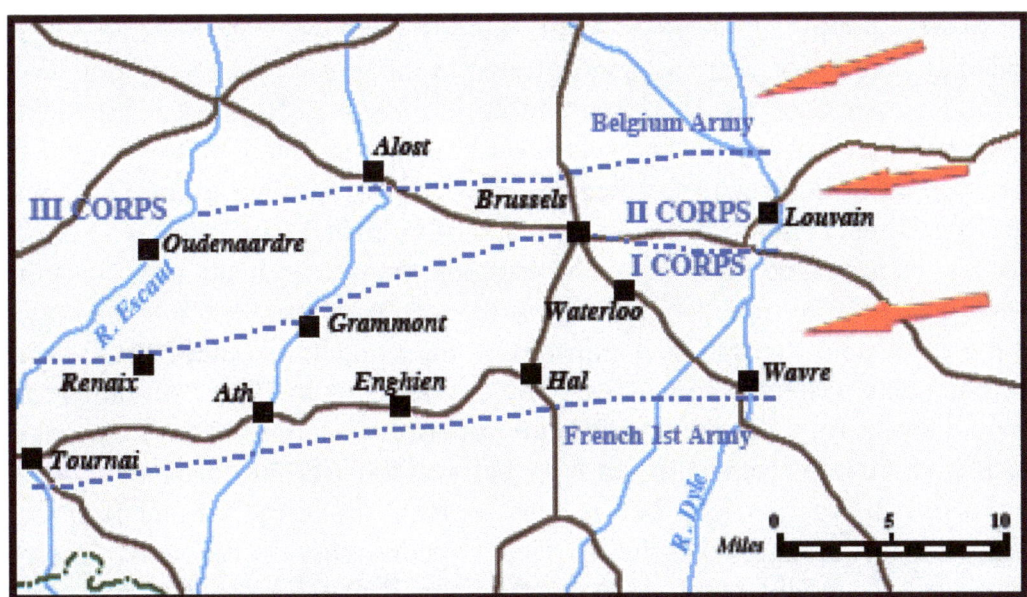

The Allied Advance to the River Dyle in May 1940

Holland, was pushed back. It soon became clear that by advancing into the Low Countries the Allies were dancing to Hitler's tune. On 13th May, the first German forces emerged from the Ardennes near Sedan, on the River Meuse. In a two-day battle, the Panzers crossed the river, despite some surprisingly stiff resistance from the second-class French defenders, and near-suicidal attacks by Allied aircraft.

FRANCE AND BELGIUM 1940

Having considered the background to the war, one should now appreciate the Regiment's initial deployments in the forthcoming campaign. In 1940, at the end of March and beginning of April, the 44th Division was sent overseas and landed at Cherbourg. Having concentrated in the area of Le Mans, they moved up the line and took over the memorable Armentières-Bailleul sector. When the German armies hurled themselves on France and Flanders, the Ist and IInd Corps, in accordance with the original plan, moved forward to the Dyle, while the IIIrd Corps, being in reserve, advanced as far as the River Escaut (*Scheldte*) and lay astride Oudenaardre. The Belgian Army, with all their neutrality shown to be a vain thing, stood then on the left, with the French some way off on the right. The strength of the army that the French, or indeed the Belgians, had been able to deploy in August 1914 did not exist in 1940. As the German panzers swept forward, the enemy's air superiority enabled them to knock out the British guns piecemeal, often long before their German ground forces had closed up. It was not long before the Germans drove the Ist and IInd Corps back, for the situation of the British Expeditionary Force was becoming desperate. It would not be long before the Royal Sussex Battalions were involved in hard fighting to the west of Oudenaardre, when the enemy crossed the River Escaut.

Initial Deployment of the 133rd (Royal Sussex) Brigade

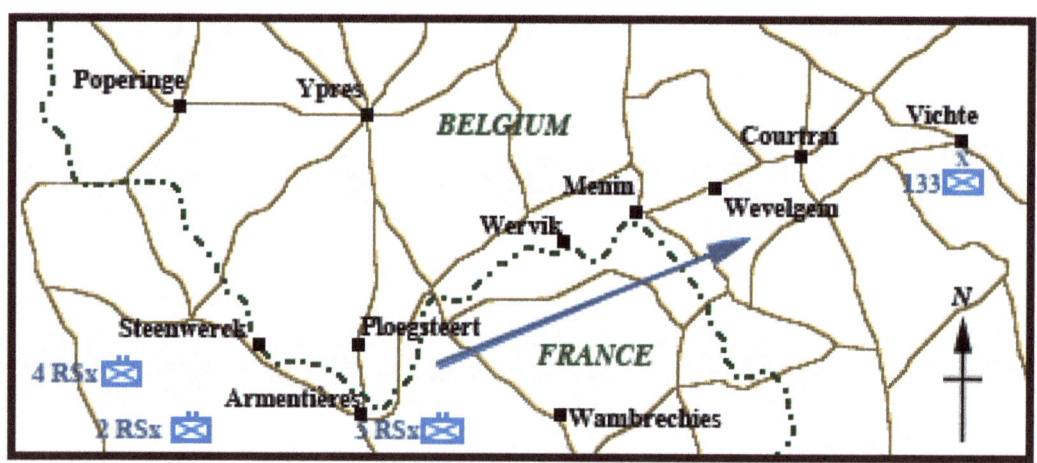

Move Forward to Vichte by 133rd (Royal Sussex) Brigade

2nd Royal Sussex. While the British Expeditionary Force had been moving up into Belgium, the 2nd Battalion, now commanded by Lieutenant Colonel P.J.M. Ellison of the Grenadier Guards, received a remarkable welcome. With the storm gathering over them, the people of Menin and Lauwe expressed feelings of the greatest friendliness. They did this chiefly by distributing flowers lavishly among the men, and the 2nd Royal Sussex went forward to its ordeal, bearing bunches of lilac. In Courtrai it was the same; cigars, cigarettes, flowers, fruit and drinks were pressed upon the troops. *"The hospitality,"* records the War Diary, *"was almost embarrassing."* Circumstances of which they were only dimly aware had begun to give the welcoming garlands a wreath-like significance; the Battalion begun moving towards Vichte and thence to Anzeghem.

4th Royal Sussex. On 10th May, the 4th Battalion had also received orders to move forward towards the Belgian frontier, which it crossed on the afternoon of 12th May, and where the Belgian population received it with the same enthusiasm. The march route was *via* Steenwerck - Ploegsteert – Wervik, and was uneventful, although B Company had to picquet Ploegstreet Wood (*memories of 1914-1918*), as a result of rumours of parachute troops. Orders were then received that the Battalion would take over certain internal security and guard duties in and around Courtrai from the 2nd Buffs. A and D Companies moved to Watermolen, the former to take over bridge guards and the latter to take over anti-parachute duties at Wevelgem aerodrome, while the rest of the Battalion remained at Watermolen. On the 14th, C Company was moved to Ledeghem to provide guards at an RAF landing ground. By 16th May, refugee traffic through Courtrai had become very heavy and the Commanding Officer had considerable dealings with the local authorities. Divisional Headquarters had given no guidance as to what action should be taken, although at this time, refugee control by the Belgian authorities was very good. That night, the Battalion was ordered to move to an area about La Croix, near Lille, although C Company still remained guarding the landing ground at Ledeghem, while D Company was detached to Vichte for refugee traffic control. The march was again uneventful but the heavy air attacks on Lille, as it was passed, were continuous. The Battalion reached La Croix at 6 am on 18th May, and following some rest, it received orders at 1 pm to march to Vichte, *via* Aelbeke, which it reached at 10 pm. The following morning, the Battalion marched to Vichte, *via* Bellegem and St Louis while the roads, which had received several bombing attacks, were crowded with refugees and military traffic moving away from the front.

5th Royal Sussex. On the German invasion of Holland and Belgium on 10th May, the 5th Battalion, under command of Lieutenant Colonel F.R.H. Morgan of The Border Regiment, who had taken over from Lieutenant Colonel Barton in January 1940, took over guard duties at vulnerable points in the area of Lillers, southwest of Armentières. By 17th May it had been moved by motor transport to rejoin the Brigade at Vichte in Belgium. However, by 8 pm that evening orders were received to march 17 miles back into France because German armour had been reported at Neuville-en-Ferrain. There, after marching all night, the Battalion was directed to return to Vichte, arriving back there in the early hours of the 19th – during its double journey, it had marched 35 miles in 24 hours.

The 2nd Battalion in France and Belgium

About the 18th of May, the 44th Division had to withdraw again into France, as the French had collapsed on the right. The Division found itself at the apex of the Dunkirk salient, with the Germans swinging round and coming in from the southwest and west. These were the German formations engaged by the 4th and 5th Battalions at Caestre and Strazeele, of which more will be said presently.

Considering the 2nd Battalion's experience, we find that though they showed all the old readiness to 'stand or fall' in the tradition of the Iron Regiment, the Army's cohesion had been weakened by vastly superior enemy strength, and actions fought by individual groups, however gallantly, can only have one end. The personal diaries of the Adjutant, Captain R.B. de F. Sleeman, Captain R.E. Loder, and Lieutenant J.F. Ainsworth give point to this, as does the official War Diary, by showing how orders either conflicted or failed to come through at all – a state of affairs which is not difficult to understand when communications are interrupted and information is delayed in consequence.

To begin with, the 2nd Battalion, unlike the 4th and 5th Battalions, found itself being constantly moved from one Brigade to another, and often without the ability to communicate with the appropriate Brigade Headquarters that happened to be commanding it at the time. Like other battalions, it also found itself embarrassed by obstructive prohibitions against 'loop-holing' houses without authority and flattening crops against concealed enemy advances. It was not until 20th May that Colonel Ellison's strong representations were successful in obtaining permission for the latter step to be taken. At this stage, the Battalion, along with the rest of the 133rd (Royal Sussex) Brigade, was deployed in a defensive position at Heirweg, and was digging-in but with a

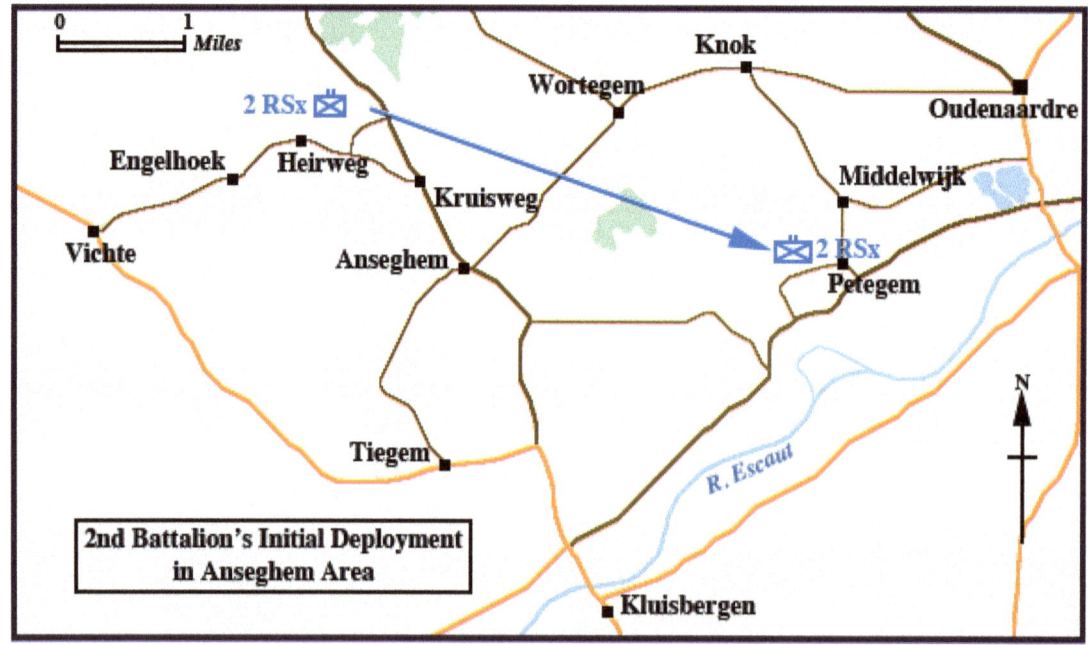

2nd Battalion's Initial Deployment in Anseghem Area

lack of materials to construct a proper defensive position. It was occupying the Brigade's reserve position; the Brigade itself being the 44th Division's depth brigade. However, the Battalion was lacking one company, as B Company had been detached for guard duties at the Embassy in Brussels, at the Divisional Headquarters, and at the road control post at Renaix.

On the following day, the 21st, after various orders and counter-orders, the Battalion was ordered to proceed as soon as possible to Anseghem, and where it was to be deployed among farms and orchards. On its arrival at 6 am, it was to join the 131st Brigade but it was not to be under command of that Brigade, as it was to receive all orders from HQ 44th Division direct. Notwithstanding this directive, at 9 am, D Company was placed under command of HQ 131st Brigade, with the rest of the Battalion following suit at 9.30 am. Immediately after, the Battalion was then ordered to proceed to the Middelwijk area. There it was required to defend an extended front of 6,200 yards but with only three companies, as B Coy was still detached. The Battalion's position was supposed to be occupied for only a few hours but they actually remained longer, troubled by lack of any defensive plan and harassed by well-directed enemy shelling. Although it was difficult to lay much line, the Signallers were maintaining what lines had been laid with great gallantry under shellfire. Furthermore, the Wireless Rear Link to Brigade Headquarters could not function, as the Battalion has not been issued with the 131st Brigade's wireless frequencies. Communications with HQ 131st Brigade were eventually established through a link via HQ 133rd Brigade; an early order from the Headquarters of the 131st Brigade was:

> *"The Battalion is to hold the position to the last man and last round BUT if heavily pressed, it should withdraw."*

While orders were issued which appeared to contradict themselves, Brigadier Whitty and Lieutenant Colonel Whistler (Commanding Officer of the 4th Battalion) visited the 2nd Battalion Headquarters just before midnight, to say that the 4th Battalion was to come up on the right flank while the 5th Battalion would come up on the left, and that efforts were being made to bring the 2nd Battalion back under command of its own Royal Sussex Brigade. This change of command had not been accomplished by the next day, but by then an enemy observation balloon was directing artillery fire on the Battalion's position, with the forward companies being heavily shelled. Battalion Headquarters was also heavily bombarded; at the height of the bombardment, one hundred shells fell in one minute and the Regimental Aid Post (RAP) was forced to move three times. In addition, the Carrier Platoon was hit by a salvo, which, besides inflicting casualties, put six carriers out of action. Sergeant Groves, who was among the wounded, would not go back to the RAP until ordered to do so; he returned to duty immediately after seeing Lieutenant Pozner RAMC, regarded in the Battalion as a most intrepid and efficient Regimental Medical Officer (RMO).

About 4 pm on 22nd May, an enemy two-pronged attack was trying to infiltrate both flanks of A Company, commanded by Captain E.G. Hollist, and was getting in between both A Company and C Company, the latter commanded by Captain R.E. Loder. Although the attack was held back with difficulty, accurate enemy shelling and mortaring continued but returning such fire was difficult as the Battalion's mortars had no sights – they had been handed in for repair before leaving England but were never replaced – reputedly, there was only one mortar sight in the whole of the Brigade. An hour later, at 5 pm, orders were received from HQ 131st Brigade to withdraw to Courtrai but confusion was caused by a similar, although slightly different order, being received from HQ 133rd Brigade. The Battalion therefore drew back, under heavy fire, to a hill immediately behind where Battalion Headquarters had been, and to the right of the 5th Royal Sussex. The situation appeared so grave that Battalion Headquarters decided to destroy by fire the Battalion's War Diaries, together with those of the 4th Battalion, as well as any other important papers that might be useful to the Germans.

Soon after nine o'clock in the evening, when the gallant Colonel Ellison had been severely wounded in the chest and carried back by his batman, the Royal Sussex Brigade again received the 2nd Battalion back under its wing. The Adjutant, Captain Sleeman, later emphasised the great work that Ellison had done throughout the battle:

> *"His persistence and determination displayed at Brigade HQ – doubtful whether the Battalion would have received any orders at all. Whilst not only was he at all times a wonderful example but his magnificent leadership and courage inspired everyone at a time when there was ample ground for depression."*

Major T. Prince, who was the Battalion Second-in-Command, assumed command of the 2nd Battalion on its arrival at Bissegem, near Courtrai. The Battalion embussed that night for Wambréchies, where it arrived at 6 am on the

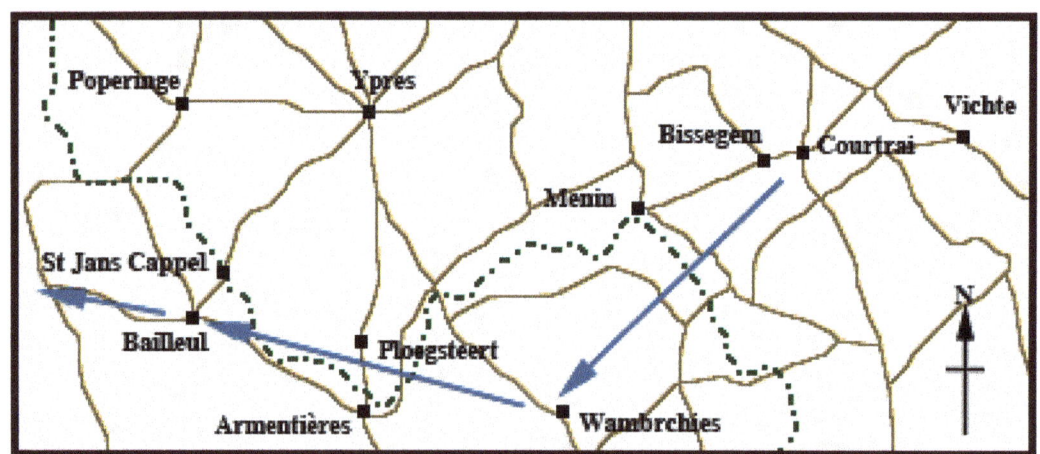

2nd Battalion's Withdrawal Route to Balleul and on to Hazebrouck

morning of 24th May; the Battalion had scarcely breakfasted when it then received orders to proceed to the coast as part of a mobile column, moving by Armentières, Bailleul and Hazebrouck. There is a memorable point about

Regimental history 2nd tending to repeat itself; Captain the Hon. Neville Lytton of the 11th Royal Sussex recorded[5] on 11th March 1916:

> *"We travelled via Abbeville and St Pol and eventually reached a little village called Morbeque, some few kilometres from Hazebrouck. My company was billeted in a delightful little farm; the men had clean straw to sleep on and, for the few days we stayed there, I think they were perfectly happy . . . "*!

Forward again to 1940, there was a slight delay in the 2nd Battalion's move to Hazebrouck as it had been given a different rendezvous to the one that had been given to the RASC[6], the corps providing the vehicles. As it waited for the transport, the Luftwaffe was passing overhead towards the coast, squadron followed by squadron. While it has been warned that it should expect armoured and air attacks *en route*, the Battalion reached Bailleul without incident, although Armentières was being bombed as they passed.

After a pause at Bailleul, during which a patrol was sent to Strazeele, the Battalion arrived at the latter place at 10 pm, but further patrols confirmed that the Germans were in Hazebrouck. A French artillery officer, making ready to depart, stated that some of the enemy were in the Forest of Nieppe, to the south. It was therefore decided to remain in the area, and the 2nd Battalion had orders to hold a position covering Strazeele, with the remainder of the Brigade being deployed to the right of the Battalion. This plan had been decided at a meeting in an estaminet[7], which was demolished by a direct hit soon after the Brigade staff had left it.

Throughout the 25th of May, the 2nd Battalion remained in occupation of the Strazeele position, which was consolidated although subjected to much dive-bombing. The only communications with Brigade HQ was through the use of Despatch Riders. It was not until noon on the 26th that the Battalion was ordered to move forward to Grand-Sec-Bois, near Hazebrouck, and relieve the 1st Royal West Kents, and fortunately at this point, B Company, commanded by Captain A.C. Davidson-Houston, returned to the Battalion. The relief of the Royal West Kents was effected that afternoon, after some delay, but the Battalion was now defending a position within the 131st Brigade's area of responsibility, while supposedly still under command of its own 133rd Brigade; the latter's Brigade Commander felt that this forward deployment by the 2nd Battalion was a mistake. Thus the former state of affairs was repeated, and information was again cut off. Late in the evening, Major Prince went back to 133rd Brigade Headquarters to report on this, and to emphasise the fact that there were enemy filtrations on the western side of Battalion's position, but there was still no one positioned on that right flank. He returned with the

---

[5] *The Day Sussex Died; A History of Lowther's Lambs*, John A. Baines, RSLHG 2012.
[6] RASC – Royal Army Service Corps
[7] Little café.

information that the 5th Royal Sussex would arrive on its right soon after midnight.

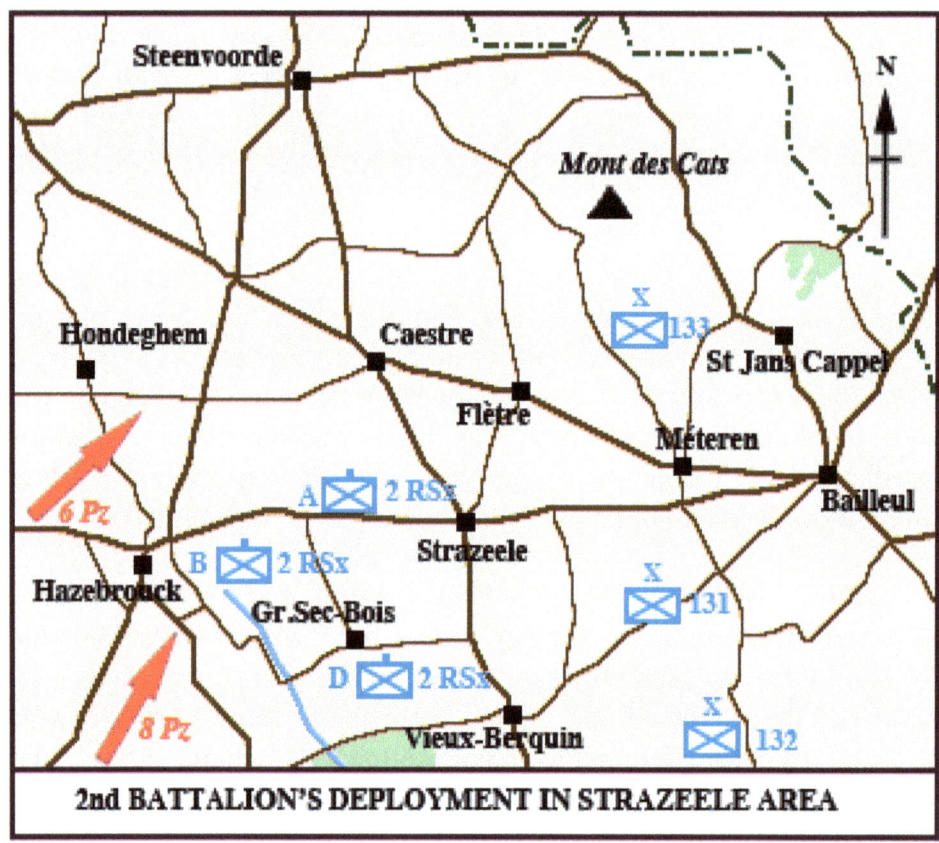

2nd BATTALION'S DEPLOYMENT IN STRAZEELE AREA

Early on 27th May, B Company, holding an isolated copse some way forward of the Battalion position, was suddenly attacked by enemy tanks and infantry, quickly surrounded and then virtually wiped out. Major Prince, who had inadvertently gone forward to visit the Company, was lost as well. Immediately after the attack on B Company, enemy tanks appeared on the Battalion's front, on the far side of the canal; regrettably, the other companies had enough problems holding their own positions and could do little to help the plight of B Company. At 9 am, Brigade HQ ordered the Battalion to recapture the B Company position although the order was later cancelled.

Major L.W. Lane, who had been commanding HQ Company, was sent for to take over command; the 5th Battalion had not arrived on the right as anticipated, and enemy tanks were proceeding to Hazebrouck and down the Hazebrouck-Strazeele road, thus not only outflanking but infiltrating behind the Battalion's position. The situation was such that the Battalion's close support artillery were engaging targets on three points of the compass; North – West – South. In the late afternoon, the Battalion was then placed under command of yet another Brigade, this time, the 132nd. It is also important to appreciate, when considering the eventual evacuation of the British Expeditionary Force, how rapidly the Dunkirk Salient was closing in on itself; the sketch map below shows the changes in the Forward Defended Localities during the 28th and 29th of May 1940.

Having now assumed command of the Battalion, Major Lane, on visiting Brigade HQ, sought definite orders, re-emphasising at the same time the dangerous situation on the right flank. He was told that the Battalion would probably have to withdraw and rejoin the 133rd Brigade the following morning. Major Lane was also informed that no organised formation was to be adopted for the withdrawal, but in the meantime they were instructed to be ready to move 'in small groups' as quickly as possible.

Hazebrouck was now occupied by enemy troops, with some having got as far as the right rear of D Company, which was commanded by Major A.K. Mumford. This report elicited a reply from Brigade HQ that French tanks would counter-attack Hazebrouck before dawn, and two battalions were coming up on the right as soon as possible. The remnants of the Hazebrouck garrison were falling back through the 2nd Battalion's position throughout that evening, and were very vague about the situation and uncertain of where to go. There was an attempt, therefore, to form some of them into a unit to defend that perilous right flank, but this was checked by counter-orders from HQ 132nd Brigade. Corporal John Brown's[8] diary gives a good indication of the situation at the time:

> *"By this time we were in a desperate fight against the Germans. A lot of men from other Regiments were coming down the road, which runs east and west through Grand-Sec-Bois. It had started to rain very heavily just after 1700 hours and eased our situation a little, about an hour later we felt even better as two Bren gun carriers came around delivering food and rum to as many men as possible; we later learnt that the Quartermaster had salvaged two jars of rum from a derelict supply lorry. About 2100 hours whilst feeding the last of the men, the carriers were shot at from the right flank by enemy machine-gun fire, which caused some casualties.*
>
> *The situation seemed different on the 28th May. We were spread very thinly as we took over and consolidated positions that had been occupied by the 1st Battalion Royal West Kent's. Behind the lines I counted about 36 artillery guns that had been incapacitated or 'spiked' because they had simply run out of ammunition. Getting supplies of anything was becoming a big problem. 2nd Lieutenant Rubie came around in a carrier when it was dark and noted that we didn't have an officer as Captain Willett had been killed the day before. The carrier came under fire from several directions and some Verey lights were sent up to try and identify the German positions. Well, the flares showed that the village of Grand-Sec-Bois was almost completely surrounded by overwhelming numbers of the enemy. Wisely 2nd Lieutenant Rubie gave the order to withdraw to Strazeele.*

---

[8] Corporal Brown enlisted into the 2nd Battalion The Royal Sussex Regiment at Eastbourne on 26th January 1931, serving in India and Egypt before transferring to the Army Reserve in 1938. He was recalled to the 2nd Battalion on 25th January 1939.

A patrol report from A Company now revealed enemy at the first crossroads and on the railway to the right rear of D Company. The promises of a French counter-attack and reinforcement of the right were never fulfilled. This open flank remained a fatal sore in the Battalion's position, for it was now in the absurd situation of being able to hold a firm forward line but with the enemy having the complete freedom to move wherever it liked on the Battalion's right flank. The situation was relieved when the Battalion was ordered, at seven in the morning of 28th May, to retire about a mile – a fighting withdrawal towards Bailleul, organised and conducted successfully by the Adjutant, Captain Sleeman, with little interference from the enemy, who were now rapidly working round to the rear.

This became very apparent when shortly after dawn on the 29th; a German patrol discovered the Adjutant of the 2nd Royal Sussex in a farmyard. *"For you,"* the officer informed him, *"der var is ober."* He produced maps of *"Englant,"* to show where they were going, and inquired ironically where the BEF was. Captain Sleeman's enormous contribution to the control and direction of the 2nd Battalion would not be told until 1944 when the then Captain Pozner RAMC and Captain & Quartermaster Hanlon, wrote a citation recommending an award of the Military Cross:

> *"For the greatest devotion to duty during the period 22nd-29th May 1940. With four Commanding Officers killed, or wounded, in succession, he carried the whole direction of the Battalion on his shoulders during a difficult withdrawal, and subsequent to a defensive position. Although suffering both from stomach trouble and a shrapnel wound to the leg, he refused to go sick. He carried on in spite of three nights without sleep, and at the end, having ordered the Medical Officer and Quartermaster to get away, he remained with one man at Battalion HQ until taken prisoner early on the morning of 29th May. His courage and example were of the highest standard throughout."*

Lieutenant Colonel P.J.M. Ellison, Commanding Officer of the 2nd Battalion when it went to France in 1940[9], also endorsed the recommendation for an award.

The remnants of the Battalion had withdrawn to Strazeele on the 28th and then on to Méteren, where on the 29th, it was well and truly dispersed. The information on what happened thereafter was provided subsequently by Lieutenant Rubie and by the Transport Officer, Captain Taylor, who had been located with B Echelon at Mont des Cats.

No orders were given to the remnants apart from being told to abandon any vehicles and head for Dunkirk. They were organised into two parties:

---

[9] Lieutenant Colonel Ellison had been badly wounded on 22nd May 1940 and evacuated to England.

No. 1 Party, under Lieutenant Rubie with 40 men and Lieutenant Pozner, the RMO, moved to St Jans Cappel and thence to Dunkirk; and

No. 2 Party, under Captain Taylor and Lieutenant & Quartermaster Hanlon, and consisting of the remnants of B Echelon at Mont des Cats, moved direct to Dunkirk.

It is also apparent that other members of the 2nd Battalion had moved back, either individually or in small isolated groups, and were similarly recovered from the beaches.

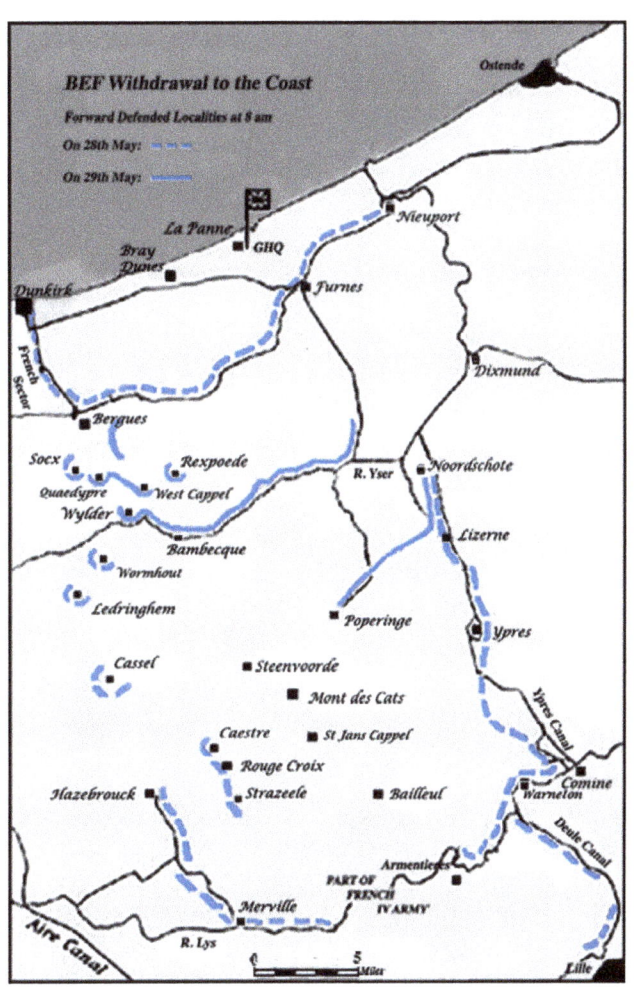

The two known Parties arrived at Dunkirk on 30th May and No. 1 Party was joined by 2nd/Lieutenant Strickland and a party of men at 6 am. The five officers and some 100 men embarked on Destroyer *No. H.73* at 6 pm and arrived at Dover at 8.30 pm. From there they moved by train to Tidworth, arriving there at 7 am on the 31st, whereupon those remaining of the 2nd Royal Sussex were directed to Perham Down Camp.

One trenchant paragraph sums up the 2nd Battalion's view of the operations:

> *"The magnificent fighting unit of three Battalions of The Royal Sussex was never properly tried; for, except on the Belgian position, where they gave us excellent support, we never fought with the 4th and 5th Battalions. Even in Belgium we were attached to another Brigade."*

This detachment from the original Royal Sussex Brigade seems always to have cut down the available information. Thus, Captain Loder, who had done great things in many trying situations and helped to reorganise D Company after Captain Willett had been killed, was launching attacks in the region of Hazebrouck, taking part in the capture of a German staff car, with maps, and dodging enemy columns on the way to Battalion Headquarters right up to 9 pm on 28th May, when he was told the real situation. By that time the Germans were all around him, and he was captured next morning, as were many others who had not been killed already. German reconnaissance planes had been free to direct shellfire, which destroyed vehicles and the means of escape.

Lieutenant Ainsworth, Battalion Intelligence Officer, speaks in his conclusions of the defensive positions taken up by the 2nd Battalion in Belgium and France. The first, round the village of Heirweg, he considered might have been held with advantage. The second, on the Escaut, taken up at short notice, had a front of 6,200 yards and, as the position's previous occupants, The Queen's, had departed before their arrival, there was no formal 'take-over'.

There were other disadvantages of terrain, but lack of satisfactory orders was the chief trouble. First they would be told to fight to the last man and last round, and while they were preparing to do this, there would come an order to withdraw. It was late on the 28th that the Battalion learnt that the British Expeditionary Force was withdrawing to Dunkirk, with the Germans closing in on either side.

Many fine things were done. Besides Captain Loder and Lieutenant Pozner, mention should be made of the magnificent work of Lieutenant & Quartermaster P.J. Hanlon in bringing up food and supplies under the most appalling conditions. There was also Lieutenant Rubie, whose leadership of the Carrier Platoon was exemplary, and he was always in the forefront of any action, and would be awarded the Military Cross – he would later be awarded a Bar to his Military Cross for his gallant action, when serving with the 49th Reconnaissance Regiment near Le Havre in September 1944. Similarly, Private W.G. Wilson, the driver of a mortar ammunition truck, which he drove to a mortar position over completely open country and evacuated both guns and crew under heavy machine-gun and artillery fire, and for which he was awarded the Military Medal. Interestingly, these were the only two Gallantry awards made in the 2nd Battalion at the time, although Captain Sleeman would subsequently be awarded with the Military Cross in 1944, while still a prisoner of war. The lack of further awards was most likely due to the fact that most of those who would have written the citations were either dead or captured, as were many of the potential recipients. Lieutenant Pozner, the RMO commented:

> *"Decorations awarded were few in relation to losses,"* and then went on to say:

> *"But in these the whole Battalion was honoured, for if their record in this campaign had not shown any victories or triumphant advances, it had demonstrated to the full, the ability of the disciplined soldier to give to the utmost that which was required of him under the most exacting conditions."*

Only five officers and some 225 men of the 2nd Battalion were eventually evacuated from Dunkirk. The Casualty Return made subsequently by the acting Adjutant on 14th June 1940 was:

	Killed	**Wounded**	**Missing**	**Total**
Officers	2	5	14	21
Men	12	58	302	372
Total	**14**	**63**	**316**	**393**

The loss of this fine Battalion was a tragedy comparable with the loss of the 35th at Almanza in 1707. Yet, after reconstitution, it was to make a major contribution to victory in the Western Desert.

The 4th and 5th Battalions in France and Belgium 1940

The exploits of the 4th and 5th Battalions are bound up with one another to a greater extent than with those of the 2nd Battalion, which, as we have seen, suffered particularly from being so much with other Brigades. At different times, the 5th had this experience too, whereas the 4th remained more constantly with the 133rd Brigade under its brave commander, Brigadier J.I.B. Whitty DSO.

There now enters upon the scene one of those singular characters who stand out with peculiar vividness against the background of world conflict. Some leaders can move their men by the furious energy, often known as 'pep', others by personal example and human understanding. Lashmer Gordon Whistler belonged to the latter type. A Harrow cricketer, a batsman with a long-armed drive who made many big scores in Regimental matches, he was eminently fitted for the rôle of *"hitting the Germans for six,"* as Montgomery was later to express it.

They had hit him first as a nineteen-year-old platoon commander with the 13th Battalion in March 1918. Wounded and taken prisoner, he had escaped as soon as he was well enough, but had been recaptured and saved from further dangerous attempts by the Armistice. He had then sailed with the North Russian Relief Force to Archangel in May 1919, journeying thence some 170 miles up the River Dwina, and returning in November. From this expedition he acquired, in the peculiar manner that happens in the services, the nickname of *'Bolo'*. Thus, it was as *Bolo* Whistler that he served with the 1st Battalion on the Rhine, with Headquarters at Dublin Castle during the Irish Revolt, and across the face of the globe in China, India, Egypt, the Sudan, and Palestine. Whether Adjutant of the 5th (Cinque Ports) Battalion in Sussex, the 2nd Battalion overseas, or Officer Commanding the Depôt at the outbreak of war in 1939, he was *Bolo* – unofficially but universally known – for many years. And thus we find Lieutenant Colonel *Bolo* Whistler commanding the 4th Battalion in the perilous pass to which the British Expeditionary Force had come to in Belgium on 21st May 1940.

Among the officers who went overseas with this Battalion was Major the Duke of Norfolk, who commanded a company. Many of the men came from his Arundel estate, so that he was of the greatest value in maintaining the important personal touch, as his father had done in South Africa. He was therefore greatly disgusted when his feet began to give serious trouble, and he concealed the fact from his Commanding Officer for as long as he could. But it was of no avail and, being firmly ordered to report sick, he was eventually evacuated from France only just in time to avoid capture.

The 4th Battalion arrived at Vichte on the 19th of May, and by 6 pm was taking up a position north-east of Steenbrugge, with the 2nd Battalion on its right and the 5th Battalion coming up a little later on the left. Digging and wiring began

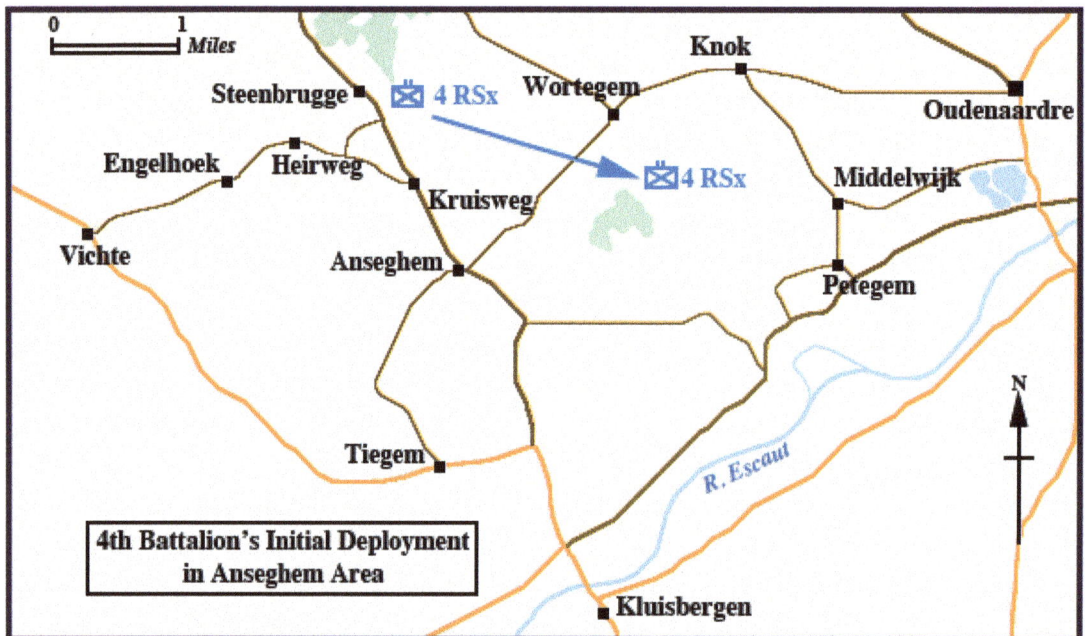

and went on continuously, with defences being improved throughout the night and following day. It was obvious that the war was coming closer; Ghent was burning fiercely and Oudenarde had several fierce dive-bombing attacks, and was also on fire. Gunfire could now be heard over the next ridge, and the landing ground at Ledeghem was evacuated by the RAF and then destroyed under orders of Captain J. Magrath, the officer who was commanding C Company.

On the morning of the 21st, at about 10 o'clock, a party of some twenty men, under an officer of The Royal West Kents, reported to Battalion Headquarters that they had been driven back from the River Escaut, and that the Germans were developing an attack about Oudenaardre. Attempts to reconnoitre a position covering the left flank were interrupted as the front began to give way. Peter Hadley, in his graphic little book[10], has supplied an animated account of

---

[10] *Third Class to Dunkirk*, Peter Hadley (Hollis & Carter), 1944.

an incident at this crisis. He had gone, with the Commanding Officer, the Intelligence Officer, and the Second-in-Command, as far as the village of Wortegem, when they encountered a disorderly mob of soldiers, grimy, bloodstained and shouting that the Boches were *"just up there by the church"*.

Picking out a Captain from among them, *Bolo* addressed him in much the same manner as Peterborough addressed Lord Charlemont at Montjuich[11], and with similar effect. Within two minutes, the officer was marching up the hill again at the head of his men. Having disposed of the matter, *Bolo* continued to stand there, coolly deciding on his plan of action.

The enemy had not in fact reached Wortegem, though there were persistent reports of a breakthrough on the left. At about 12.30 pm, the Battalion was ordered to move forward to an assembly position at Anseghem, and arrived there at about 5 pm. The village was being shelled at the time and several casualties occurred; Captain G.A. Watkins of D Company was killed together with Private T. Hemmings, the first of the men to be killed. The Battalion occupied the high ground between Anseghem and Knok, just to the south of Wortegem, with the 5th Battalion on its left. Despite being under heavy shellfire, the 4th Battalion lost no time in digging in, building a trench system of such strength that Colonel Nix was able to recognise much of it when visiting the spot seven years later. While they did so, various 'last survivors' of forward units came trickling back, and were promptly formed into platoons by the Commanding Officer, who retained them in the area. All the time, a German 'plane circled over the place, and any movement brought down accurate shellfire. Amongst others, Captain W.K. Hubbard of HQ Company was wounded, thus making him the third Company Commander casualty of the day.

The Regimental Aid Post was severely shelled and had to move; the Medical Officer, Captain F.S. Smith, did much gallant work, was wounded himself, and was subsequently awarded the Military Cross.

The troops at this stage found it hard to appreciate the problems facing the Royal Air Force, as German aircraft 'spotted' unopposed, and even the imperturbable *Bolo* sent a message to Brigade: *"Please may I have half a Hurricane for half an hour?"* Later, the comparative absence of German aircraft over the beaches at Dunkirk provided a great vindication of the RAF, whose valour had helped make the evacuation possible.

---

[11] Just before the brilliant *coup-de-main* by which Montjuich was taken, a body of enemy troops was reported as advancing from the city: *"the troops were seized with panic and Lord Charlemont, Peterborough's second in command, retreated with the rest. When the Earl of Peterborough came hurrying back, he snatched the half-pike from Charlemont's hand and, with a torrent of abuse, brought his officers to their senses and waved them back to the fort."*

The 4th Battalion's effective digging was carried out on the instructions of the Divisional Commander, who had told the Commanding Officer to take up a position on the south side of the village. He wished the Battalion to stand in

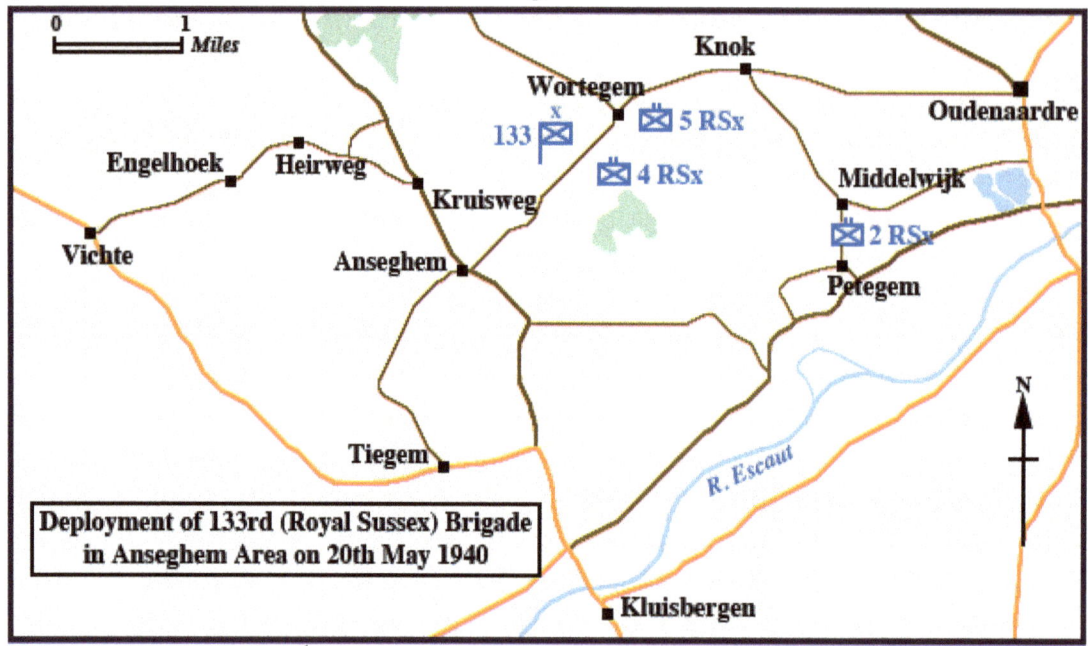

Deployment of 133rd (Royal Sussex) Brigade in Anseghem Area on 20th May 1940

reserve behind the 2nd Battalion, which was then forward on the River Escaut. Heavy shelling made deployment difficult, but the Battalion was in position by dark, save for C Company, which having vacated the landing ground after it had been destroyed, were then placed in control of refugees at Courtrai. However, on the 22nd, an attack developed on the Battalion's front and the shelling of the lines became heavier. The 2nd Royal Sussex had been withdrawn through the 4th Battalion, while troops from other forward positions, mainly from the Queens and Royal West Kents, had also begun to make their way back but these were organised into platoons under their own officers, and remained in position with the 4th Battalion. The attack continued all day and eventually, the enemy penetrated into a wood that lay on the left flank between the 4th and 5th Battalions. By this time there was little or nothing between the 4th Battalion and the enemy, and both flanks had gone; at 4 pm, Brigadier Whitty ordered a withdrawal behind the Lys at Courtrai.

The withdrawal was duly carried out at 10 pm, with the evacuation of the position being covered by the Carrier Platoon and a machine-gun company of the 1/8th Middlesex. The 4th Battalion made the long march by night and, at dawn, found Courtrai a city of the dead – shops with shattered windows, broken wires trailing over pavements – and only their own feet waking the echoes. The Belgians were in position covering the river; the last bridges were being demolished as the Battalion moved in. A small party of British troops had been cut off beyond the river and were rescued by Lance-Corporal Dench; he swam across to the enemy's side several times, and was afterwards Mentioned-in-Dispatches.

As C Company had rejoined at Courtrai, the 4th Battalion was now complete once more. That night, while quantities of British transport were coming

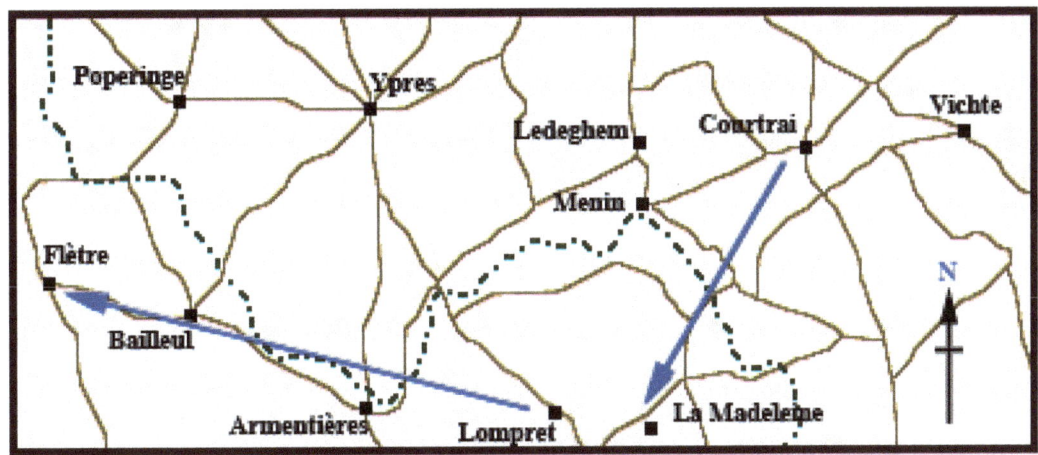

4th Battalion's Withdrawal Route to Flêtre

through, they marched via Menin to Gheluwe, embussed, and at 2.30 in the morning of the 24th arrived at Fort de Lompret. From there, the Battalion then marched ten miles to the Lille suburb of La Madeleine, the tall figure of the Commanding Officer at its head.

They were not allowed to remain long in Lille; indeed, they moved off at 9 am without a pause for breakfast, and finally, after debussing outside Flêtre at two o'clock in the morning of the 25th, marched to a defensive position at the neighbouring village of Caestre. Here the Battalion took up a line facing westwards – it will be remembered that the Germans were swinging round and coming in from that side – with the 5th Battalion coming up on its left. The 4th Battalion prepared to stand its ground, setting to work once more on defences. One battery of 65 Field Regiment RA, under command of Capt F.S. Shrimpton was in support, and the Brigade Anti-Tank Platoon and one platoon of medium-machine-guns were under command. Later in the day, four 2-pdr anti-tank guns came to the village under Major Christopher RA, and subsequently

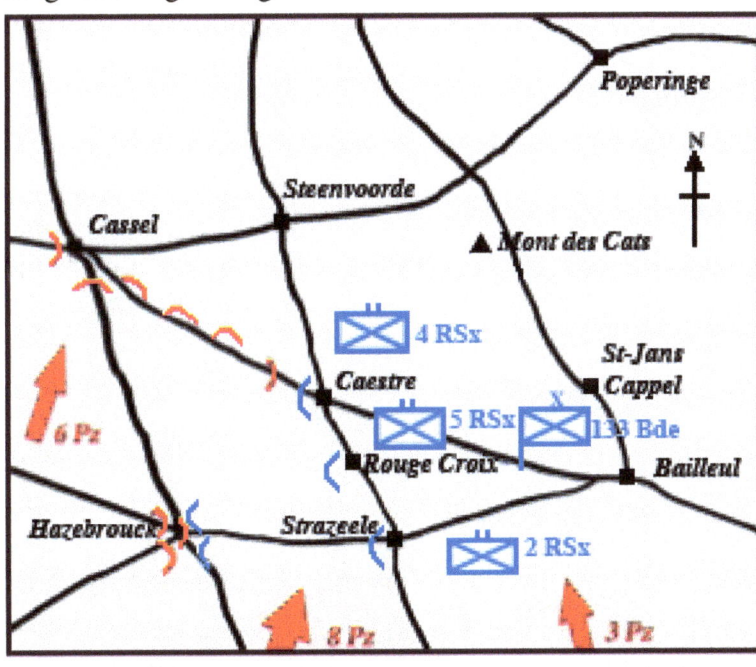

133rd Brigade – General Situation Around Caestre on 27th and 28th May 1940

took part in the defence. Little was known of our own troops and very much less of the enemy. Cassel was on the right and Hazebrouck on the left front, the latter burning hard and being bombed frequently.

German panzer formations opened heavy fire on the position, and Hadley, then a platoon commander, tells how he was ordered to pick a fighting patrol of ten men and report to Battalion Headquarters:

> *"I found the CO standing in the middle of the street, with a positive hail of explosives coming down all around us. Don and I, in common with others standing by, made no secret of our distaste for this sort of thing, and crouched down unashamedly at the side of the road at the whistle of every approaching missile; but the CO merely stood there with his hands in his pockets, laughing at us, for all the world as if he was in the Royal Enclosure at Ascot."*

The shelling developed in intensity, but the troops had dug themselves in and casualties were light. It was about noon on 27th May that twenty German tanks, both light and medium, were reported to be approaching. The men withstood the attack in splendid style, while the Brigade Anti-Tank Platoon, led by 2nd/Lieutenant E.P.R. Jourdain, destroyed several tanks. C Company, commanded by Captain J.S. Magrath, and the left flank of B Company bore the weight of the attack, and, supported by the 65th Field Regiment RA, this small 'pocket of resistance' forced the enemy to withdraw, leaving eight tanks on the field, with their surviving crews as prisoners. The sight of these panzers lying disabled in front of their positions gave the 4th Battalion a unique tonic[12] and would spare them from further armoured attack. Both Captain Magrath and 2nd/Lieutenant Jourdain were each subsequently awarded the Military Cross for their leadership and gallantry in this action.

Sixty or seventy German 'planes dived and circled round the village that evening but, strangely enough, dropped no bombs. In the meantime, the Battalion began preparing for more tank attacks with bottles full of petrol, with men posted in the upper floors of buildings in order to discharge them more effectively.

The 28th of May was a day of shelling, which severely limited traffic movements, so that Lieutenant & Quartermaster Angell had to provide rations from 'local purchase'. At one period, six French medium tanks that appeared on the scene, were placed under the command of the Battalion, and moved forward a short way on to the previous day's battlefield. They did not linger, however, and at ten o'clock that night, Brigade orders arrived for the Battalion to withdraw from Caestre, which the Germans had now decided to by-pass, and it moved back ten miles through Flêtre to Mont des Cats. All transport was

---

[12] *Destination Dunkirk*. Gregory Blaxland, The Military Book Society, London 1973.

accordingly rendered unserviceable, except two vehicles per company. The Battalion reached the Mont at dawn, picking up a solitary prisoner on the way.

The men were very tired but still full of fight. It was now known that the Belgians had given in, and the blaze of fires, near and far, indicated the magnitude of the disaster in which they were involved. It was, therefore, not surprising that most units gathered at the Mont des Cats were both weak and disorganised, but the 4th Royal Sussex, the last to leave at 11 am, after holding the southwest approach and suffering from much shelling and low flying bombing attacks, came out steadily. The Battalion's orders were to move to an Assembly Area west of Poperinghe, in formation if possible but – if not – to make independently for Dunkirk.

The 4th Battalion experienced a variety of adventures in this process. D Company withdrew round the southeast corner of the hill, did not pass the Start Point, and reached Dunkirk in two parties. On the way to the Assembly Area, the road was shelled and dive-bombed, and A and C Companies, moving independently across country, missed the Assembly Area through having no maps, with A Company rejoining the Battalion on the beaches. From the assembly area, the route followed was Proven – Roesbrugge – Hondeschoote – Bray Dunes. C Company encountered blown bridges and had to cross a flooded countryside by improvised rafts; on reaching the beaches, it was retained for guard duties by Divisional Headquarters. The remainder of the 4th Battalion were some of the last troops to reach Bray Dunes. Altogether, after leaving Mont des Cats at eleven in the morning of 29th May, the Battalion marched all day and all the next night, arriving at Bray Dunes on the morning of the 30th. It embarked during the day and evening, either from Dunkirk Mole or the beaches, except for 300 men under Major Nix, who did not embark until dawn on the 31st of May. Hadley describes how, with half of B Company, he fell in with the 5th Battalion near Roesbrugge-Haringhe, and marched with them to the coast.

The detachments of the Battalion disembarked in England on 1st June and having been processed, were despatched to various collecting centres. It started to reform at the Infantry Training Centre Camp at Oxford on the 5th of June. A Battalion Return made on 20th June 1940 showed that the 4th Battalion suffered the following casualties during the campaign:

	Killed	**Wounded**	**Missing**	**Total**
Officers	2	5	3	10
Men	19	49 (a)	31 (b)	99
Total	**21**	**54**	**34**	**109**

Notes: (a) 18 of the known wounded, were also missing.
(b) 3 of the missing were believed to have been killed.

Sir John Smyth[13] makes an interesting and most pertinent comment in his book *Bolo Whistler*[14] about the evacuation from Dunkirk:

> "And so ended a very great adventure for the 4th (Territorial) Bn of the Royal Sussex regiment. The CO, Bolo Whistler, who won a well-deserved DSO for his leadership, not satisfied with the numbers of his battalion which had been evacuated, went back, like Oliver Twist, to seek for more: and like Oliver Twist, didn't receive great encouragement. But it was a very gallant and characteristic gesture. Secrecy hung over this Bolo operation and the story was never published; but among those who knew, 'The Man who went Back to Dunkirk' became part of the Bolo legend. It is curious however that Bolo's official record of service shows him as having returned to the UK from the BEF in France, not on May 30th, 1940, with his battalion, but two days later, on June 1st, with a battalion of the Manchester Regiment. It was on that day that the 42nd East Lancashire Division left Dunkirk: and Bolo may well have known that a whole company (D Coy) of his regiment was missing.
>
> Brigadier Ashworth, later Colonel of the Royal Sussex Regiment, and Bolo's Adjutant in 1940, who considered him 'a born leader and a wonderful commander to work with', is convinced that Bolo went back to Dunkirk on the same destroyer that brought him over and had a good look round the beaches at Bray to see if he could pick up any of his missing men before he finally returned to the UK. So it may not have been merely a legend after all."

Bolo Whistler's return to Dunkirk was also corroborated by Brigadier J.J. McCully DSO who subsequently commanded the 5th (Cinque Ports) Battalion, and later the 4th/5th (Cinque Ports) Battalion after the amalgamation of the two Territorial Battalions on 1st January 1943, following the Battle of El Alamein.

The 5th Royal Sussex had shared with the 4th Battalion in the operations round Caestre when it became a 'pocket of resistance', and were also evacuated from the beaches. They too had suffered the same discouraging experience of being shelled accurately by means of unopposed air observation, which made communications extremely difficult. The Germans overran part of the Battalion's position but C Company stood firm, and the enemy's advantage was not exploited. There was the same general feeling of bewilderment about the campaign, since information as to what was going on was so meagre. The men fought well in the subsequent retreat to Courtrai, though they suffered more casualties than the 4th Battalion, and twelve vehicles were destroyed.

---

[13] Brigadier Sir John George Smyth, 1st Baronet, VC MC PC was a British Indian Army officer and Conservative Member of Parliament. Although a recipient of the Victoria Cross, his army career ended in controversy, although the unjustified findings against him were later rectified.

[14] *Bolo Whistler: The Life of General Sir Lashmer Whistler; a study in leadership.* John Smyth, 1967

On the 20th May, the 5th Battalion had moved up to the front line on the high ground overlooking the River Escaut, and there had to dig trenches on the forward slope in full view of the enemy. The whole area was constantly under accurate shellfire, with Battalion Headquarters at Wortegem being hit six times. The situation was obscure and little information reached the Battalion; an expected attack by the enemy at dawn on the 22nd May was forewarned but never materialised.

During the afternoon, orders were received that the Division would withdraw through Courtrai and that all units would be over the River Lys by 7 pm on the 23rd, when the bridges would be blown. Before the withdrawal, enemy infantry overran some forward posts but they did not exploit their success. By the

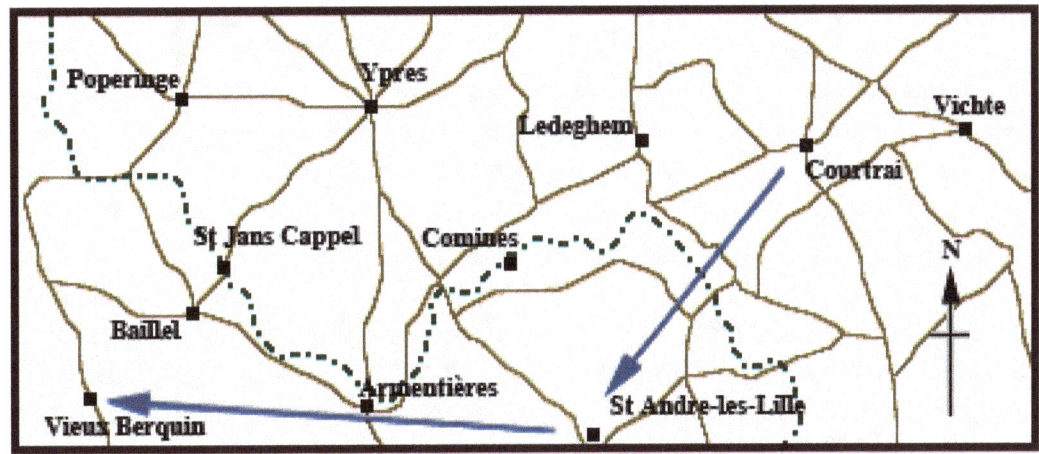

5th Battalion's Withdrawal Route to the Strazeele Area

morning of the 24th, the Battalion was resting in an empty hospital for incurables at St André near Lille, and so far, had suffered 160 casualties. That night the Battalion was ordered to march to Croix du Bac and come under command of the 132nd Brigade, although the order was later cancelled and they were required to return to St André. Nevertheless, the following morning they proceeded once more to march to Croix du Bac, and from there the Battalion marched to Vieux Berguin, near the Forest of Nieppe, whereupon they reverted to command of the 133rd Brigade; similar to the 2nd Battalion, there was sometimes confusion as to which Brigade was commanding the 5th Battalion. At midday on the 27th, orders were received to move at once to Strazeele, where the 5th Battalion was to reinforce the 4th Battalion in its battle against enemy tanks at Caestre. Major Alex Grant, the Battalion Second-in-Command, who went forward to select positions, left a vivid account of the battle that followed:

> *"D was the leading Company and was ordered to move straight through the village to Caestre to assist the 4th Battalion, but they had already moved into their defensive positions on the north side, so A Company was sent down the road instead, to be followed by B, C and D Companies. As the head of A Company cleared the village, enemy tanks were observed advancing from the west, distant about 800 yards. A*

Company were unaware of this as the hedge was thick on the roadside. The Brigade anti-tank platoon had only one gun but it came into action and destroyed at least one tank. Two Artillery two-pounder anti-tank guns, which were in the village, came into action on the road where one was hit. By now eight tanks were moving round the north side of the village and four more round the south side.

The Battalion in the village occupied houses and, with a machine-gun platoon of the 8th Battalion The Middlesex Regiment, engaged the tanks with Bren gun and rifle fire. By now, however, A Company was 500 yards from the village. The leading platoon took cover in some houses but the rest were obliged to take shelter in the roadside ditches. The tanks burst through the hedges and, straddling the long straight ditches, opened up with machine-gun fire which killed or wounded 67 of A and D Companies. The tanks also shot up some lorries and trucks on the Clyte Hill road. The tanks were supported by armoured field guns and mortars. This action started about 1300 hours, and about 1530 hours the tanks withdrew to a position about 2,000 yards back, leaving the village in our possession."

The 5th Battalion's front then lay between Caestre and Rouge Croix; C Company was on the left in Rouge Croix, B Company in the centre and D Company on the right, trying to keep touch with the 4th Battalion in Caestre, while A Company occupied a position in reserve between B and D Companies. The Battalion had had little artillery support, no proper anti-tank guns, and only three Bren guns per company. No reserves lay behind them, and rations were short. Major Grant recalls that a few biscuits and two eggs were all he had for three days. He considers that the stand made at this point contributed in no small degree to the evacuation of hundreds of troops already waiting on the beaches. The Carrier Platoon, under 2nd/Lieutenant Austin, was dug in on a forward slope on a front of a quarter of a mile. An artillery forward observation post was spotting from this position and by dusk at least eight enemy tanks had been put out of action.

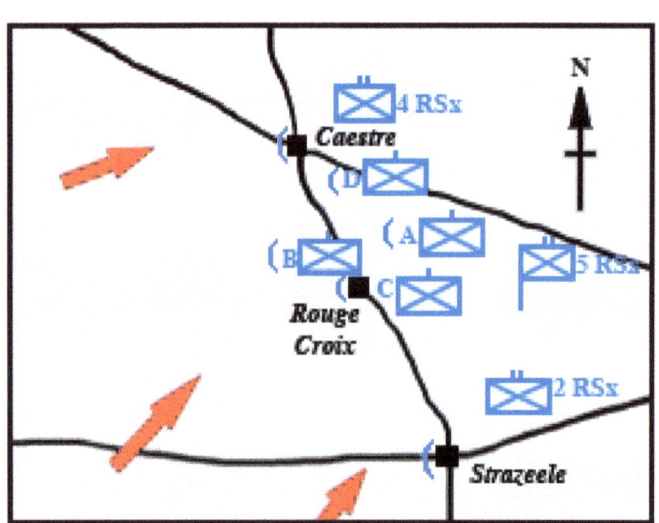

5th Battalion's Deployment in the Caestre and Rouge Croix Area on 28th May 1940

Throughout the morning of the 28th of May the Germans increased their shellfire, especially during the early afternoon when their infantry launched an attack in heavy rain against the 4th and 5th Battalions. At first, the 4th Battalion was more heavily pressed, but later DF(SOS)[15] signals went up all along the line of the 5th Battalion. The rain gave place to low-lying mist, and some of the forward positions on the right were overrun, and so B Company, with some of D Company, were pulled back. C Company at Rouge Croix was completely overwhelmed but the Carrier Platoon made a most effective counter-attack and rescued many of the Company who had been captured, and drove the enemy from the position, thus allowing the Company to reoccupy its former positions. 2nd/Lieutenant Austin was subsequently awarded the Military Cross for this gallant counter-attack with the Carrier Platoon; only himself and one of his drivers remained, all others being killed or wounded, but by their magnificent efforts, the line of the Strazeele-Caestre road was kept intact.

Other counter-attacks were also mounted as mentioned in Major Grant's diary:

> *"Later the enemy attack was resumed in greater strength and by dusk most of the roadway to the crossroads south of Rouge Croix had been lost. It must be understood that the Companies had no depth. The forward positions were on one side of the road facing west and the supports on the other, the road being on a small ridge with the ground falling away slightly to each side. Furthermore there was nothing behind them for miles except a very weak A Company. Battalion and Brigade HQ were some 500 yards back. At about 2100 hours Brigadier Whitty put in a counter-attack consisting of one platoon of Buffs, some Queen's, a rifle platoon of 8th Middlesex and the Brigade platoon of cooks, runners, batmen, etc, on to the Rouge Croix position which restored the situation for a while, although by nightfall some of the houses were occupied by Germans and some by our men."*

Orders were soon received from HQ 133rd Brigade to withdraw to Mont des Cats, which towering in the midst of the plain and crowned by a monastery, had been a familiar landmark to many veterans of the Great War. When the 5th Battalion arrived there at about 8 am on the 29th May, the whole hill was crowded by troops with their guns and transport. The Battalion dug in and occupied a forward defensive line from which they could see the enemy guns taking up positions in the distance. These guns began to register an hour later. At 10 am, a low bombing attack by some twenty Stukas caused heavy casualties among the transport. Then came orders to destroy all transport and withdraw towards Dunkirk, starting at 10.30 am.

Enemy shellfire was rapidly increasing when elements of HQ Company set off on the main road to the coast. Because all roads were under air attack, parties of some twenty to thirty men, each under an officer, were told to make their way independently to the coast. The 5th Battalion, with the 4th behind them, marched through Proven and Roesbrugge where, during a halt that evening, Brigadier Whitty and the Brigade Major (Marshall) joined them. Gun and

---

[15] The call for immediate defensive artillery fire on pre-recorded priority targets.

machine-gun fire was heard on each flank and the bridges were blown at about 8.30 pm. The final progress of the Battalion's withdrawal to Dunkirk during the 30th of May is best described from the words of Major Grant:

> "The march was continued throughout the night past blazing parks of cars and stores, each bridge with its defence and demolition party standing by until, on passing over the last bridge, the long straight causeways to the beach were reached. The low land on each side of these roads had been flooded and the roads themselves were one solid mass of vehicles and guns. It was with the greatest difficulty that the infantry could squeeze through and units became even more separated.

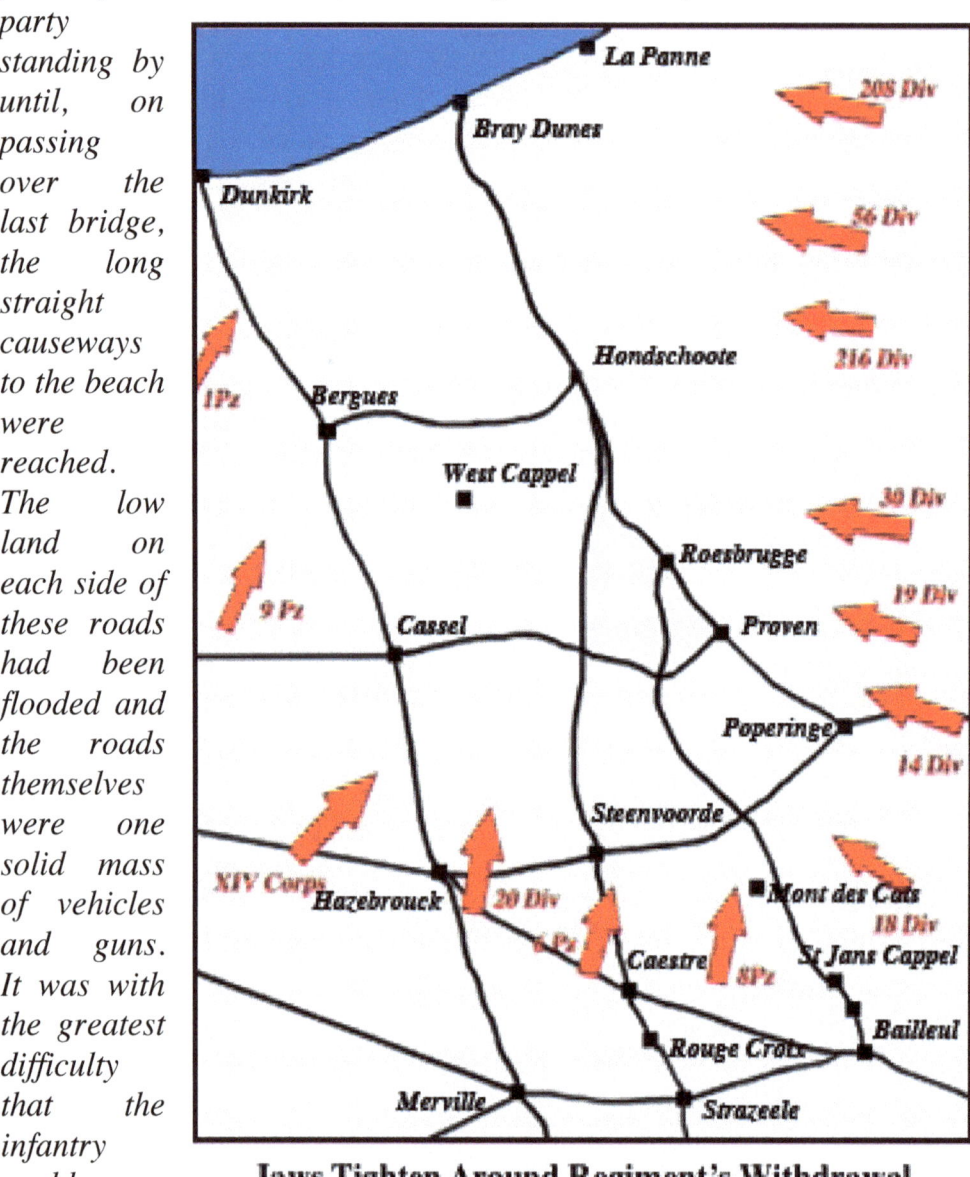

Jaws Tighten Around Regiment's Withdrawal Routes to Bray Dunes

> However, on reaching the beaches, the Military Police were able to direct men to the rendezvous of their unit near a large hospital at Bray Dunes. Here eventually eight officers and some 130 men of the Battalion were assembled. Trenches were dug in the sand, but fortunately a low-lying cloudy sky prevented any interference by aircraft. The Embarkation Officer allotted two parties to the Battalion

> *at different times; each party duly paraded on the beach and embarked in small boats, canvas skiffs, etc, and rowed out to the ships."*

Major Grant was left in charge of the rear party which sailed at 7.30 pm in the *Golden Eagle* and reached England without further incident. On arrival in England on 1st June, the Battalion was scattered in various camps throughout the country but began to reform at Reservoir Camp in Gloucestershire on the 5th of June. Some 12 officers and 500 men had eventually got back to England, but during the fighting in France and Belgium, the 5th Battalion had suffered approximately 354 casualties. Towards the end, it had been almost impossible to get all the wounded back to the coast and many had to be left in houses in the care of the inhabitants. All the missing officers and many of the men, some of whom were wounded, eventually turned up after the war.

To which of these two Battalions, C.R. Mepham of the Royal Corps of Signals, was attached is difficult to say. His account[16] fits in with much of Hadley's but he also describes digging pits in the sand, then pushing and pulling boats along while up to the waist in water, and finally rowing out to a troopship, where men were packed beneath the deck, scarcely able to turn round. Since Hadley mentions Ramsgate as the port of arrival, and Mepham landed at Sheerness, it is possible that the latter was with the 5th Battalion.

All in all, the Dunkirk campaign was a harrowing experience for the Royal Sussex Brigade. While constantly on the move with hardly time to draw breath, and faced with frequent changes in the situation, it speaks well for the spirit of the three Battalions that when called upon to face the enemy, they gave such a good account of themselves. The Brigade in France and Belgium had lost much, but possibly even more had been gained. The experience, if bitter, had been valuable. The virtual loss of the splendid 2nd Battalion meant a great task of reconstitution; nevertheless, at the same time there had been built up the tradition of the 133rd Brigade, composed of Royal Sussex Battalions, which had yet to play a decisive part in the turning of defeat into victory. Furthermore, throughout the campaign and especially at Caestre and afterwards, the example set by the Brigade Commander was a great strength to all those who came in contact with him.

The dominant figure in this part of the Regiment's adventure was assuredly *Bolo* Whistler. He had kept a firm control of his 4th Battalion throughout, and it was doubtless his outstanding skill at the defence of Caestre that gained him his first Distinguished Service Order.

The 6th and 7th Battalions in France 1940

Meanwhile the 6th and 7th Battalions had been doing things elsewhere. Both Battalions had gone to France in April 1940, principally deployed on the

---
[16] *From Belgium to Dunkirk*. C.R. Mepham (Stockwell), 1944.

defence of the lines of communication.

The 7th Battalion, commanded by Lieutenant Colonel R. Gethen MC, largely untrained and poorly equipped, was to hold up the highly organised, well trained and motorised spearhead of the swiftly advancing German Army for a critical period of time. Besides being brief and almost suicidal, it nevertheless exercised a general effect out of all proportion to the numbers of men standing in the path of the victorious Germans. It took place at St Roche Station, west of Amiens, from the 18th to the 20th May.

The 7th Battalion was formed in late-1939 and was based at Dyke Road Barracks in Brighton. The strength of the Battalion in about March 1940 was 376 all ranks and it moved to France in April 1940. The Advanced Party departed on 6th April 1940, embarking at Southampton on the *SS Clan MacAlister* on 8th April, and arriving at Le Havre on the following day. The Main Body left Brighton on 18th-19th April, embarking at Southampton on the *SS Ben-my-Cree* on 21st April, and arrived at Le Havre the next day. The strength of the Battalion on 28th April had risen to some 620 all ranks, having received a further 131 reinforcements, found mostly from The Dorsetshire Regiment and The Duke of Cornwall's Light Infantry. On the 7th Battalion's arrival in France, A Company was detached to guard the ammunition dump at Argueil, while the rest of the Battalion went on to camp at Rosay, some 25 miles northeast of Rouen.

Both the 6th and 7th Battalions, as part of the 37th Brigade, were then ordered forward to the Amiens area to help stem the advance of Hitler's invading Armies - their Brigade Headquarters remained with the main Divisional elements, while the Brigade's third battalion, the 2nd/6th East Surreys, was detached on duty elsewhere. Two trains were diverted to transport the Royal Sussex Battalions; the first contained the 7th Battalion and the 263rd Field Company RE, while the 6th Battalion moved in the second train with the 264th Field Company RE.

Early on 17th May, after A Company had come back under command, the 7th Battalion boarded a train for Abbeville, although this was subsequently redirected to Lens, and then to Amiens. About 3 pm on Saturday 18th May, as the warm sun was shining through breaks in the clouds, the 7th Battalion's train braked for a signal check near to Amiens St Roche Station. Lunch was being prepared in the rear wagons and some men got down from the train and passed the time picking flowers at the trackside. As the signal cleared and the train started to move, they jumped back on, still clutching the flowers they had gathered, with no idea of the destruction which was about to come upon them.

As the train moved into the station yard, enemy planes appeared from between the clouds and dive-bombed the train, destroying the locomotive and the officers' coach with the first salvo. As the bombing and strafing continued, the men took cover wherever they could, including beneath the wagons of a nearby ammunition train. As a result of this bombardment, many were either killed or wounded. Although the exact numbers are not clear, the Battalion appears to have suffered some 60 to 80 casualties, of which some 25 were killed; a newspaper article in 1940 suggested that the Battalion might have suffered about 100 casualties.

Following the attack, the 7th Battalion had detrained and reorganised in a wood some 700 yards away, near Ailly-sur-Noye, while a French ambulance helped to remove the wounded. Among these was the Adjutant, Captain John McCully, who was evacuated to England; a very fortunate circumstance for he was an able officer and subsequently went on to command, with great distinction, the 5th Battalion in North Africa, and following the Battle of El Alamein, to command the combined 4th/5th Battalion. Meanwhile, the 7th Battalion remained in the wood throughout that night and next morning, Colonel Gethen, after seeing that they had 'cleaned up' and breakfasted, went into Amiens, where he learnt that no more trains were available. In effect, the 7th Royal Sussex, as well as the 6th Royal Sussex, were not only both cut off from their Brigade Headquarters but also from each other.

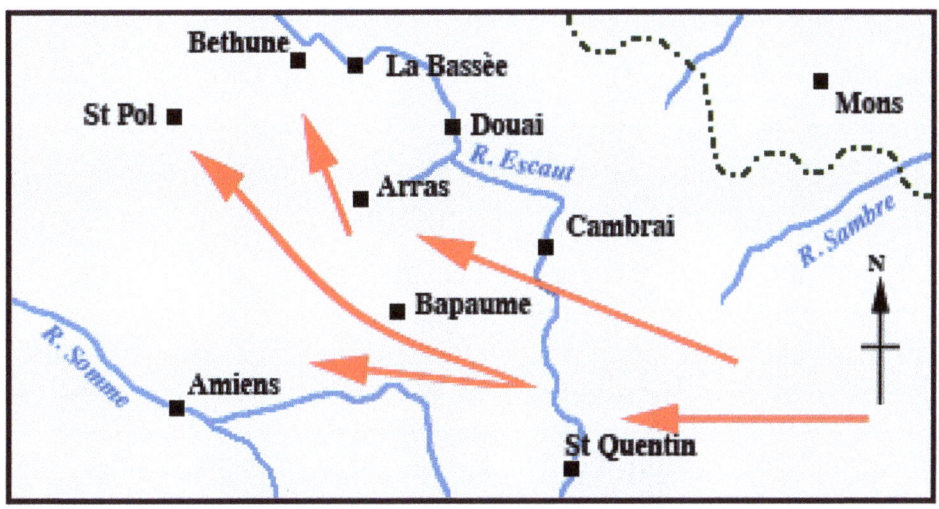

German Advance to the Sea

Major James Cassels MC, the Second-in-Command, had been advised that it was intended to move the Battalion out of the wood and, during the Commanding Officer's absence, he reconnoitred some high ground on the Amiens-Poix road. Meanwhile, Captain Brook, a GSO 3 (Grade 3 General Staff Officer), had visited the Battalion but left no instructions. When Colonel Gethen returned at 10 o'clock, the Battalion began moving by platoons to the high ground, marching via the station and the Great War Memorial, up the Amiens-Poix road to Chateau Blanc. A principal purpose of the move was to provide dispersal against possible bombing attacks – a timely decision, since the wood was heavily bombed at noon - and the bombing continued for two hours, being directed as well at trains containing reinforcements and refugees. The latter were also arriving by road, pouring down in such numbers that it was decided to erect a roadblock against the general stampede of people. Colonel Gethen also stopped a French tank and persuaded it to remain.

Early next morning, the Battalion positions were re-adjusted to meet the air attack. The Commanding Officer moved A Company again to a position north of the Amiens-Poix road, and forward of B Company, which was astride the road. Lieutenant Jackson, who had taken over A Company after Captain Fallowfield Cooper had been wounded, organised shaving and washing at a farm in front of his area, and chose a site for the cookhouse. Meanwhile, Colonel Gethen had been in touch with the French Commandant at Amiens; being in a 'French Zone' he judged that his Battalion now came under French command. However, the French Commandant had no orders to give, and contented himself with introducing two staff officers who had arrived from Sedan during the night. They glibly assured Gethen that the gap had been closed, and isolated units that had broken through, had been cleared up; *"there were no Germans between us and Sedan"*, they said.

The bombing of Amiens began soon afterwards, and by noon on the 20th the Germans were in the town. Jackson, who had learnt this from a reconnaissance patrol he sent out, comments drily: *"fast moving from Sedan to Amiens overnight"*![17]

The 7th Battalion prepared as well as they could for the uneven battle; still without orders, equipped with only rifles, with 50 rounds per man, two to three Bren light-machine-guns, and two 2-inch mortars equipped with smoke bombs only, it found itself facing a German Panzer Division.

In the early afternoon, the enemy became active on A Company's front. Machine-guns opened up, three tanks appeared 300 yards away, and artillery, mortars and small arms caused several casualties. Somehow, the Company had managed to put one of the enemy tanks out of action and this made the Germans very cautious, and they made little attempt to advance on the position. Colonel Gethen had sought to relieve the situation by advancing HQ Company, B Company and 'train details', relying on D Company to conform from the right flank. These efforts seem to have been unavailing, for Lieutenant Jackson, who had suffered four flesh wounds, emphasises that he saw nothing of any other company, except for a lorry-load of D Company men, following a track that run diagonally across the front and being fired on by both sides, until it caught fire. He feared that none of the occupants could have survived.

All through that afternoon, the Germans pounded the British positions, advancing only very slowly, in the apparent belief that they were dealing with a highly trained and fully equipped force. This misconception, once created, was certainly effective in slowing the Germans advance but the cost, in terms of lives lost and injuries suffered by the Battalion, was colossal. At four o'clock the battle developed, and continued for an hour, when the German tanks advanced and overcame HQ and B Companies. A Company held out for five hours until after 6 o'clock, and it was not until late that night that the Germans could feel that all resistance was at an end. Lieutenant Jackson was subsequently awarded the Military Cross for conspicuous bravery in an isolated

---

[17] It is 120 miles from Sedan to Amiens.

position.

In the evening, and appreciating that they had run out of any realistic options, the Commanding Officer told the remnants of the 7th Battalion to withdraw and, at 7.15 pm, gave the order for those left to surrender.

Lieutenant Jackson relates that a German officer met him with courtesy, said that the Battalion had made a heroic stand, and offered to send him to hospital in his car. He declined and marched in to Amiens with the remains of A Company but was dizzy from the loss of blood by the time they arrived. Whilst in captivity, he met Regimental Sergeant-Major Eames, who told him of the death of that rare character, Major James Cassels. According to his account, when the Germans overran Battalion Headquarters and called upon James Cassels to surrender, he remained seated and did not raise his hands. He was promptly shot dead.

Over the course of the three days (18th-20th May), 131 men of the 7th Battalion lost their lives and many others were wounded, of which a number subsequently died of their wounds. Of the 165 who were taken prisoner, a further 5 died in captivity. Although a good number of men escaped the battlefield and got back to England, to all intents and purposes, the Battalion was destroyed at Amiens. Of those who escaped, the majority made for Rouen, then on to Blain, near Nantes, and thence to Cherbourg. On or about 7th June, what was left of the 7th Battalion, having collected as many stragglers as possible, embarked at Cherbourg for Southampton on board *HMS Duke of York*. There remains the academic but debated question of whether the Battalion should have 'stayed put' as it did, or made for some other point. Colonel Gethen, who was also taken prisoner, had summed up the situation to his company commanders on the 19th of May, in these words:

> *"Our original orders were to proceed to Lens. That is impossible. We have no orders to go back – therefore we stay where we are."*

And stay they did, facing the full weight of a German Panzer Division, and perhaps the verdict on that action may be left finally to the enemy. Ober-Leutnant Richter, interviewed by Lieutenant Colonel Gethen and Captain G.H. Cook, at whose *Oflag* he later chanced to take the parade, told them that he had been with General Rommel's Panzer Division in France, and remembered very clearly the opposition encountered from a small force of British troops near Amiens on 20th May 1940. He said that the Panzer Division had travelled 70 kilometres since dawn on that day, and this was the first serious opposition they had met. He spoke highly of the gallantry shown by this small force, and admitted that, in consequence of the action, his Division had been unable to proceed until daylight on 21st May.

General Rommel had been in command, and it was to him that Colonel Gethen had been handed over as a prisoner. This was not the last time that Rommel was destined to encounter that Sussex obstinacy epitomised by the words, *"we won't be druv"*. On a subsequent occasion it was to exercise a decisive influence on his career.

The Royal Sussex Regiment was awarded the unique Battle Honour of *Amiens 1940* for the 7th Battalion's heroic defence and sacrifice in this action.

Of particular note are the exploits of Lance-Sergeant Archibald Tilling of the 7th Battalion. On the morning of the 20th May, as the Germans increased their attack, he was hit in the thigh but continued for some time to fire on a machine-gun post. He eventually crawled to a temporary Field Dressing Station (FDS) but an hour or so later, they were surrounded by German tanks and were forced to surrender. While most of the prisoners – the walking-wounded - were removed under escort, four of the wounded were left under armed guard at the FDS. That night, Tilling, who was determined to escape, eluded the guard, crawled down the road in the ditch and eventually found an abandoned bicycle, upon which he free-wheeled for about two miles into the next village. He was taken later to a French hospital, and through the machinations of the French networks, eventually arrived in Marseille, having had the bullet in his thigh removed *en route*, and there he came under the care of the American Consul. The US system then declared him to be a Polish citizen, and allocated him a Polish passport and visas to Portugal and Spain. Although this fell through, various negotiations with somewhat suspect characters, which in turn never materialised, he finally walked over the Pyrenees into Spain, where he was then arrested. After various deliberations and negotiations, he was then sent to Gibraltar *via* Madrid in December 1940, and from where he was evacuated to England. Lance-Sergeant Tilling, quite deservedly, was subsequently awarded a Distinguished Conduct Medal for distinguished services in the field.

On their return to England, the remnants of the 7th Battalion did not continue for long as an infantry battalion but, in due course, were converted into gunners as the 109th Light Anti-Aircraft Regiment, Royal Artillery (TA), and their Headquarters was once again at Brighton. As gunners, they returned to France on D Day+4.

The last Royal Sussex Battalion to leave France in 1940 was the 6th Battalion. Mobilized at Horsham under Lieutenant Colonel Keith Wannop, it went overseas on 20th April. On the 18th of May, the Battalion left its camp at Abancourt, 20 miles west of Amiens: *"nice white tents in an open field 200 yards from a main railway line,"* records Major Richard Tolston, and entrained an hour before the camp was bombed. Like the 7th Battalion, with whom they were brigaded, they were supposed to be making for Lens. Brigadier R. Wyatt, a former 4th Royal Sussex officer, commanded the Brigade; *"a most reasonable man and commander,"* says the chronicler, *"in every way, except that he insisted the military term 'outposts' should be 'posts-out'."*

The 6th Battalion, similarly poorly equipped and insufficiently trained, was originally being entrained to move forward ahead of the 7th Battalion but a loading delay on the train caused the 7th Battalion's train to pass them and go on ahead. The 6th Battalion, therefore, found themselves held up outside Amiens while the 7th Battalion's train was being bombed. The 6th eventually got through Amiens but stopped at Ailly and took up a defensive position in the nearby woods. At this time, while the 7th Battalion was fighting its famous action with Rommel's Panzers, communications were interrupted, and the general situation was unknown.

After two days of uncertainty, Colonel Wannop commandeered a train and the Intelligence Officer, the then Lieutenant Tolston, found a French engine driver, although the latter did not stay long. Because of this, Lieutenant Tolston, who had attended a one-day locomotive course, took over the train and it went southwards to within a few kilometres of Paris, and subsequently, past Chartres into Brittany; Lieutenant Tolston noted at the time, *"I drove a train here – the men hated it."* The Battalion then detrained and marched until it came to Blain, where the Labour Corps was preparing the Base Ammunition Depot for destruction. On the day before the French signed the Armistice, the Battalion received orders to be ready to move to St Nazaire, and on the actual day it marched off, the men were fortified by packets of cigarettes, flung to them by NAAFI employees in passing trucks! At noon in St Nazaire the Battalion heard of the surrender, and were told that the Germans were at Le Mans.

A member of the 6th Battalion, Private Cecil Davis would later recall:

> *"While we were queuing to get harbour-side, the Luftwaffe were making bombing runs. The German ground forces were no more than an hour away. We were crouched along the streets, keeping tight against the buildings so enemy aircraft couldn't see where we were. Our company was in the rear and we were keeping a sharp lookout for any advanced German units.*
>
> *There was a swing-bridge we had to cross to get to the SS City of Mobile, which was waiting to take us out. But the French, who had by now capitulated, wouldn't let us set foot on the bridge, and blocked our way. The Germans had sent an order that any French caught assisting the British would be in for it, so they weren't going to help. We couldn't believe it – these were our allies!*
>
> *Our company commander had a row with the French and he said to us: "Come on lads, get across bridge!" We made a rush and swept the French aside, belting along the bridge and clambering aboard the Mobile, the last ship left to take us to freedom. The Germans arrived at the bridge just as we got to the other side. We were that close to being nabbed.*
>
> *There were 90 of us crammed on the deck, and I was a Bren gunner for light aircraft defence on the stern of the ship. We were dive-bombed by Stukas who dropped bombs on us but we saw them off with small-arms fire.*

> *To leave St-Nazaire, the Mobile had to go out stern first, towed by a French tugboat. The idea was they'd swing us round in the river to point us downstream and out to sea. When we were broadside across the river, two French sailors from the tugboat chopped the tow rope, casting us adrift. Cast aside by our so-called friends!*
>
> *The ship slewed round a hit a sandbank. Luckily it swung itself about and away we went. But when our ship hit the sandbank, it got a 12 ft split in the hull. We had to use half our power to pump the water out and the other half to propel our ship along, and we limped back to Plymouth. We arrived back two weeks after the Dunkirk evacuation, about the last ship out of France. But at least we were home."*

The 6th Battalion got away on 18th June, just before the enemy arrived in strength, and landed in England, hungry but otherwise unharmed. The 6th Battalion did not go overseas again as a battalion, although many men from the 6th went overseas as Drafts to the Regiment's other Battalions.

With France under the Nazi heel, the defences of Britain were manned against seemingly inevitable invasion. The various Battalion moves are too many and involved to give in detail, but Captain Langham remarks at one point: *"we were jolly thin on the ground, I can tell you."* The 2nd Battalion, in course of renaissance, was at Rye, the 4th at Hastings, and the 5th, appropriately enough in Langham's view, at Bexhill and Normans' Bay.

A grievous loss, at the year's end, was that of Major General Cecil Malden, newly appointed to command the 47th Division, who was killed by a land-mine, while inspecting beach defences. He had served with distinction in the 1st Battalion on the North West Frontier, had been instrumental in maintaining that Battalion's high reputation for efficiency after the Great War, and, subsequently, had held various staff appointments, being Director of Military Training at the War Office from October 1939 until the day before his death. Though regarded by some as a martinet, he had in fact a sympathetic nature, which grew more evident as men learnt to know him better. He had been a hockey-player of international class and the mainstay of the Regimental team.

For its actions in France and Belgium in 1940, The Royal Sussex Regiment was awarded Battle Honours for *Defence of Escaut, Amiens 1940, St Omer-La Bassée, Foret de Nieppe*, and **North-West Europe 1940,** the latter Honour being emblazoned on the Colours. The Battle Honour *Amiens 1940* is unique to the Royal Sussex and no other regiment was awarded it.

Gallantry Awards for France and Belgium 1940

The following awards were made to individuals in The Royal Sussex Regiment for the campaign in France and Belgium in May 1940:

Distinguished Service Order (DSO):

Lieutenant Colonel L.G. Whistler	4th Battalion
Lieutenant Colonel F.R.H. Morgan (Border Regt)	5th Battalion

Military Cross:

Captain C.H. Jackson	7th Battalion
Captain J.S. Magrath	4th Battalion
Captain R.B.de F. Sleeman	2nd Battalion
Lieutenant F.M. Smith RAMC	4th Battalion (attached)
2nd/Lieutenant I.M. Austin	5th Battalion
2nd/Lieutenant J.B. De Manio	7th Battalion
2nd/Lieutenant E.P.R. Jourdain	4th Battalion
2nd/Lieutenant P.H. Rubie	2nd Battalion
2nd/Lieutenant E.C. Sevenoaks	7th Battalion
2nd/Lieutenant P.E.X. Turnball	4th Battalion (GHQ LO)

Distinguished Conduct Medal:

Company-Sergeant-Major W. Connell	4th Battalion
Sergeant D.E. Hollands	7th Battalion
Sergeant A.C. Knapp	5th Battalion
Lance-Sergeant A. Tilling	7th Battalion

Military Medal:

Lance-Corporal R. Binnington	4th Battalion
Private H. Croft	2nd Battalion
Private W.G. Wilson	5th Battalion
Corporal W.H.E. Goodhall	7th Battalion

Croix de Guerre 1940 with Palm

Major P.J.L. Powell and Lance-Bombardier Crossfield of the 7th Battalion were both awarded with the Belgium Croix de Guerre 1940 with Palm for their service in 1940, although they were actually serving with the 109th Light Air Defence Regiment RA when the Honours were awarded in 1945. Major Powell's award was the Chevalier of the Order of Leopold H with Palm.

Mentioned-in-Despatches:

Nineteen officers and twenty men from all the Regiment's Battalions in France and Belgium were Mentioned-in-Despatches.

Seven officers and men of the 7th Battalion were later Mentioned-in-Despatches in November 1945 for their actions at Amiens in 1940. These were gazetted after they had been released from being prisoners-of-war, as to have done so whilst in captivity would have left them open to reprisals from their German guards.

Similarly, RSM J.E Eames of the 7th Battalion was later awarded an MBE (Military) for his actions at Amiens, having escaped with some others on 20th May 1940 but being recaptured twenty-fours later by a German armoured car.

Escapees

Lieutenant R.J. Fuller of the 5th Battalion had been captured in May 1940 and was in a prisoner-of-war camp near Warburg in Germany. With two others they made their escape on 30th August 1942 and hiding by day and walking by night, they eventually crossed the Dutch frontier on 14th September. They were eventually put in touch with an organisation, which arranged for their escape through Belgium and France. Lieutenant Fuller was subsequently awarded the Military Cross for this gallant and distinguished service.

Sergeant S.H. Cooke of the 2nd Battalion was captured at Hazebrouck on 27th May 1940 and was imprisoned in Stalag VIII B (Lamsdorf) in Germany for the whole of his period of captivity. He made five attempts to escape before finally reaching Warsaw in the summer of 1944. He was well cared by the Poles but in August 1944, he decided to join the Russians, who were then advancing in the direction of Warsaw. After long interrogations and imprisonment by the Russians, who needed a great deal of convincing that he was English, Sergeant Cooke was finally handed over to the British in Moscow on 22nd September 1944. He was subsequently awarded the Distinguished Conduct Medal for his action.

THE REFORMATION OF THE 133RD (ROYAL SUSSEX) BRIGADE

On its arrival at Tidworth on 1st June 1940, the strength of the 2nd Battalion was three officers and 225 men but by the 28th of June, through Drafts from various sources, including 100 men from the 4th Battalion, its strength had risen to 22 officers and 917 men. During this period, Lieutenant Colonel Kirkby MC had taken over command of the Battalion. The considerable achievement of rapidly restoring the strengths of battalions had been repeated with the 5th Battalion at Gloucester, which had received drafts totalling twelve officers and 425 men to raise it to its full complement. The 4th Battalion needed fewer reinforcements as, fortunately, it had suffered less casualties in France and Belgium.

On 28th June, the Brigade Headquarters and all three Battalions moved from their separate locations to reform as a Brigade in Yorkshire. The 2nd Battalion was based at Selby, the 4th at Goole and the 5th at Knottingley. Initially deployed on guards and vulnerable point duties, the whole Brigade spent a considerable period carrying out intensive training and undertaking a wide range of anti-invasion exercises. The 133rd Brigade then returned to the southeast of England and was deployed on coastal defence; the 2nd Battalion moved to Rye in November 1940, the 5th Battalion to Bexhill in December 1940 and the 4th Battalion to Deal in May 1941. The Battalions were moved around the east of Kent on various schemes, training exercises and operational deployments for a year or so, and the Brigade became a highly capable, battle-worthy and respected formation. Nevertheless, it is interesting to observe that one of the orders in a 5th Battalion Operational Instruction in May 1941 states:

> *"All officers and NCOs will synchronise watches with BBC Time at 2100 hours on 18 May 1941."*

While on duty near Hastings on 16th June 1941, Corporal D.E. Wood and Private S. Talbot of the 5th Battalion were each awarded the George Medal in recognition of their conspicuous gallantry, courage and initiative in entering a minefield at Fairlight to rescue a wounded soldier and carry him to safety.

In May 1942, the 133rd (Royal Sussex) Brigade would receive orders to move to Liverpool to embark on ships for an unknown destination.

SITUATION IN NORTH AFRICA FROM 1939 TO 1941

The 1st Battalion in Egypt

The 1st Battalion had been stationed in Egypt since 1937 but the years of 1939 and 1940 had a considerable influence on its future standing and war-fighting capability. During these years, great changes took place in its personnel, equipment and organisation, which stood it in good stead for the great conflict that was pending.

The Battalion, since its move from Jerusalem in September 1937, had been stationed in the Garrison Town of Moascar, which lies beside the Suez Canal in Egypt. Just before Christmas 1938, B Company rejoined the Battalion after completing a year on detachment in Cyprus, thus bringing the Battalion up to its full strength. The Garrison, commanded by General Brooks, with Major Kennedy as the Brigade Major, consisted, in the main, of two British battalions: 1st Battalion The Royal Sussex Regiment and the 1st Battalion The Essex Regiment. The Essex Regiment, commanded by Lieutenant Colonel Paxton, was responsible for the northern half of the Garrison area, while the 1st Royal Sussex, commanded by Lieutenant Colonel W. Holderness MC, was responsible for the southern half.

Life in the garrison was the normal happy peacetime existence of most foreign stations, with the usual amount of training, lectures, route marches, courses *etc*, plus a variety of sports and pastimes, including swimming, and yachting on the Canal and Lake Timsah, and dances at the French Club. In fact, a year's posting to the Canal, in normal circumstances, by a battalion returning to the UK from the Far East was considered to be a good one.

The clouds, however, were starting to gather over Europe and of this the Battalion was all too conscious, if only because a number of the officers had served with the 2nd Battalion at Mersa Matruh and in the Sudan in 1936, at the time when Mussolini had started to cause trouble. The Battalion was also fully aware of the Italian transports passing through the Canal packed with troops on their way to the Eritrean region, whose closer acquaintance, in less happy circumstances, the Battalion was to make later on.

The 1st Battalion's first cloud came in April 1939 when B Company was ordered to Suez to protect the oil refinery area from suspected sabotage. The Company was housed in the slaughterhouse buildings, adjacent to the refinery, and life for the next six weeks or so was extremely unpleasant. Apart from any possible Foreign Agents, who did not put in an appearance, the Company had to contend with myriads of flies, which did, plus the stench of the refinery, not to mention the bugs and the high humid temperature.

About this time, C Company was sent to guard the vast ammunition dump at the Tura Caves, south of Cairo, another of the salubrious Egyptian hideouts. It was with much relief that both these detachments returned to Moascar in June 1939.

On the Declaration of War with Germany on 3rd September 1939, the 1st Battalion, which had mobilised itself a week before the Declaration, moved to Suez and the 1st Essex to Port Said. Some rear details, and the families, were left behind in Moascar, and specific tasks such as closing the Battalion Accounts were put in hand, including organising the Station against any possible gas attacks, which might occur.

During the first year, owing to postings, promotions, escapes to jobs in Cairo (the *'Gabardine Swine Trail'* as it was labelled) and many other demands, and particularly after the immediate outbreak of war, the Battalion had been stripped of no less than three-quarters of its officers. This fact is made amply evident by comparing the names of officers on the strength of the Battalion in September 1939, with those on the strength in October 1940; in addition, a very large proportion of the trained other ranks had also departed.

In the summer of 1940, the officer strength of the Battalion was very fortunately boosted by a large Draft from the UK and, even more fortunately, a large proportion of them came from such famous units as the Artists' Rifles, the Honourable Artillery Company (HAC) and other Territorial Army regiments, who were thus versed in the art of soldiering, although they had no experience of desert conditions or life in the Middle East. However, these particular ingredients were to be added in the immediate future. Among the intake was the new Commanding Officer, Lieutenant Colonel J.M.H. Edye DSO OBE MC (a veteran of the Great War and, at the time, aged 46 years), who arrived some time in June.

Entry of Italy into the War

On 11th June 1940, and following the fall of France, Italy declared war on Great Britain. Crossing the Egyptian frontier at Sollum on 13th September, the Italians captured Sidi Barrani on the coast by 18th September. Here they halted and built a series of separate fortified camps, stretching southwards into the desert for a distance of over twenty miles. The Italians occupied these with approximately five divisions.

The British forces in the Western Desert at that time were the 7th Armoured Division, the 4th Indian Division, and the Matruh Garrison. The latter defended the small port and railhead at Mersa Matruh, while the 4th Indian Division was in a strongly defended position some twelve miles further east around Gerawla. A few miles to the south of the 4th Indian Division was the 7th Armoured Division, ready to counter-attack should the Italians try to take Matruh and advance down the coast road to Alexandria.

Since the Italians showed no intention of advancing further east, plans were made to take the offensive and drive them out of Egypt. The 7th Armoured

The Sidi Barrani Operational Area in September 1940

Division and the 4th Indian Division would move westwards in December 1940, preparatory to attacking and capturing the chain of enemy fortified camps in and around Sidi Barrani.

Preparation for Desert Warfare

Meanwhile, back at Suez, Italy's entry into the War was demonstrated to the 1st Royal Sussex by an abortive attempt to bomb the refinery. The bombs were released at such a height, presumably in fear of the Battalion's non-existent anti-aircraft defences, that they fell a considerable distance away from the target. Their total 'bag' was one poor camel innocently grazing in the desert nearby; grazing on whatever camels seem to find in such arid regions. It was assumed that raids of a more serious nature would shortly follow this attack, and as a result, those families, which had drifted 'Suezwards', hastily returned to Quarters in Moascar and, eventually, as the threat increased, were evacuated to South Africa in October 1940.

It was also in October 1940 that the 1st Battalion joined the 7th Indian Brigade, commanded by Brigadier B.R. Briggs, and began its long and very happy association with the famous 4th Indian Division, and which was to add most gloriously to the Battalion's long fighting record. The Battalion moved into the Mena House area of Cairo where heavy and intense desert training was to be the order of the day. Insufficient credit has been given to Lieutenant Colonel Edye, the new Commanding Officer, for welding the Battalion together and introducing it into an Indian formation, a sensitive task, not made any easier by his age, his weak eyesight and other physical handicaps, and not lightened by his Second-in-Command. The introduction to the Indian culture, within what was a largely Indian[18] formation, needed a conscientious and understanding approach by British troops, as this simple Indian code of social intercourse demonstrates:

> *"Your chief concern is not to endanger your comrade.*
> *Because of the risk that you may bring him, you do not light fires after sunset.*
> *You do not use his slit trench at any time.*
> *Neither do you park your vehicle near the hole in the ground where he lives.*
> *You do not borrow from him, and particularly you do not borrow those precious fluids, water and petrol.*
> *You do not give him compass bearings, which you have not tested and of which you are not sure.*
> *You do not leave any mess behind that will breed flies.*
> *You do not ask him to convey your messages, your gear, or yourself unless it is his job to do so.*
> *You do not drink deeply of any man's bottles, for they may not be replenished. You make sure that he has many before you take his cigarette.*
> *You do not ask information beyond your job, for idle talk kills men.*
> *You do not grouse unduly, except concerning the folly of your own commanders. This is allowable. You criticise no other man's commanders.*
> *Of those things, which you do, the first is to be hospitable and the second is to be courteous. The day is long in the desert and there is time to be helpful to those who share your adventure. A cup of tea, therefore, is proffered to all comers – it is your handshake and your badge of association. Over the tea mugs the good-mannered guest transacts his business expeditiously, gossips shop for a little, and gets him gone.*
> *This code is the sum of fellowship in the desert. It knows no rank or any exception."*

A new development in the disposition of an infantry battalion at this stage was the Carrier Platoon, of which mention has been made already in the campaigns in France and Belgium. They were designed primarily as machine-gun carriers, used to support and maintain the principle of fire and manoeuvre within a

---

[18] Each of the Brigades within the 4th Indian Division consisted of two or three Indian or Gurkha battalions and one British battalion.

battalion. It seems, however, that this design was seldom realised in practice, and the Carrier Platoon performed a diversity of duties, ranging from that of a light screen shielding Matilda tanks[19] to that of serving as porters to the rifle companies.

After the completion of training at Mena, the Division moved forward and the Battalion became part of the defensive area known as the *Baggush Box*, on the coast some 7 miles east of Mersa Matruh, where the 2nd Battalion had been in 1935-36. During Wavell's advance to Sidi Barrani, the 7th Indian Brigade would not arrive in the forward area in time to participate in the battle, apart from the Anti-Tank Platoon of the 4th/16th Punjabis. The rest of the Brigade took over lines of communication duties and protection of dump areas, with a forward battalion at *Charing Cross,* 7 miles west of Mersa Matruh. Although in a reserve rôle, the Brigade was poised to exploit any situation should it be required. This, however, was not to be its fate for, at the very last moment, after the successful conclusion of the Sidi Barrani operations, the 4th Indian Division was withdrawn from the Western Desert and received orders to proceed to the Sudan. Nevertheless, before leaving for the Horn of Africa, one should not forget that the successful operation at Sidi Barrani electrified the world; the march of the hitherto invincible Axis powers had been halted by a devastating defeat. At a cost of less than 700 casualties, the 4th Indian Division had destroyed four Italian Divisions and taken more than 20,000 prisoners; the 4th Indian Division had put the Western Desert on the 'Front Page'.

---

[19] The Matilda was the Infantry or 'I' tank and weighed about 27 tons with a top speed of 15 mph. It had a range of some 50 miles on internal fuel tanks, and its armour was quite respectable for its day, with some 78mm at the front, and 20mm on the thinnest plates. The main armament was a Quick-Firing 2-pdr for which 93 rounds were carried, while mounted co-axially was a 7.92mm machine-gun.

OPERATIONS IN ERITREA

On 4th July 1940, the Italians had invaded the Sudan and occupied Kassala, some two hundred miles east of Khartoum, and also Galabat further to the south. This was then followed up with an invasion of British Somaliland.

It was from Eritrea that Mussolini had based the expansion of his East African Empire. Four years had passed since Abyssinia had been struck down, but in its hinterland the Duce's writ still ran somewhat precariously. To hold the fierce intractable tribesmen in check, the cream of Italy's fighting men had been shipped to East Africa. Among the quarter of a million troops in garrison, when Italy declared war on Britain, were her finest colonial service brigades, Alpini, Bersaglieri and Grenadiers – well-disciplined soldiers hardened by the rigours of irregular warfare. Having taken Abyssinia, the Italians then crossed the frontier into the Sudan before they entered British Somaliland - and to the south glistened the rich prizes of Kenya, Uganda and Tanganyika – a more than dazzling prospect for the Italian empire builders. Bit by bit the dream was to perish. British officers had busily stirred up revolt among the Abyssinian patriots so that Emperor Haile Selassie was able to return to his kingdom. The Italians would be driven out of the Sudan and plans were then speeded up for their destruction in Italian and British Somaliland. But that still left Eritrea, the most firmly established Italian foothold in East Africa.

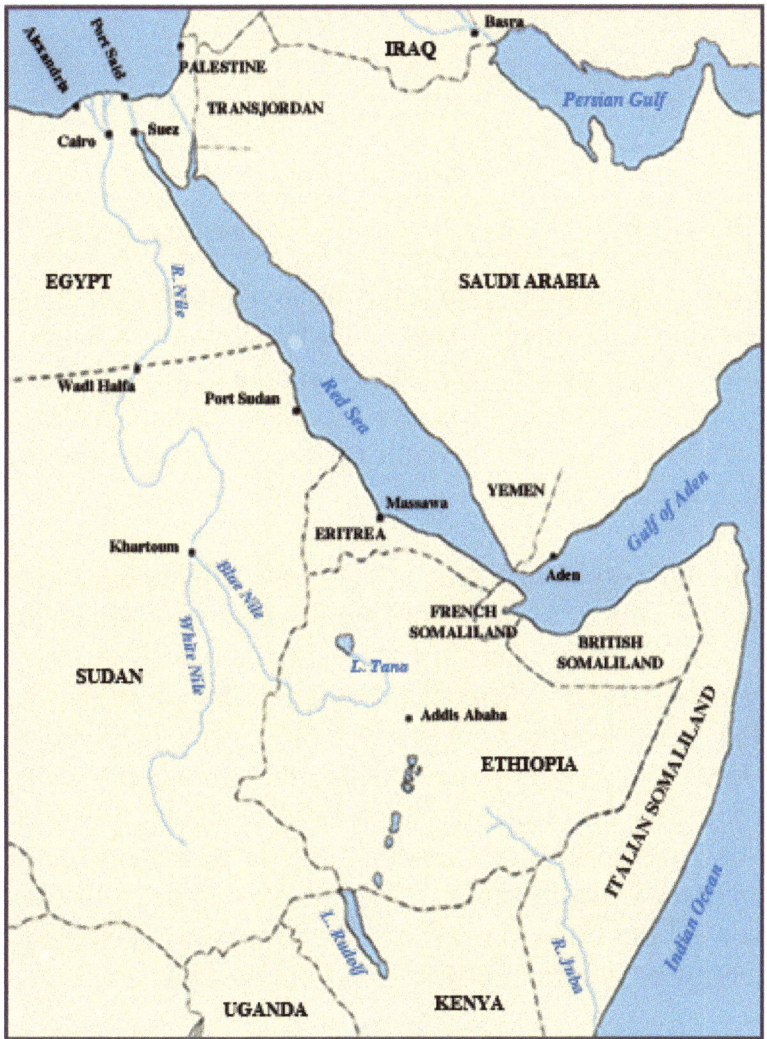

There are few less accessible spots on earth[20]. Only the port of Massawa offers entry from the Red Sea, and this harbour is ringed by miles of coral reef, blocked by clusters of offshore islands and served only by a tortuous channel – an impossible landing site for an amphibious operation. Behind this bleak and desolate foreshore stands the central keep of the mountains, the eastern wall high and grim, its bare rocks slashed only by the precipitous ravines which bear a spate of storm water for three months in each year and are bone dry thereafter. At a height of 7,000 feet, the capital town of Asmara snuggles among the peaks. To the northwest, a formidable mountain range supports the interior plateau high above the broken lands and sandy wastes, which spread westwards towards the Nile. In a hundred miles there is only one crack in this wall. At Keren, a small dusty upland town where the trails come in from the north, a deep gash in the mountain face provides a twisty passage through which the railway and motor road drops sharply into the valley, which leads to the Sudanese border.

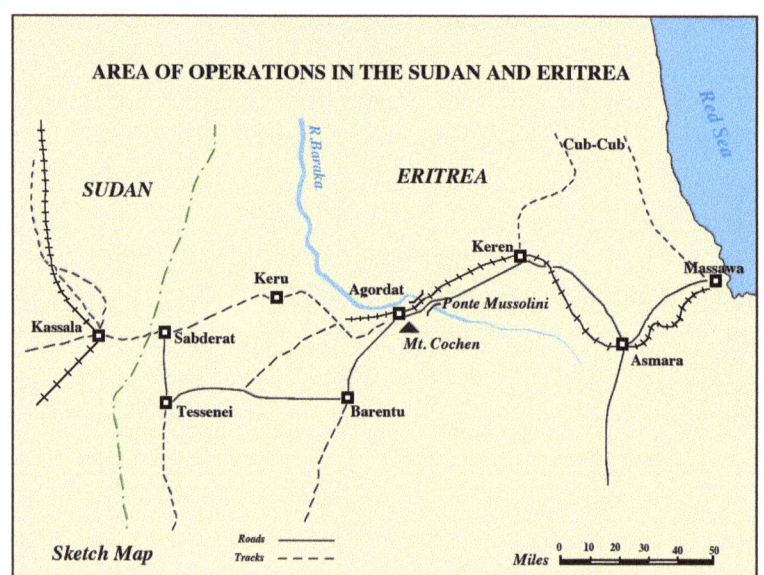

With the Massawa and Keren gorges blocked, unscaleable heights await the invader on all approaches to Eritrea, save on the south where passable roads follow the grain of the land into Abyssinia. The security of such an eyrie influenced Italian strategy profoundly. After the disaster at Sidi Barrani and the headlong flight of the Italian forces from Kenya, the enemy prepared to sustain his resistance in East Africa by retirement behind these mountain walls, which he deemed to be impregnable. In British high-level planning, however, the cleansing of Africa held first priority. Even before Sidi Barrani revealed how shakily the Italian military structure stood, it was decided to seize Eritrea. With scarcely less disdain of the odds that he had exhibited in the Western Desert, General Wavell entrusted two Indian Divisions with the task[21].

The 5th Indian Division had been moved from India to the Sudan in the autumn of 1940, and was joined by the 4th Indian Division in January 1941. Plans were then put into operation for the liquidation of the Italian East African Empire. To do this, South African forces were to advance into Italian Somaliland and

---

[20] As described in the *Fourth Indian Division* by Lieut. Colonel G.R. Stevens OBE.
[21] Ibid.

Ethiopia from the south, while the 4th and 5th Indian Divisions attacked Eritrea from the Sudan - in Churchill's words, *"to clear the back door to the Middle East"*. The final objective was to be the capture of the Italian Red Sea port of Massawa.

On Boxing Day 1940, the 1st Battalion embarked at Suez for Port Sudan, and with the rest of the 7th Brigade, arrived there in early-January 1941. It was thus that the Battalion opened operations against enemy territory at a time when the Italians had enjoyed unbroken success against the territory of others less capable.

On the 19th January 1941, the advance of the 4th and 5th Indian Divisions began, but it was not until the 8th April that Massawa was captured. The Italian defence was based on the natural fortress of mountains, which guarded the entrance to the Keren Plain and the road to Asmara, the capital. For over seven weeks, under the most unusual conditions, British and Indian troops fought to break through the enemy's defences. Although the strength of the forces engaged was not as great as in many other battles of the war, this battle must rank as one of the grimmest. Everything was against them: the terrain, the climate, the inadequacy and unsuitability of their equipment for the conditions confronting them, and the fact that they were outnumbered by three to one.

Although an approach through the port at Massawa was not tenable, in the rocky massif behind it stood the prime objective, the capital at Asmara. Therefore, the only hope of taking Asmara was to attack from the west, and there was only one road to reach it; the road through the town of Keren, and hence the importance of the forthcoming Battle of Keren.

Brigadier Briggs, commanding the 7th Indian Brigade, had been pressing for permission to start his own operation against the frontier post at Karora, prior to a thrust towards Keren. However, Lieutenant General Sir William Platt, the 'Kaid'[22], who had long been aware of the attractions offered by such an advance down the Red Sea coast, was extremely dubious about his ability to maintain anything more than a very small force along this route – certainly nothing as big as a brigade group. Sources of fresh water were scanty, the road was little more than a track, and there was a chronic shortage of vehicles. Nevertheless, as the Italian Commander-in-Chief, Generale Luigi Frusci, was known to be unusually sensitive to this route; even in January, the idea of a diversionary force, which might lead the Italians into thinking the real threat to Asmara was coming from the north, had a considerable attraction. The alternative of supplying Briggs by sea was eventually reckoned to be just

---

[22] A colloquial abbreviation for 'Kaid El'Amm': - leader of the Army – a title which General Platt was justly proud. He was invariably known as 'The Kaid', rather than 'The Army Commander' or 'Commander-in-Chief'. General *Bolo* Whistler would also have the honour of being appointed as 'The Kaid' of the Sudanese Defence Force in 1948.

feasible but only if his force was restricted to one brigade group (its overall strength did in fact total something over 6,000).

Briggs's force, known as the 'North Force', which when assembled turned out to be a completely cosmopolitan conglomeration – a Commonwealth and Allied compote. To Briggs's own two battalions of the 1st Royal Sussex and 4th/16th Punjabis (the 4th/11th Sikhs had already been detached to another force), would come a battalion of the French Foreign Legion[23], itself a heterogeneous mixture which even included nine Italians, all of whom were subsequently killed in the fighting against their own countrymen, together with a Senegalese battalion[24], which had Free French officers. The 'Force' also included other divers and miscellaneous Sudanese and Indian units.

The 5th Indian Division had been operating in the Sudan since the previous September and had the distinction, in this part of Africa, of opening the war against the Italians on a major scale when, on the 6th of November, it attacked the Sudanese fort of Gallabat. When the two Indian Divisions began the invasion of Eritrea on 19th January, the 4th took a northerly dirt road, which led to Keru, while the 5th took a more southerly route, on a good motor road leading to Aicota. Both Divisions were in pursuit of the hurriedly withdrawing Italians.

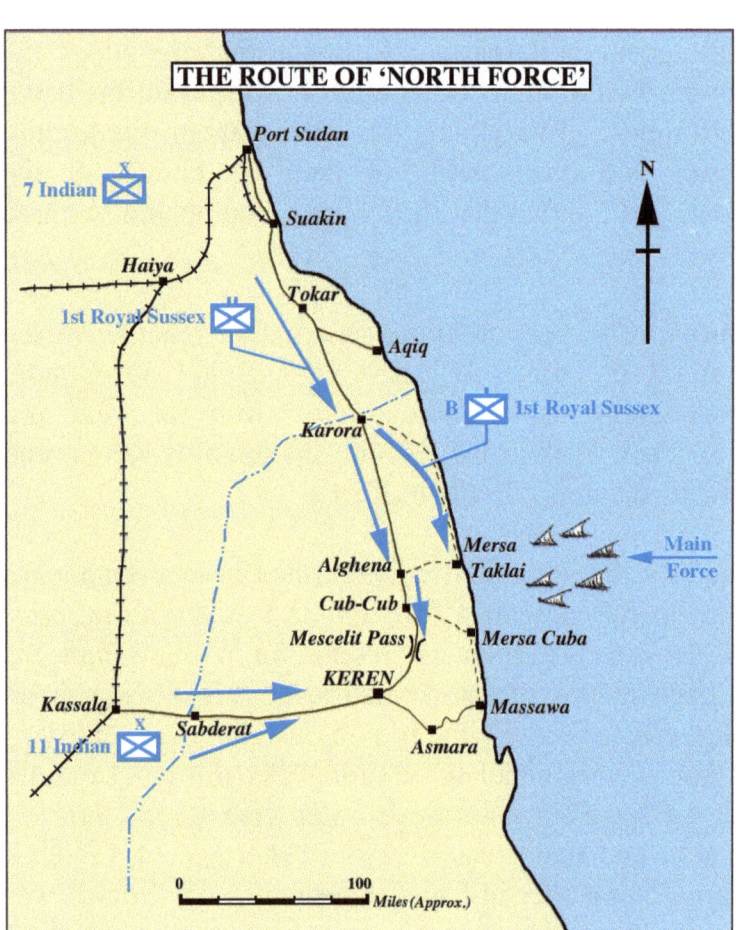

As part of this, it had been decided that as the line of communications by land was too long and tenuous, the 'North Force' needed to open up a port and advanced base on the coast at Mersa Taclei. This commenced on 2nd February with a small column, under command of Major G.E. Phelps[25], which was tasked with capturing this port; a tiny fishing village which had been selected from the map as the most

---

[23] The 14th Battalion Etranger, which had seen service in Norway.
[24] The Troisième Battalion de Marche (Tchad) from French Equatorial Africa.
[25] Major Phelps would later command the 1st Battalion in May 1944, taking over from Lieutenant Colonel J.B.A. Glennie DSO after the Battle of Cassino.

likely place at which an advanced base could be set up, and where the rest of Briggs's force could be landed and supplied. The column consisted of B Company 1st Royal Sussex and the Battalion's Carrier Platoon, plus the anti-tank platoon of the 4th/16th Punjabis; a Regiment that was to become the 1st Battalion's close comrades-in-arms in many a hard fight to come. While a company group may appear to be a very small force for a task of this importance, its size was limited entirely by the resources available, and the fact was that there was only enough transport to lift two companies of the Battalion at any one time. Meanwhile, the rest of the 1st Battalion was to capture the frontier town of Karora, with the intention that the two objectives would be taken simultaneously.

The Mersa Taclei objective was some 40 to 50 miles away across trackless dunes and dry watercourses, and the column took a night and a day to get within striking distance of it. The maps were inaccurate and, being printed on linen, became more useful for wiping the sweated brow than for guiding troops across the desert. They had set off at dusk, and progress was slowed down at first by the tufty scrub, deep wadis and rocky outcrops – something of a test for the vehicles, but particularly for B Company in their three-tonners. As they cleared the foothills, the going improved – until next evening, when rain set in heavily for most of the night. Late in the following afternoon, the column halted on the coast, four or five miles north of Mersa Taclei. The Carriers were leading, and, having sighted the enemy, gave chase and opened fire – killing two camels, which belonged to some apparently innocent nomads. The latter were placated by tins of bully beef, and with a chit for two new beasts; the chit being honoured two days later by camels captured from the enemy garrison!

A platoon was now sent forward to gain information concerning the enemy defences. This platoon did more, and in fact drove the enemy from some buildings covering the flat beach on the northern approaches. Driving off a counter-attack, they remained to harass the garrison. Besides these buildings, Mersa Taclei consisted of a large fort-like structure with a tower, a lighthouse, and a cluster of sheds around it. Leading from this was a track, cutting through a low escarpment, which described an arc round the port; in normal times the port was a fishing village with a little coasting trade.

At first light, the column had moved up and deployed, ready to attack. Then the Punjabis' 2-pdr anti-tank guns opened up with solid shot at the tower and High Explosive at the enemy on the beach and escarpment. Meanwhile, the carriers were moving round to the escarpment flank, and literally swept up two outposts by sheer surprise and a couple of sharp Bren-bursts. They then 'leapfrogged' into successive fire positions to support the Company as it advanced; for his initiative in this action, Corporal S.J. Deville, whilst in command of a carrier, rounded up a machine-gun post thus saving many casualties, and was subsequently awarded the Military Medal. The carriers' fire was so accurate and so close to the leading sections that the enemy riflemen and machine-gunners, harassed on the flank, never effectively engaged the front. Thus, the attacking force suffered no casualties in the initial assault, while the enemy had half a dozen killed, twice as many wounded, and some sixty were taken as prisoners. As the Company advanced methodically through the post, the carriers worked round to the rear, cutting off the enemy's retreat across the open country to the south. Although it was only a minor encounter, the Mersa Taclai operation demonstrated what could be achieved when a company and its supporting carriers properly exploited the principle of fire and manoeuvre.

Apart from some bombing by Italian aircraft, the Karora objective was taken by the rest of the Battalion, according to schedule, and without incident. This allowed the dhows to land French reinforcements at Mersa Taclai and, amongst other things, to unload NAAFI stores, which meant there was no shortage of tea, sugar and tinned milk for the rest of the campaign!

The first troops to disembark were the battalion of the Foreign Legion and the Senegalese battalion known as 'Battalion Garby'. As B Company set off on a thirty-mile march to rejoin the rest of the 1st Battalion at Nagfa, the Senegalese troops were met by a chorus of catcalls from the Company's column of lorries. The allies later became firm friends of The Royal Sussex, who, however, could not repress their amusement at the Senegalese battalion's practice of balancing all their equipment on their heads when on the march, including their boots! Neither they nor the Foreign Legion showed any scruples as to whose ration-dump supplied their rations, but the 1st Battalion proved too wary for even these experienced foragers. The Foreign Legion were veterans of Narvik, and had been in England; nevertheless it was always good policy, when on outpost duty, to return through their lines and enjoy a delicious meal of venison, vegetables and wine - which seemed to flow in abundance – in marked contrast to the lack of beer in the Battalion. They also had a tough but nevertheless attractive Frenchwoman as an ambulance driver; as one officer remarked, *"a strange and very welcome sight"*.

On the day after the fall of Mersa Taclai, the Battalion seized Alghena, and three days later, the column went forward 80 miles and found itself opposed by the Italians at Cub-Cub. The Italian blocking force was of battalion strength – the 112th Colonial Battalion - with a number of mountain artillery guns holding a ring of low hills behind the village. Brigadier Briggs was determined to manoeuvre the enemy out of its position and a mobile column consisting of C Company and a carrier platoon was despatched on an encircling move to cut the Italian lines of communications, while the Senegalese Battalion sent two companies on a shorter hook round the right flank. The C Company group was delayed for 48 hours by the soft sand, impassable *khors*[26], and because of the inaccurate handkerchief maps. They eventually cut the road three miles south of Cub-Cub, one of their captures being an Italian field cashier with two large chests of *Lire*.

---

[26] Dried river beds.

Despite the lack of water and the soft and treacherous stretches of road, the international aspect of the force produced its own problems too. Different races, different nationalities and different religions demanded five different types of rations – British, Indian, Sudanese, French[27] and Senegalese – whilst French equipment complicated the ammunition supply. All these issues tended to slow progress and the fact that the force was able to make the rapid advance, which it did, may be regarded as an administrative triumph. As the Official History of the campaign records:

> *"Administration is not the drab servant of the art of war - it is rather of war's very essence. Armies and air forces can only operate with what the lines of communication succeed in delivering . . . ."*

This maxim can be said to have been never truer than at the coming battle at Keren, particularly in respect of Briggs's force.

On the morning of the 22nd of February, the attack on the enemy positions at Cub-Cub began. The guns of 25th Field Regiment RA and elements of the 4th/16th Punjabis, which had arrived from Alghena, supported the Frenchmen. The objective was cleared by that evening, and the victors took 430 prisoners plus a number of artillery pieces, while the attacking force suffered 40 casualties. There remained a varied assortment of booty, ranging from operatic records to tins of asparagus. The records and a portable gramophone found a home in a carrier, and proved very popular, but by the end of the campaign, the Carrier Platoon had grown weary of Italian opera. However, the most important prize were the wells at Cub-Cub, which had been left completely undamaged; even the Italian engineer who serviced the pumps remained at his post.

Pressing on, the column reached Mescelit from which it was possible either to advance against Massawa or to strike at the rear of Keren, where a frontal assault was then in preparation by the 11th Indian Brigade. Following a period of rest, the Battalion, as part of the 7th Indian Brigade's diversionary operation, then adopted harassing tactics, containing eight battalions of the Italian's colonial infantry and a substantial group of field guns in the neighbourhood of Enghiart, until Keren fell.

Pulling out of the Battalion's positions in the Engiahat area, near Mescelit and north of Keren, was by no means an easy matter, owing to the terrain. As an example of these difficulties, A Company, which was commanded at the time by Major Phelps, was in a position up in the mountains to which not even mules, had any been available, would have gained access. All the ammunition and supplies, such as there were, had for the past month arrived by porters, who

---

[27] The French were notorious for helping themselves to any extra rations that came their way. On at least one occasion they consumed three days' rations in one; on another occasion, a fatigue party sent to draw water from the only available well, drank up their entire loads on the return journey!

faced a stiff climb of over two hours from the base to A Company's position (a platoon from one of the other companies provided this porter service). Bully beef, biscuits and, worst of all, only one bottle of water was the daily ration. Communications with Battalion Headquarters, some 3 miles away as the crow flies, was by lamp at night and by helio in daytime. When orders to withdraw were received, the Battalion concentrated and moved eastwards towards the coast, and then followed the coastline south in the direction of Massawa.

Owing to a shortage of transport, this was a 'ferried' move – *i.e.*, half the troops were lifted at a time by three-tonners and leapfrogged forward in 10 mile tranches; a total distance of some 60 miles over atrocious tracks, with no chance of 'dashing forward' to the attack. After a slight skirmish at Emberini, the 1st Battalion arrived, as the light was beginning to fade, at a position about 4 miles south of Emberini. Here orders were received to launch a dawn attack on Massawa, some 5 miles south-southeast of the Battalion, and timed so as to coincide with that of the forces moving directly on the town from the west. By now it was pretty dark and as there had been no opportunity to plan the operation by daylight, it was decided to line up the companies as best one could, to advance over the intervening ground on a compass bearing of 155° and, with luck, overcome the enemy in the ensuing engagement.

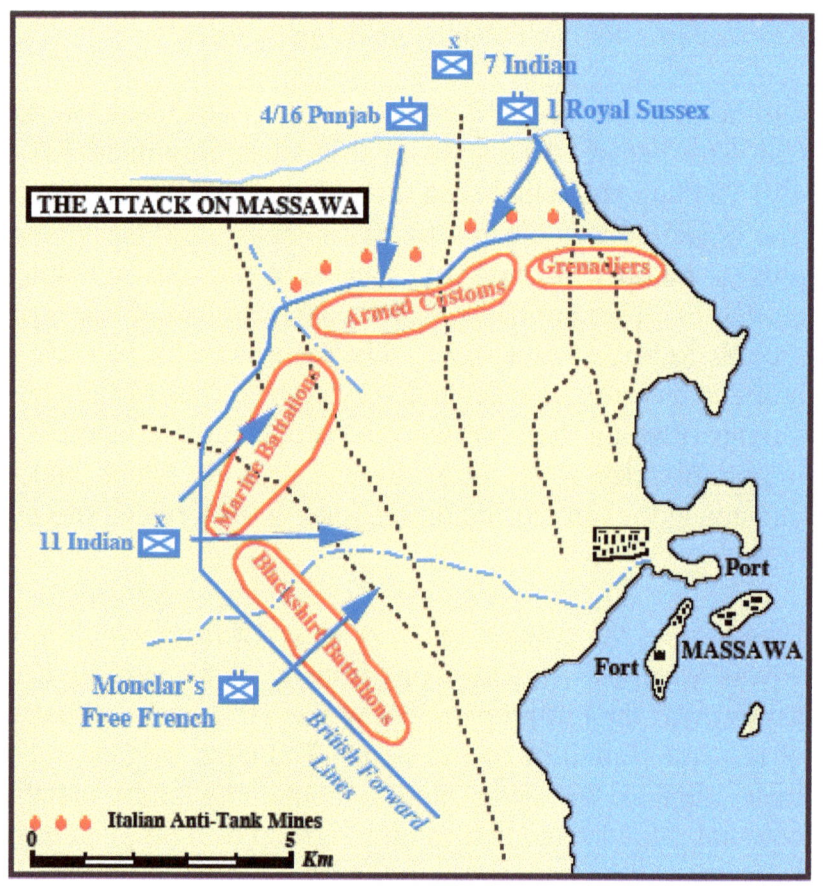

The initial plan was for three companies to dash forward to induce the Italians to surrender but a 'do-or-die' order from Rome encouraged the Italian forces to be slightly more belligerent.

The 1st Battalion crossed the Start Line some time after midnight and advanced on Massawa with the 4th/16th Punjabis; the night was clear and, fortunately, moonless, with the bright shining stars helping the companies to keep direction. Despite heavy shelling from batteries of naval 4-inch guns, all seemed to be going well when the leading company on the right encountered an enemy patrol in the dark, which raised the alarm. This resulted in a hail of fire, *'flaming onions'* (produced by anti-aircraft guns in the ground role) being much in evidence and the whole scene being well lighted up by quantities of star shells, searchlights, Verey lights, *etc*. This pyrotechnic display lasted till dawn, by which time the companies found themselves pinned down in very open country, and up against the main defences. At this stage, the Battalion was without any artillery or anti-tank support; the former had run short of ammunition, and the latter (4-pounders) were among the very first casualties. To complicate matters further, there was no communication with Brigade Headquarters as the line had been cut and the Battalion's wirelesses (No. 18 Sets), which were not very good at the best of times, were soon put out of action. By about 10 o'clock in the morning the situation was nasty; it was already very hot, ammunition was running short, the men had not had a meal for nearly 24 hours and, worst of all, water bottles were, in most cases, empty. The situation was not improved by the arrival on the scene of a troop of medium enemy tanks, presumably on a reconnaissance mission as, fortunately for the Battalion, they withdrew after a few shots from the Battalion's only surviving anti-tank protection, the Boys Anti-Tank rifle.

Eventually, a message was got through to Brigade Headquarters, and the Brigade Commander decided that as no help was available (the Battalion's Carriers under Ben Dalton had crept as far as Brigade Headquarters on their last drops of fuel, and the gunners were down to their last few rounds of ammunition), the Battalion was to remain in position as best it could, and withdraw under cover of darkness, and he issued orders to this effect. When the Commander of A Company got back to Battalion Headquarters with these orders in the early afternoon, they were suddenly greeted by a show of white flags all along the enemy front – never was a sight more welcome! The 1st Battalion was extremely fortunate to escape in this action with only relatively few casualties; regrettably, young Paget, a promising young officer, was among those killed. Massawa subsequently fell through the action of units of the 5th Indian Division.

After the fall of Massawa on 8th April 1941, some 550 officers and 10,000 Italian and native troops laid down their arms on the following day. The 1st Royal Sussex spent a fortnight helping to clear up the mess in the town, but soon orders were received for the 4th Indian Division to start moving to Port Sudan for embarkation and return to Egypt; the men were not sorry to go.

For its gallant action in the Eritrean Campaign, The Royal Sussex Regiment was awarded Battle Honours for *Karora-Marsa Taclei, Cub-Cub, Mescelit Pass, Keren, Mt Engiahat and Massawa,* with the principal Honour emblazoned on the Colours being **Abyssinia 1941**.

Gallantry Awards for Eritrea 1941

Military Medal:

Corporal S.J. Deville   1st Battalion

Mentioned-in-Despatches:

Five officers and eight men of the 1st Battalion were Mentioned-in-Despatches.

THE WESTERN DESERT IN 1941

Thus it was that the 1st Royal Sussex, as part of Wavell's famous 45,000, helped to overthrow the Italians in Eritrea and Abyssinia; but the real test of their mettle came after the forces in North Africa had been seriously drawn upon to assist the Greeks against the invading Germans. This decision had been communicated to General Wavell and his staff at the very moment they were planning advances to Benghazi, Tripoli and beyond. The effect was to place severe limitations upon the North African campaign. Benghazi was to be the final scope of the advance and then only if it could be done *'on the cheap'*. The British intervention in Greece was based on the supposition that it would delay the German attack on Russia, but this theory, when measured in terms of fighting divisions, is open to considerable doubt.

Wavell, therefore, was now faced with General Rommel's Afrika Korps and six fresh Italian divisions, while his own force consisted of two British divisions besieged in Tobruk, and only another five infantry brigades and part of one armoured brigade to defend Egypt – a corporal's guard to do the work of an army. It was fortunate that the rapid conquest of East Africa had freed the 4th and 5th Indian Divisions to return and reinforce North Africa.

Towards the end of April 1941, the 1st Battalion had returned by sea to Suez, and then on to the Western Desert, and back to the *Baggush Box*. But it now had a new Commanding Officer, Lieutenant Colonel G.C. Evans DSO, a soldier of the highest courage and enterprise. As a Major in The Royal Warwickshire Regiment, as well as having been the Brigade Major of the 11th Indian Brigade during the recent campaign in Eritrea, he had been specially selected to take over command of the 1st Royal Sussex on its return from Eritrea to Egypt.

Although the Battalion was not involved in the operations around Halfaya (Operation BATTLEAXE), which had not only failed to relieve Tobruk but had revealed that the enemy was better armoured and possessed superior anti-armour fire-power, the anti-tank and carrier platoons of the 7th Indian Brigade had been formed into composite companies, and they played an active part in these operations. The Carrier Platoon, under Lieutenant B. Dalton, was surprised to find itself in the rôle of protective screen to the Matilda tanks assaulting Fort Capuzzo, which in turn were even more surprised in the first encounter with the German 88mm guns[28]. The tanks suffered heavy losses, and the engagement was broken off after the second day. In the main attack, the Carrier Platoon had sufficient speed and mobility to suffer little damage from the enemy, but in covering the withdrawal, they were hotly peppered by a group of German Mark IV tanks, and lost three carriers. However, during the long

---

[28] The German 88 mm Flak gun (Flugabwehr-Kanone) was one of the most highly publicised, famous and feared weapons of the Second World War. It was primarily an anti-aircraft gun adaptable to general artillery use where it performed with distinction in the anti-tank rôle.

trek back to base, the ingenuity of Sergeant Rassel and Corporal de Ville, allied to the Platoon Commander's acquisitive enterprise, enabled them to make good the main part of these losses.

This first clash in the Western Desert with the Afrika Korps brought to a head the strong controversy over tank tactics and tank function. Many considered that the British cavalry regiments, now mechanised, to be still wedded to the *arme blanche*. They were disposed to regard their tanks as iron horses, expendable as battle offered. Others considered the tank as a specialised weapon of auxiliary and limited function, only to be employed in conjunction with other arms. A great deal of acrimonious yet valuable discussion ensued over the proper integration of infantry, armour, anti-tank guns, artillery and air forces. The common ground for agreement was the rueful admission that the enemy had better tanks and a new and devastating anti-tank gun, and that Rommel's men had been trained for armoured combat in accordance with a definite tactical doctrine. Until British forces could produce equal weapons and equal training, the panzers promised to remain masters of the desert. The Royal Sussex would suffer unduly at El Alamein from the lack of sound infantry/tank training and cooperation.

General Sir Archibald Wavell would be required by Winston Churchill to hand over command to General Sir Claude Auchinleck in July 1941. Interestingly, Rommel rated Wavell highly, despite Wavell's lack of success against him, and he carried an annotated translation of his book *Generals and Generalship* in his pocket throughout the North Africa Campaign. Indeed, Auchinleck would later say of Wavell:

> *"In no sense do I wish to infer that I found an unsatisfactory situation on my arrival – far from it. Not only was I greatly impressed by the solid foundations laid by my predecessor, but I was also able the better to appreciate the vastness of the problems with which he had been confronted and the greatness of his achievements, in a command in which some 40 different languages are spoken by the British and Allied Forces.*

For most of the 1st Royal Sussex, the period after Operation BATTLEAXE was a waiting stage in the desert campaign, which continued for some time. They, and the rest of the 7th Brigade, initially took part in various minor operations, and also spent time deployed at the Siwa and Giarabub oases; in the main, this involved escorting an Indian labour force, which was stocking the supply dumps near the two oases for future offensive operations. These oases were ancient settlements some 200 miles deep in the desert on the Egyptian-Libyan border. One of them, Giarabub, was straight out of the pages of P.C. Wren – a real *Beau Geste* fort, white and crenellated. Around it were a few Libyan houses and nearby were several date palm groves. In the oasis was a mosque with the sacred shrine of Mohammed Ben Senoussi; founder of the Senoussi sect. A Punjabi diarist recorded at the time, *"The men soon made themselves very comfortable in the date gardens."* While this might have suited the

Punjabis, the 1st Royal Sussex held other views; there is an amusing story of a private in the Battalion who, tired to death of flies, brackish water and the monotony of his diet, at length received a food parcel from home – the first for six months. It contained dates from Siwa!

At this time, C Company, under Major A.C. Bryant took part in long desert patrols northwards, with 25-pounders, 2-pounder anti-tank guns, and South African armour in support. They were based on Melfa, east of Giarabub.

Late in October the 1st Battalion and the rest of the 7th Indian Brigade returned from the oases, at a time when the Eighth Army came into being. With Syria, Persia and Iraq pacified, and the Greek adventure over, it was now possible to seize the initiative, even though Rommel's armoured strength was still superior. On the 8th of November, the Brigade received orders to move to Sofafi, some twenty-five miles southwest of Sidi Barrani, and it was clear that a big offensive was pending.

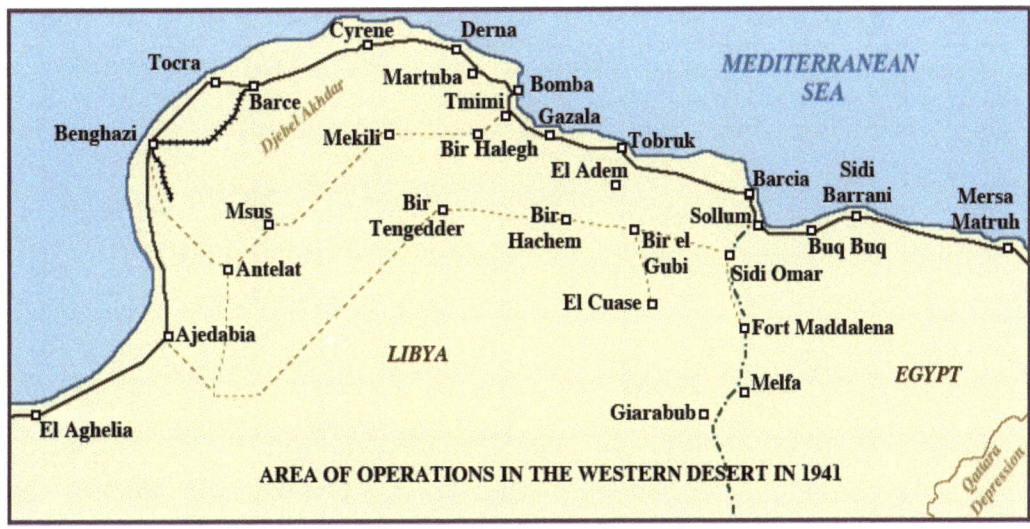

Operation CRUSADER, the second large British Western Desert offensive, opened on the 19th November 1941. The enemy had established a series of heavily defended positions on the Egyptian-Libyan frontier, along the line of the frontier wire between Sollum on the coast and Sidi Omar, some twenty-five miles to the south. The British garrison in Tobruk was holding out against Axis attacks, and in the area between the enemy-held frontier and Tobruk was the bulk of Rommel's armour. The object of the British offensive was the destruction of the Axis forces in Cyrenaica, thereby relieving Tobruk.

The British Eighth Army was composed of 30th Corps, containing the armour, and the 13th Corps. In outline, the plan was that, after crossing the frontier south of Sidi Omar, the 30th Corps should advance northwest and destroy Rommel's armour, while the 13th Corps mopped up the enemy frontier defences. The 4th Indian Division was part of the 13th Corps, and its 7th Indian Brigade was given the task of capturing the strongly defended position at Sidi Omar.

Accordingly, on 19th November, British armour moved forward again into Cyrenaica, supported by aircraft. The 4th Indian Division, displaying its Divisional sign of the Red Eagle (also known as the *Punjabi Hawk*), moved in the van of the advancing army, with the 1st Royal Sussex leading. The two Corps thrust their way into enemy territory, keeping to the desert before swinging northwards around Rommel's defences. The action that followed became known as 'The Battle of the Omars'.

As the 7th Indian Brigade embussed and moved off, the desert was covered with a variety of lorries, camouflaged in different shades of light grey suitable to blend with the surroundings. Mr Sean Fielding[29] described the scene:

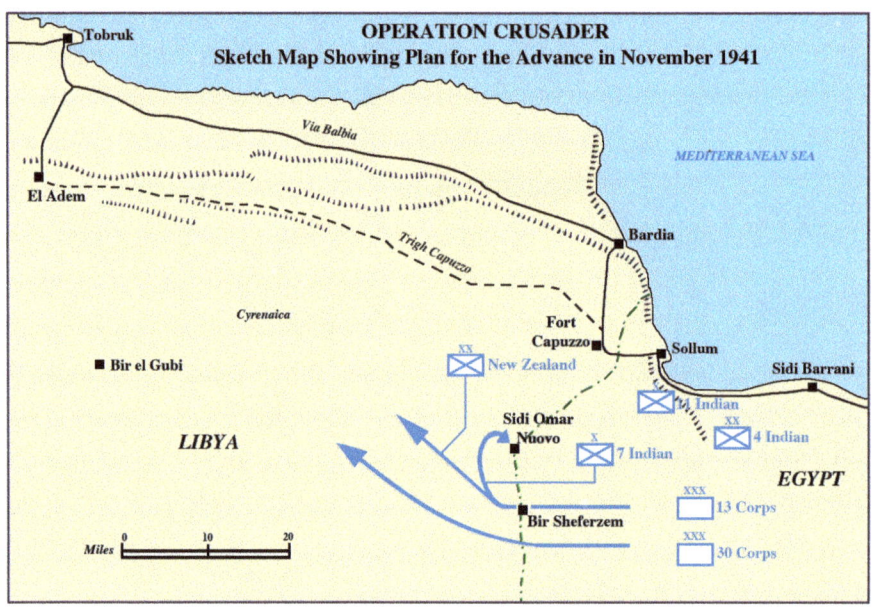

"Everywhere there are eager faces. Convoy commanders sitting up aloft their trucks like sunburned gods – their sun-compasses pointing a black sliver of shadow towards the Boche.

Despatch-riders bumping incredibly through the dusty rutted tracks. Officers in groups, their maps on their knees, listening to their orders.

Lorried infantry waiting, waiting, waiting. Guns, their dust covers off, marching through the infantry and off to a flank in majestic indifference."

That same night, the 1st Battalion had to take Bir Bu Deheua, about ten miles north of the Omar defences and right behind the enemy. The objective was reached without opposition, and the next phase was to attack the Omar defences on the frontier in order to deprive Rommel of a base for operations across the rear of the Eighth Army. These defences were built on two slight humps on the Libyan Plain, fifteen miles south of Capuzzo. They consisted of

---

[29] Colonel Sean Fielding, who conceived the idea of the *Soldier* magazine while serving in the Western Desert, and later, became Editor of The Tatler and Daily Express.

two defended areas on the frontier, two miles apart, well prepared for all-round defence, and supported by German gunners manning 88mm and Italian 75mm guns. It was because of the great width of the position that all four of the rifle companies would have to be used in the attack, leaving nothing in reserve. In addition, deep trenches, without parapets, made artillery observation difficult, and to the east, north and west, the perimeters were heavily mined. Five miles to the northeast, other strong defences began.

Battle of Sidi Omar Nuovo

The 4th Indian Division's plan was to attack Sidi Omar Nuovo from the north with the 1st Royal Sussex, while the 4th/16th Punjabis attacked Libyan Omar, just over 2 miles to the west. While it was known that the enemy had had a long time to prepare his defences, and that consequently they should be very strong, it was vital to know the extent of the minefields, particularly on the approaches that would be taken by the Battalion's supporting tanks. Patrols were sent out nightly to gain this information but even as late as the morning of 22nd November, the day on which the assault was to be made - all reported that there were, *"No sign of mines."*

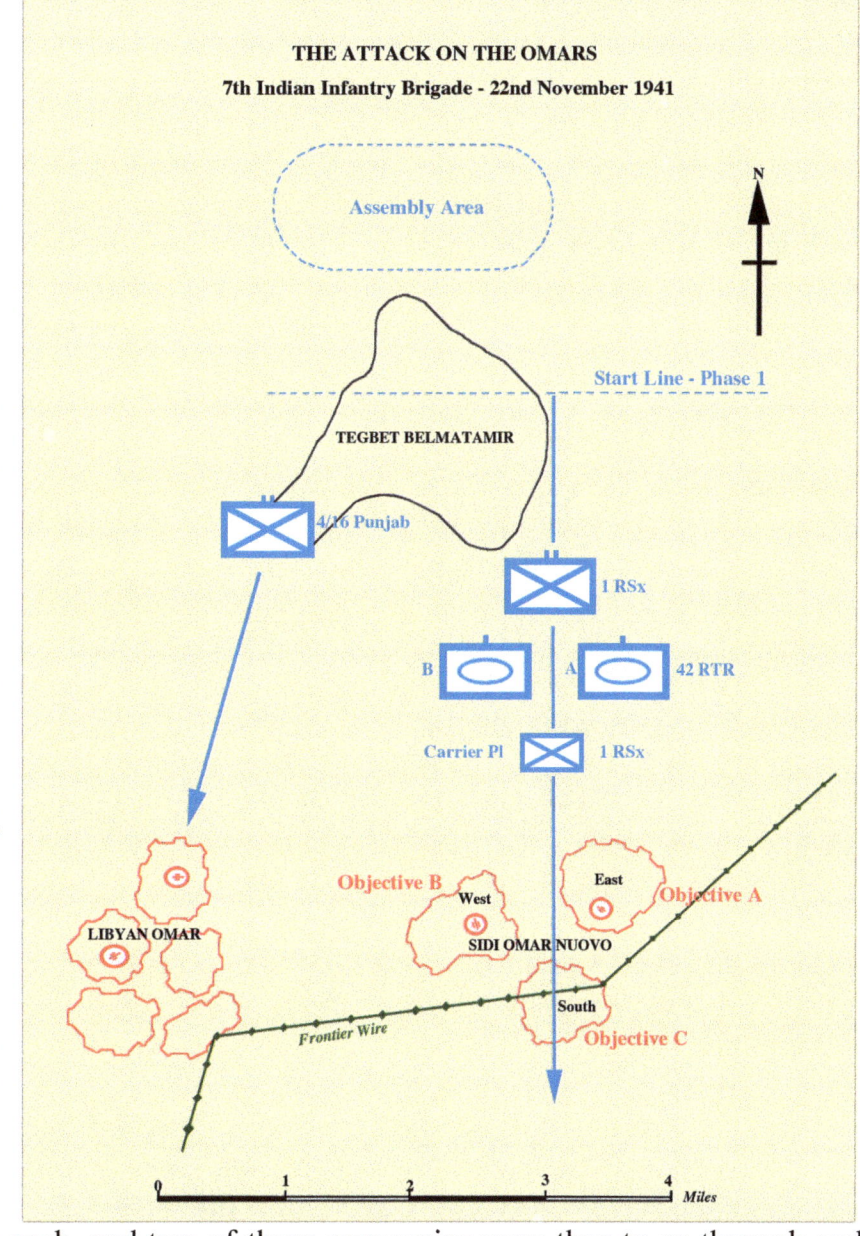

The 1st Battalion's plan was to attack two defended localities, A and B, with two companies each, and two of these companies were then to go through and take C, the third objective. The attack began at noon on 22nd November with an artillery concentration, preceded by a bombing-attack by three aircraft. The Battalion's armoured carriers went in front, with two squadrons of tanks from 42nd Royal Tank Regiment in support, with the Battalion itself in lorries. A mortar detachment mounted in carriers, was to move in close support of each inner flank company, with an anti-tank troop from 259th Anti-Tank Battery RA in rear of both columns. Two artillery field batteries, W and X, were in support for the attack. The unpleasant surprise waiting for the Battalion on this occasion was that the ground they were to cover, which had been clear the day before, was now mined – a tribute to the rapidity with which the enemy could work. Fortunately, the mines had been laid so hurriedly that some had not been armed. The enemy was also strongly supported by its 88mm and 75mm guns, and the Battalion group had never met the tanks that would be opposing them. As the 1st Battalion got ready in the assembly area, the carriers and tanks could be seen going forward under heavy shell-fire, and the Brigade Headquarters, a few hundred yards behind the start line, received a 'full ration' as well. Nevertheless, when the Battalion moved up to the line, every man was in good heart and high spirits, cheering the Brigadier when he came to see them off and wish them good luck.

Lieutenant D.W. Gaylard led the way with the Bren carriers, two of which were blown up almost immediately - yet he not only brought the tanks up to their first objective but led them on to their second, showing great courage and coolness in doing so. For this and other gallant actions during the battle, Lieutenant Gaylard was subsequently awarded the Military Cross. The 1st Battalion crossed the start line at zero hour, and the troops debussed only 400 yards short of the enemy positions. In fact, the Battalion crossed the start line a little late, soon after noon, by which time the artillery concentration had finished. The men went forward unhesitatingly, despite the losses in company commanders; sometimes they went forward in front of the tanks, several of which were blown up on the mines, although some got through. There were many examples of individual courage and coolness under fire, both in the fighting itself and in the recovery of casualties, and many acts of gallantry must have passed unnoticed in the heat of battle. Strong point by strong point were cleared and by 2.20 pm, Objective A had been captured while it appeared that Objectives B and C were half captured. This meant that three companies held a position on an isolated hill, behind which were 300 enemy, equipped with heavy mortars and machine-guns, and still offering a determined resistance.

Lieutenant Colonel Desmond Young MC, an Indian Army Public Relations officer who was there at the time, provided a vivid story of the approach and subsequent action:

> *"As we crossed the desert that morning, we could hear the rumble and crashes as the artillery and bombers laid on. The little carriers of the Royal Sussex lead, followed by the tanks with their pennants flying. Immediately behind the tanks came the leading*

> *companies of the infantry in lorries. Behind them, Brigade Headquarters. Then came the remainder of the Royal Sussex, and following, more tanks, lorries and carriers for the 4/16 Punjabi attack, until as far as the eye could reach the plain was filled with fighting machines speeding into battle. I had just said, "Trafalgar must have been like this" when a whizz and a crash showed the enemy ranging on us. On the horizon upright black streaks marked the telescopic ladders of his artillery observers. We had had no hope of concealing ourselves on a plain as flat and bare as a billiard table."*

But it was soon clear that the assault was held up everywhere. The rising ground to the left and slightly south was assumed to be part of the Battalion's last objective, and heavy enemy mortar fire was falling on it. Although some men were moving about, others were lying on the ground with mortar bombs bursting among them, and were unable to advance further. While the distance made it difficult to identify the troops, it was assumed that they were the remnants of A and D Companies. Over to the right, where B and C Companies might have been, there was a good deal of sniping from the enemy trenches, and it was clear that neither company had succeeded in capturing their objectives. The other immediate concern was that there were only three hours of daylight left and thus it was imperative that the position should be captured before darkness fell. But the companies were heavily handicapped; only two tanks were still serviceable, while all the other tanks that were visible were knocked out and burning fiercely, their ammunition exploding inside them. At that stage, Captain Frank Day, the Battalion's Intelligence Officer, appeared with the Brigade wireless truck in tow, so at least communications could be re-established with Brigade Headquarters. Captain Day was then sent forward to establish contact with C Company to see what could be done to finish off the third objective; this objective had been partly sited on rising ground and most of it lay on the other side of the ridge, facing south. Although the Battalion's attack had come from the north, the enemy was apparently well placed to fire in that direction also.

When the Commanding Officer, Lieutenant Colonel Evans, was able to reach the bottom of the slope he found a wounded Captain P.M.J. Harrison, Second-in-Command of B Company. His Company Commander, Major R.E.S. Shinkwin, was farther up the slope with a mixture of troops from A, B and D Companies. He, too, was wounded. Major Johnson, D Company Commander, the officer who had given up his staff job in Cairo to rejoin the Regiment, had been killed. So also had Major Deacon, the Commander of A Company, immediately killed as he had debussed. Another officer who had been killed was Lieutenant C.H. Covington of C Company. He died with particular valour. As he led his platoon into the attack, a burst of machine-gun fire caught him full in one knee. His leg was completely shattered. But he did not stop. Hopping on his sound leg, he struggled forward, urging on his men, and he got to within fifteen yards of the final enemy trenches. Only then was he stopped, but it took a bullet through his head to do so.

While Major Shinkwin and his troops were just below the crest of the slope, they were unable to go on because of the intense enemy fire from machine-guns and mortars. Major Shinkwin had already tried to get round the flanks but without success, and the men on the slope were in a grim situation. All the time they were held there, unable to advance, their numbers were dwindling as more and more of them were killed or wounded by the heavy and accurate fire. Something had to be done quickly – and in doing so, Major Shinkwin calmly walked back amidst a hail of bullets, found one of the remaining tanks and led it on foot to deal with the opposition. Earlier, two of the Battalion's mortars, had been installed in two armoured carriers with a minimum of crew, so that if the situation arose, they would be able to go right forward in the face of enemy fire. As such a situation had now arisen, one of these carriers went rumbling up the slope, with Major Shinkwin's tank, and with this extra support, B Company was able to capture the last defended area by about 5.15 p.m. But it was at considerable cost and only as a result of the considerable gallantry on the part of the men:

> Corporal A.W. Talmey, already suffering from several wounds, continued to fight and lead his men forward, and when unable through weakness to go further forward himself, he gave covering fire with a Bren gun and so enabled two men of his section to get forward and capture an enemy post. For his courage and devotion to duty, Corporal Albert Talmey was awarded the Distinguished Conduct Medal;

> Sergeant E. Conroy, a platoon sergeant in B Company, although painfully wounded through the mouth carried on leading his platoon until the objective was taken. Sergeant Ernest Conroy was awarded a Military Medal for his gallantry and determination;

> Corporal P. Brennan was in charge of stretcher-bearers and seemed to be oblivious to the enemy fire as he tended the wounded. After one mortar bomb exploded, wounding two men, he rushed forward to help them, although he knew that already the enemy had put down something like thirty large mortar bombs in the area where they lay and more were likely to arrive. Corporal Brennan was awarded a Military Medal for his gallant actions;

> Private S.B. Young, the No. 2 of a Bren gun, immediately took over the gun when his No. 1 had just been killed. He maintained his gun in action and, although exposed to heavy fire and fierce opposition from the enemy, he opened fire himself whenever the opportunity arose. For his bravery and devotion to duty, Private Stanley Young was awarded a Military Medal; and

> Private J. Cunningham's section was held up by a Breda[30] machine-gun, and alone and in the face of heavy fire, he went forward and put the post out of action with a grenade. For his initiative and courage, Private Cunningham was awarded a Military Medal.

Both Shinkwin and Harrison remained in action until the position was properly consolidated and secure; only then were they evacuated to the Regimental Aid Post. Major Shinkwin and Captain Harrison were subsequently awarded Military Crosses for their gallant actions and leadership.

Meanwhile, C Company was still trying to capture the remaining part of the northwestern area; a position that was alive with enemy snipers. On his return to Battalion Headquarters, the Commanding Officer was informed by Captain Day that there were only fourteen men left of C Company, and that CSM Moore was in command as all the officers had been killed or wounded. Major Pollington, the Company Commander, had been hit in the chest shortly after the assault began. Thus, two company commanders out of the four had been killed and the other two had been wounded. A very quick action was required, and once again, Captain Day was sent forward with the one remaining tank with instructions to tell CSM Moore to do as best he could – and what a best it was! The sight of the little tank put new life into the remnants of C Company, which had been subjected to heavy and accurate fire of every type. With the tank leading, they rushed forward and swept over the rest of the defended area - there was no holding them - they cleared the position, taking no fewer than three hundred prisoners and capturing a large assortment of enemy weapons.

Some seventy-five percent of the Battalion came from Sussex and it had gone into action a little less than 400 strong; it turned out that they were to be outnumbered by something like five to one. Their objective had a frontage of about two miles and a depth of nearly a mile and a half. The troops had done magnificently; no less than 12 officers were either killed or wounded in the first 200 yards after debussing, and the battle had been fought very largely by the non-commissioned officers commanding platoons and sections, who had led their men with outstanding skill and courage. Many individual soldiers had shown extraordinary resource when they found themselves in a tight spot. By 5.30 pm, when it was dark, Lieutenant Colonel Evans was able to report to the Brigade Commander: *"Omar Nuovo is in our hands."* Lieutenant Colonel Evans was subsequently awarded a Bar to his DSO.

---

[30] The Fucile Mitragliatore Breda modello 30 was the standard light machine-gun of the Italian Army during the Second World War. In infantry battalions, one Breda 30 was issued to each section, so an infantry company would normally have about eight light machine guns.

The Battalion never knew how many of the enemy were killed but they had taken sixteen hundred of them prisoner, and had captured two batteries of 75mm guns, two 88mm guns and a large number of anti-tank guns and automatic weapons. But the 1st Battalion had paid heavily for its victory. Just under half of those who had gone into action had fallen as casualties; four officers and thirty-nine men were killed; seven officers and seventy-one men were wounded, and three men were missing, believed killed. The tanks had also suffered heavily.

Axis Prisoners Taken at Omar Nuovo
Photograph: Imperial War Museum

The 4th/16th Punjabis had already begun their assault on Libyan Omar but there was still much for the 1st Battalion to do before the men could get a badly needed rest. The Battalion had to be reorganised and the position consolidated against counter-attack, and the ammunition replenished. The dead and wounded had to be collected, and this was no easy task as they were scattered over a very wide area. On that first night, they were able to bring in all but one of the wounded and in twenty-four hours, the RMO, Captain Babty RAMC, treated no fewer than eighty-seven casualties. As for the dead, not one was found who had died other than with his face to the enemy, and most of them had died within a few yards of the enemy's trenches. The officer situation was particularly serious as none were left in A or C Companies, and in each of B and D Companies only one very junior officer remained.

The importance which the Germans attached to the Omar Nuovo position, so valiantly rested from them, was soon demonstrated when Rommel staged a panzer raid in strength behind the British lines. Following two days of heavy shelling, the tanks began their attack on 25th November. As they came forward, the 4th Indian Division's artillery held its fire until the panzers were close enough to be destroyed, and those few that survived fell back followed by harassing artillery fire. Despite continuous bombing attacks, which caused considerable damage, the Battalion held firm and through a regime of intensive patrolling, took the fight back to the enemy and succeeded in bringing in more than 1,000 prisoners.

An American correspondent, Quentin Reynolds, who inadvertently became involved in the action was so deeply impressed by what he saw that, besides writing an article on the campaign, he told the *Daily Express* that he thought the Royal Sussex were the real heroes of the Western Desert, and in a broadcast on the Libyan campaign, he went on to say:

> *"They were out of a book, this regiment. It might have been written by Kipling. I have never seen fighters like it in my life. Every night they would go out and bring in Huns and Ities. I was with them all the time; and their only one thought was to attack and pursue, and their only thought was to get close with the bayonet. All these were the fightingest men I have ever seen in my life.*
>
> *It was a little regiment called the First Royal Sussex, and they showed that they are quite fit to stand with the great British regiments of the past."*

But the battle was by no means over; it was not until the 30th of November - a week later - that Libyan Omar was captured after a very gallant defence. However, without the capture of Omar Nuovo, the situation might have been a great deal more serious than it was. Omar Nuovo became a haven into which poured various formation headquarters and isolated detachments to take refuge until the surge of German tanks had receded.

The next serious action came in December, when the Battalion was suddenly ordered to fill a gap nearly three miles wide, between the 22nd Guards Brigade and the 5th South African Brigade. Opposite this gap, and preparing to attack, were no less than two Panzer divisions. The Battalion occupied the position by night and dug themselves in so skilfully that, despite being shelled by the artillery of both enemy divisions, they suffered very few casualties. Unfortunately, one of the casualties was Captain Bapty, the RMO, and he had to be evacuated. He had done excellent work at the Omars, tending the wounded under heavy shellfire, and for this he was subsequently awarded the Military Cross. In the event, the enemy attack did not materialise and on the following night, patrols were sent out and brought back valuable information. This enabled the British armour to follow up the retreating panzers at first light, and inflict severe casualties.

Pursuit to Benghazi

The pursuit of the enemy, beaten in the Tobruk battle, began on 17th December with the 5th and 7th Indian Brigades carrying out a series of enveloping moves westwards – along the line of Gazala, Martuba, Derna and Barce. Outside Gazala, the Battalion was visited two or three times a day for three days by squadrons of Stukas, until the troops began to look on these visitations as a matter of routine, but they always gave them a hot reception! The plan was for the 7th Indian Brigade. *"to rush on to Carmusa and then turn to Martuba and Derna, while the 5th Brigade cut across their tail directed on Jovanni Berta*[31]*."* This sounds like Chesterton's 'Road to Roundabout' until one looks at the map and then the adroitness of the enveloping moves becomes clear. In effect, it was arranged that 7th Indian Brigade would work up the track to Carmusa and

---
[31] Generally referred to as *Giovanni Berta*.

having cut the by-pass there, would wheel east and seize Martuba, where extensive airfields were located, thereafter exploiting across the high plateau towards Derna. 5th Indian Brigade, on reaching the Carmusa by-pass, would strike in the opposite direction towards Giovanni Berta, a market town 23 miles from Carmusa, and thereafter, thrust on to the Lamluda crossroads, from whence the main highways led through the Djebel. This short cut involved both Brigades in difficult treks across rocky and broken terrain, in vehicles rickety and crotchety after a hard campaign. Nevertheless, the sight of rolling uplands, of grass and trees, the presence of abundant water and of fruitful grounds, was sufficiently stimulating to launch everyone on this adventure in good heart. The Germans were known to be in full retreat and the Italians, after their heavy battering, were not expected to provide serious opposition. At all events it succeeded; Carmusa was reached on the morning of the 18th, at about 11 am, and while the 4th/16th Punjabis secured the Derna by-pass, the 1st Royal Sussex raced back twelve miles along the road to Martuba, capturing an Italian tank with its crew, one heavy gun, some lorries and more Italians. They rushed on to the airfield, destroyed three aircraft, and secured large dumps of

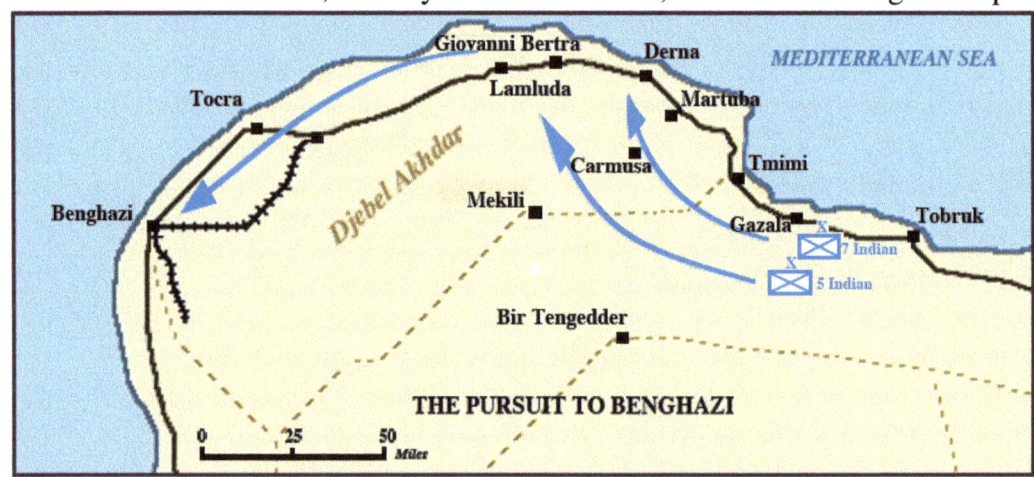

bombs and stores. The 4th/16th Punjabis also attacked and captured an airfield near Derna complete with transport-planes, bombers, fighters and a great deal of booty. Meanwhile, the 1st Battalion discovered a large hutted camp at Martuba where a meal, just prepared, had been left uneaten. Deeply shocked, they hastened to repair the omission! Although not called upon to take part in any big action during this phase, the Battalion suffered a number of casualties, caused by the enemy air attacks.

From Barce, the 1st Battalion had moved onwards, out of the desert and into the green and pleasant hilly country of the Djebel Akhdar, the fringes of which pushed northwards into the Mediterranean, and by the 29th of December it had reached Benghazi. By the end of 1941, the conquest of the Djebel was complete, and there can be no doubt that the 4th Indian Division had a major share in the victory, which brought the Eighth Army to Benghazi. It is even possible that an end might then have been made of Rommel in the Gulf of Sirte, if other events had not called once again for reinforcements to be sent elsewhere.

In Benghazi, the 1st Battalion found shops and cafés run by either the Italian civilian population or by Arabs. Life there was very different to what it had been in the past few months – then the Battalion had lived out in the open without any cover and everyone was exceedingly fit – in Benghazi they lived inside, billeted in houses and in very few days most of the Battalion had streaming colds or feverish chills.

About ten miles south of Benghazi, the Germans had begun to lay a minefield running eastwards from the coast. It was decided to make use of this to provide against the possibility of a rapid German advance from Agedabia, which lay about ninety miles south of Benghazi. The Battalion spent much of its time improving the minefield and getting to know the country thoroughly. It was fortunate that it did.

Gallantry Awards for North Africa in 1941

A month after the Omar Nuovo operation, it was learned that eleven members of the Regiment had been awarded the decorations shown below. However, there is no doubt that many other deeds of individual heroism had gone unseen.

Bar to Distinguished Service Order:

Lieutenant Colonel G.C. Evans	1st Battalion

Military Cross:

Captain R.E.S. Shinkwin	1st Battalion
Captain P.M.J. Harrison	1st Battalion
Lieutenant D.W. Gaylard	1st Battalion
Captain L. Bapty RAMC	1st Battalion (attached)

Distinguished Conduct Medal:

Corporal A.W. Talmey	1st Battalion

Military Medal:

Sergeant E. Conroy	1st Battalion
Corporal P.C.A. Brennan	1st Battalion
Private J. Cunningham	1st Battalion
Private S.H. Young	1st Battalion

Mentioned-in-Despatches:

Seven officers and ten men of the 1st Battalion were Mentioned-in-Despatches.

SITUATION IN NORTH AFRICA IN EARLY-1942

Although the 4th Indian Division alone had taken several hundred prisoners and destroyed many aircraft and heavy German tanks in a matter of a couple of months, the Axis forces were far from beaten. There was then an additional factor; with Japan's entry into the war in December 1941, troops that should have been coming to reinforce the Middle East were now being diverted to meet the new menace in the Far East, with Australia requesting the early return of two of her three divisions to defend their own country. The Eighth Army, therefore, was faced with extremely extended lines of communication, stretched out across hundreds of miles of the North African desert, but with insufficient troops to sustain it. The forces strung along the Djebel crescent were in a particularly vulnerable position; a situation which gave General Rommel a perfect opportunity.

By 28th January 1942, Rommel had struck with such success that, before midnight, he was closing in on Benghazi and the 7th Indian Brigade was cut off and surrounded. It was fortunate that the Brigade had been organised in mobile columns on a more or less self-sustaining basis. It was also equally fortunate that the leaders of these columns – Brigadier Briggs of Headquarters Group, Lieutenant Colonel Goulder of Gold Group and Lieutenant Colonel Evans of Silver Group, were all men of wide desert knowledge and great determination. It is interesting to note that although Brigadier Briggs issued only general instructions for the operation, all columns adopted similar tactics in making their getaway, even though each was required to make its own way back across the desert. Finally, the breakout proved once again the soundness of the old adage that fortune favours the audacious; the escapees had good luck because they took long chances. The situation was graphically described in *The Tiger Kills*[32], an extract of which is shown below:

> *"The booming guns at Coefia, the soaring flares along the line of the escarpment, told the 7 Brigade Commander all that he needed to know. He was cut off, surrounded, and in the greatest peril. As he studied his map, the desert called with no uncertain voice. If the enemy could be dodged in the coastal corridor, his brigade might escape.*
>
> *This night of storm was made for adventure. The pelting rain drove the enemy into close leaguer and blurred the sentries' eyes. The darkness was a dense curtain, although later there would be a moon. If dawn broke with the columns beyond the Agedabia-Antelat trails, the danger would be over. That meant 75 miles before daybreak across rough country.*

---

[32] One of the three books written about the Indian Divisions in Africa. The other two were: *The Tiger Strikes* and *The Tiger Triumphs*.

At 2000 hours all plans had been laid. A message was sent to Lieut-Colonel Lavender at Coefia asking him to arrange his own route if he could break away. A similar message went to Lieut-Colonel Peake of the Royals. (A message likewise was despatched to Divisional Headquarters but was never received.) The following signal then sped to Gold and Silver Groups: 'Road cut. Groups must make own way over desert. Carry only personnel and weapons. Conserve petrol by destroying surplus vehicles. Good luck everyone'."

The 1st Royal Sussex formed most of the 'Silver' Group, under its own Commanding Officer, and had with it C Squadron Central India Horse, 31st Battery 25th Field Regiment RA (25-pdrs), two troops of 171st Light Anti-Aircraft Battery RA, 259th Battery 65th Anti-Tank Regiment RA, and the anti-tank platoon of the 4th/16th Punjabis; its overall strength being about one thousand. However, most of the Battalion's administrative vehicles, mainly those from B Echelon, were to move with the Brigade Group, which included the Quartermaster, Major Charles Pocock, who had with him all of the Officers' Mess supplies for safe keeping! Although Silver Group had been fully refuelled before leaving Benghazi; the unrelenting cross-country route across the desert was to have a significant effect on the column's consumption of fuel, particularly

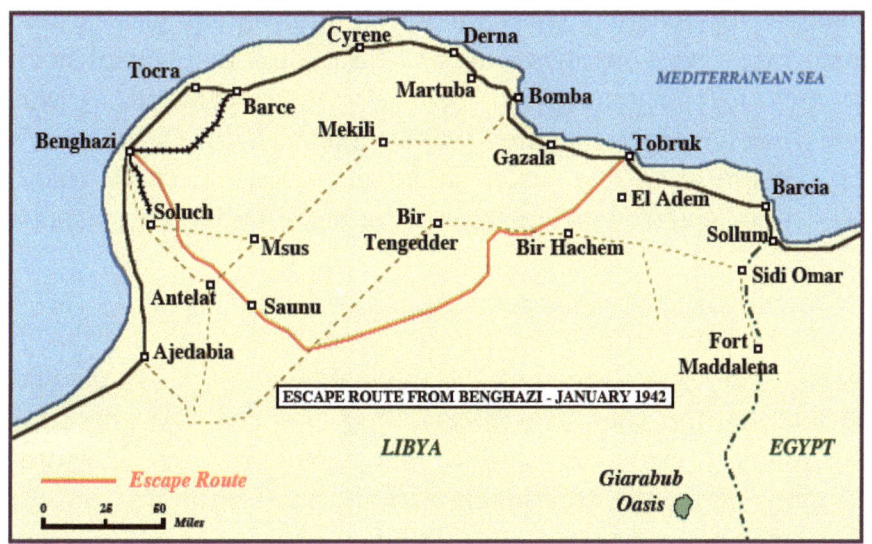

on the heavy users like the carriers and the 'Quads'[33], the large artillery vehicles that towed the guns. Fairly early on, some vehicles that could be taken no further – some were unserviceable and being towed – had to be destroyed silently *en route*.

The column had fallen back slowly throughout the day, disengaging after hard fighting and withdrawing behind minefields. By the light of the moon, the column had set out over the rough ground and at about 11 pm, at Nauughia Station, it picked up C Squadron of the motorised Central India Horse, which had been watching the gap in the minefield; the obstacle that the Battalion had improved earlier. The next morning, it had covered some sixty miles although it was discovered that one platoon of D Company had been lost overnight,

---

[33] The Morris Commercial C8 FAT (Field Artillery Tractor), commonly known as a *Quad* was used by British and Canadian forces to tow artillery pieces, such as the 25-pounder gun-howitzer and the 17-pounder anti-tank gun.

together with a troop of 25-pounder guns. However, in the course of the night, as a *quid pro quo,* the column had picked up an officer and five men of The Welch Regiment and four light anti-aircraft gun crews with their weapons. In was now that the critical stage of the journey began in earnest, and the column was formed up in wide desert formation, with two hundred yards between each vehicle, laterally and in depth; the overall formation being some two thousand yards wide and about three thousand yards deep. The Central India Horse led as the reconnaissance group, with the Carrier Platoon on the left flank, providing a guard against possible attack from the escarpment, which rose some six hundred feet above the coastal plain. The going was fairly good, although a little heavy after the rain, and the column was able to make about ten miles an hour.

The plan of escape was to make for the frontier oasis of Giarabub, a distance of some two hundred and eighty-five miles. By going so far south and so deep into the desert, it seemed fairly certain that the column would avoid any strong enemy formations; it was likely that the enemy would be much more active in the Djebel area to the north, concentrating on Benghazi and the long British lines of communication. By reaching Giarabub, the column should also be able to find water and stores; combat supplies that the 1st Battalion had helped stock there during the previous September-October. In the meantime, it was impossible to light fires at night in case it drew attention to the column's presence in a very hostile area, and when halted in a position of all round defence, all meals were taken from the emergency rations – bully-beef, biscuits and water.

As the column proceeded in a southwesterly direction, it was evident that it was drawing too close to the escarpment - a navigational error, which was intensified by the fact that the column was travelling at speed. At about the same time as the compass error was noticed, an enemy column of motor transport started coming down the escarpment and appeared to be heading for Benghazi. The Carrier Platoon was despatched to deal with it and as it closed, it was noticed that about a mile ahead of the transport column there were two German Mark IV tanks, moving along the base of the escarpment. Appreciating the potential problem, the Carrier Platoon slipped in behind the tanks and went straight for the motor transport; a column from the Italian Trieste Division and which consisted of twenty lorries, two staff cars and three motorcyclists. As the carriers were going in, one of the last lorries turned about, dropping its tailboard to disclose a 50mm anti-tank gun. Sergeant W. R. Rassel, the platoon sergeant, went straight for the lorry, zig-zagging to avoid the shells from the anti-tank gun, and then opened fire killing first the gun layer and then the crew commander. The three motorcyclists were also despatched with bursts of Bren gun fire. In the short, sharp action, the Carrier Platoon killed thirteen Italians and wounded a fourteenth. They destroyed eight motorcycles, five troop-carrying lorries and a diesel lorry and trailer loaded with eight hundred gallons of diesel oil. The other vehicles, which vanished over the hills, were badly riddled by Bren gun fire. The tanks gave no trouble

– they made off fast towards the north as soon as the carriers had started to attack! When the Carrier Platoon rejoined the column, it brought back a diesel lorry and twenty-seven Italian prisoners, including one officer. Sergeant William Rassel was subsequently awarded a Military Medal for his courageous and offensive spirit - a heroic and offensive action undertaken by the carriers when meant to be in a state of retreat.

In spite of this small battle almost within sight of Antelat, no general alarm was given and Silver Group was able to cross the trails, negotiating the dangerous gap without discovery. Retribution, however, was in the air. Two Messerschmitts flew low over the column and, contrary to orders, an anti-aircraft gun opened fire, and while one was hit but not brought down, the other 'plane returned to machine-gun the column. There were a number of casualties but the worse thing was, the column's identity and location had been made known. An hour later, six Italian bombers attacked the rear of the column and 2nd/Lieutenant W.P. Mayers and eleven men were killed and sixteen more wounded. At 3 pm, two low-flying Messerschmitts carried out a third attack and caused further casualties, although no more were killed. With complete calm and outstanding efficiency, Lance-Corporal F.W. Hall, the Battalion's Medical Orderly, assisted the RMO in dealing with and evacuating the casualties. For two days and nights he never left the wounded, attending to their wants and keeping them cheerful. For his outstanding devotion to duty, Lance-Corporal Frank Hall was also awarded a Military Medal.

The column then moved deeper into the desert and when it was some 60 miles to the southeast of Saunnu, it halted at 6 pm that night to eat. It was decided that, despite their tremendous achievements, the carriers, which consumed a great deal of fuel, would have to be left behind in the desert as there was no longer sufficient petrol for them to continue. At 7.45 pm the column resumed its travel and undertook an all-night march. The moon was bright and the going was good and by 5.30 am it was eight miles short of where it had hoped to reach by daylight, and it was still using far more petrol than had been anticipated. It was therefore decided to reduce the vehicles in the column to the bare essentials needed for troop transport. The Quads, the vehicles that towed the guns and which consumed so much petrol, were to be driven into a wadi where, among the folds in the ground, they would remain undetected. The guns themselves had their breech-blocks removed, and then the guns were to be buried in the sand. The intention was that once more petrol was acquired at Giarabub, the gunners would return and recover the guns and Quads. As this action was being carried out, a truck appeared on the skyline and, following investigation, it turned out to be a young officer of the Green Howards. He had been sent out on a patrol from the 150th Brigade of the 50th (Northumbrian) Division, and which was positioned about thirty miles to the north at Qaret el Auda in the Menny Massiv.

On the morning of the 30th of January, the whole of Silver Group formed up, still with its Quads and guns, and began the last few miles of the journey, arriving at Tobruk on the 31st. The rifle platoon and the troop of guns, which had gone adrift in the withdrawal, had made their own way across the desert to Tobruk and rejoined the Battalion two days later. The column had sustained fourteen killed and twenty-four wounded in the air attacks but the Battalion's carriers had cost the enemy fourteen dead and taken thirty-five prisoners.

The other two columns had also made it through successfully although the B Echelon troops with the Brigade Column did not fare so well. Many of them were captured, which meant that a considerable amount of administrative stores and equipment also fell into enemy hands. Only four vehicles made it to Tobruk – a company's 'Cooks' lorry, two Water Carts and the MT's 'Spare Parts' lorry. Some of the Brigade Column troops tried to make good their escape before they were captured and a hundred or so officers and men set off on foot across the desert. They had a hard and eventful trek across country – the road distance for their journey was something over two hundred miles - and many of them got through. One of the individuals was Private Hewlett of The Royal Sussex Regiment; Hewlett had lived on snails, been helped by Bedouin tribesmen and, as a result of his gruelling trek, had to spend three weeks in hospital in Cairo. However, he recovered and then joined the Long Range Desert Group, but unfortunately was killed in operations later.

The success of the breakout from Benghazi was shown when the 7th Indian Brigade tally was taken. Over four thousand officers and men had slipped through the enemy net and returned safely to fight again. They also brought back with them some eight hundred vehicles. *The Tiger Kills* well summarises the operation"

> *"The break-out from Benghazi showed British and Indian troops at their best. From the moment Brigadier Briggs gave the command, every heart rose to the tonic of a bold decision. They were audacious and it paid handsomely. Gold Group leaguering for the day in the midst of hostile forces; Headquarters Group cutting across the Agedabia-Antelat trails in the midst of the swarming enemy transport; Silver Group turning to strike venomously at a careless enemy; these were the daring acts, which won their reward. High resolve was allied to good practical management, and every man responded with a supreme effort. General Auchinleck made courage the keynote of his short stirring speech on March 7th, when he reviewed the refitted 7 Brigade. 'You got through because you were bold. Always be bold', he said."*

For its gallant action in these early campaigns in the Western Desert, The Royal Sussex Regiment was awarded the Battle Honours of **Omars** and *Benghazi*.

Gallantry Awards for North Africa in early-1942

Military Cross:

2nd/Lieutenant G.P. Bidder1st Battalion

Military Medal:

Sergeant W.R. Rasell1st Battalion
Lance Corporal F.W. Hall1st Battalion

Mentioned-in-Despatches:

One officer and two men of the 1st Battalion were Mentioned-in-Despatches.

THE TURN OF THE TIDE IN THE WESTERN DESERT

The 1st Battalion's remarkable adventures in the Western Desert were only the beginning of many further anxious months, during which Tobruk fell, and Rommel drove the Eighth Army back into Egypt until it stood at bay. The situation in North Africa in 1942, therefore, was one of extreme peril. However, the 7th Indian Brigade had no part in these latter operations; they were sent to Cyprus, and there the Battalion had a period of rest and training. During this period, Lieutenant Colonel C.E.A. Firth (The Gloucestershire Regiment) took over command of the 1st Battalion from Lieutenant Colonel Evans.

The new Commander of the Eighth Army, General Montgomery, arrived on the 12th of August 1942. Following a detailed examination, it was revealed that one point of vital importance to the whole line was virtually undefended. This was the ridge of Alam el Halfa, in rear of the El Alamein line but commanding a large area of desert. Here lay the key to the whole defensive system and any 'right hook' movement by Rommel must capture this feature to achieve success. Since there was a shortage of troops, Montgomery gave orders for the 44th Division to be sent up at once. Thus the 133rd (Royal Sussex) Brigade comes once more on to the scene.

In fact, the 44th Division had sailed from England at the end of May 1942; during the 26th to 28th of May, the 2nd and 5th Battalions, together with the Brigade Headquarters, had embarked at Liverpool in the *USAT[34] Santa Rosa*, while the 4th Battalion was on board the *USAT J.W. MacAndrew*. Captain Langham, a former 5th Battalion officer then serving with the 2nd Battalion, described the conditions[35] on board:

> *"It was a new experience for many of the officers and men, the majority of who had joined the Regiment since 1940. To the veterans it was almost two years to a day since the survivors of the pre-war battalions had landed at various south coast ports from Dunkirk. There was even a handful of old Regulars who had travelled in troopships before the war. Yet even these were as much surprised as the youngest-joined soldier by the conditions they found aboard.*
>
> *For Santa Rosa was an American ship belonging to the Grace Line and employed in peace as a luxury liner cruising from New York to the Caribbean and South America, carrying some 300 first-class passengers. Now she was taking on 2,400 soldiers consisting mainly of the two Battalions and Brigade HQ, together with 120 Light A.A. Battery RA, 133 Brigade LAD, 18 Field Butchery RASC and other details. The troops were stuffed into every nook and cranny. The holds*

---

[34] *USAT* - United States Army Transport.
[35] Swedes at Sea, *Roussillon Gazette*, Vol. 34, No. 3.

contained no cargo; they were filled with men sleeping on wooden bunks tier upon tier, and muddled in somehow . . . . .

. . . . We were escorted by the US aircraft carrier Wasp and two battleships – Nelson and Rodney – besides destroyers, and we felt pretty important . . . . "

The 44th Division had sailed for 'an unknown destination' but while it was still at sea, the news that Tobruk had fallen resulted in its being 're-routed' for Suez, apparently at the Prime Minister's express command. They landed at Suez on 24th July and, as Captain Langham expressed it at the time:

"Many of our hearts beat faster as we landed in that country which knew the Roussillon Plume so well, and we of the 2nd, 4th and 5th Battalions were proud to join our distinguished brethren of the 1st in the Western Desert, where they had covered themselves in glory."

Montgomery had good reason for demanding that the 44th Division should be sent up, for he had toughened and trained them himself on the Sussex and Kent beaches, until they had '*sighed with relief at the prospect of parting from the little man and his weekly training 'run-walks' for all ranks – even cooks and clerks – in full battle order.*' There was a quaint touch of humour in the fact that they were now meeting '*the little man*' again; meeting him, moreover, with unexpected pleasure for his appearance had a heartening effect.

Shortly after disembarkation at Port Tewfik near Suez, the 133rd Brigade moved to El Khatatba where extensive training took place in desert warfare. This training was in preparation for action in the Western Desert but was terminated early in order to move forward into reserve defensive positions.

Battle of Alam el Halfa

The 133rd (Royal Sussex) Brigade was given the key position on the Alam el Halfa Ridge, and on 16th August was deployed in order, from west to east: 4th Battalion, 2nd Battalion, Brigade Headquarters, and 5th Battalion. The 5th Battalion had also detached two Companies to support other Brigades; C Company was detached to 23rd Armoured Brigade, with D Company in support of 22nd Armoured Brigade. None of the Battalions had any experience of desert warfare, unlike the 1st Battalion, which was still in Cyprus, although preparing to return to North Africa.

On its voyage round the Cape, the 4th Battalion's Commanding Officer, Lieutenant Colonel *Bolo* Whistler, fell ill and was admitted to hospital. This was bad news but, as Captain Langham has put it, *"the mighty warrior was not going to be defeated by a mere microbe – not he!" While we were hacking away at the rock of the Alam Halfa Ridge, we suddenly heard he was back among us and once more in command of the 4th."* Colonel Whistler had contrived a passage in the next convoy from the Cape, reached Cairo in the middle of August, and learnt that the 4th Battalion was moving up from its concentration area into the desert the same afternoon.

The lack of defences on the Alam el Halfa Ridge meant that everyone had to set to work and dig in against time, and in very difficult terrain and conditions, for there was no knowing when Rommel's attack might come. Digging in that rocky soil was extremely difficult. According to Captain Langham, *"The picks were continually being sent back to the sappers to be straightened and re-tempered, while the company crowbars, having been bent into large hooks by hefty Sussex hands, were cast aside as no longer serviceable."* Explosives were really needed for the task, but the sappers were too busy getting the guns dug in to assist the infantry in this respect. Gradually, all infantry vehicles, less the company commanders' trucks, were withdrawn from the position, and these too had to be concealed, where possible, in vehicle pits.

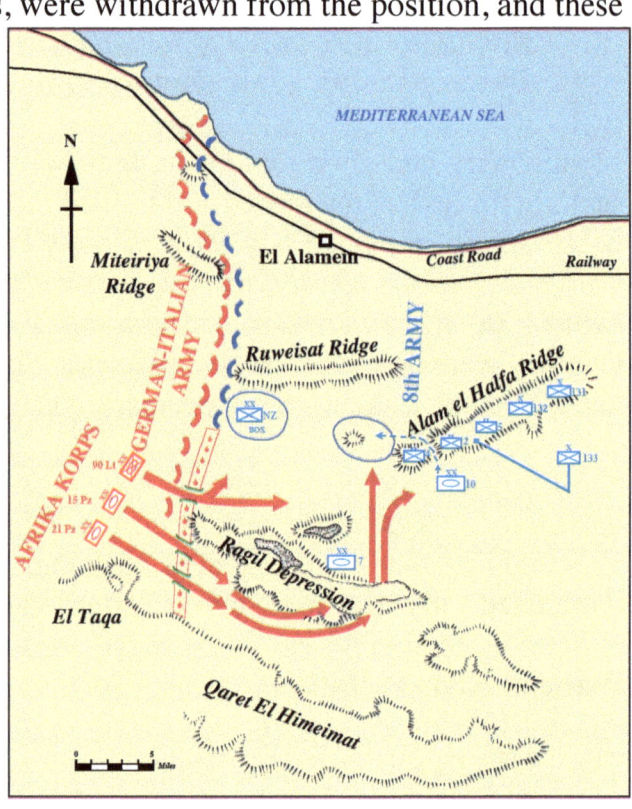

On the 20th of August, Mr Winston Churchill, who, as Lord Warden of the Cinque Ports was also Honorary Colonel of the 5th (Cinque Ports) Battalion, carrying on the tradition of William Pitt the Younger, visited the 5th Battalion in the line, accompanied by Generals Alexander and Montgomery. This was something more than the usual *'just to get to know you'* visit; morale was already high but the visit had the effect of making each member of the Battalion feel that something was really happening, and that the days were coming when the British forces would be in a position to take the offensive.

As the anxious August days went passed, the defenders grew more confident. However, even though Rommel's communications were now stretched out as badly as the Eighth Army's had been at Benghazi, he very confidently announced to his troops on 29th August that they would be in Alexandria within two to three days. Two nights later, he attacked.

Just before this vital assault, the Commander of the 133rd Brigade had fallen ill, and on 24th August, his command was taken over by Lieutenant Colonel Whistler, who came straight from commanding the 4th Battalion. Therefore, for the decisive battle of Alam el Halfa, a Royal Sussex officer led the Royal

Sussex Brigade, with one of his Staff Captains also being from the Regiment – indeed, it was virtually a family affair! In the meantime, Major C.F. Nix assumed command of the 4th Battalion.

Montgomery had anticipated that the enemy's main thrust would be made in the south, towards the Alam el Halfa Ridge, and was anxious that this should happen. Bearing this in mind, *Bolo* Whistler was concerned that the minefield defending the ridge had insufficient density, and while it was improved, he considered it still to be of the absolute minimum. There was also an important gap in the minefield, for resupply forward, but the gap, known as 'Queen's Gate', was only to be closed with permission from the Corps Commander – a classic dichotomy for the 'on-the-spot' ground commander in the successful control and execution of a reserve demolition.

Shortly after midnight on the night of 30th - 31st August, Rommel launched his attack as anticipated, with a formidable assault using 15th and 21st Panzer Divisions, the 90th Light Division, and the 20th Italian Corps. There were three simultaneous thrusts with the heaviest in the south. As dawn broke, the entire desert south of the ridge looked to be covered with German tanks and transport. At about 7.30 am, the German tanks dashed forward, heading for the gap in the minefield. Permission to close the Queen's Gate gap was finally obtained and was given to Corporal Barson, the section commander, just as five enemy tanks appeared and begun firing up the gap. Under heavy fire, the section and the sappers closed the gap but, regrettably, Corporal Barson and two others were killed and three more wounded. Captain Prodgers, who was in command of that part of the vital area, did very good work in getting the wounded in under fire, and then later the dead were brought in and buried by the Padre.

Meanwhile, the battle that was to decide so much in the Second World War was approaching its climax. To their south, the Battalions could see that the enemy's axis of advance was directed towards their ridge and thence northwards to the Ruweisat Ridge, in an attempt to roll up the line from south to north. Both sides had surprises waiting for them: the Germans were unprepared for the exact ranging of every feature by the British artillery; the British were unprepared for the German Mark IV special tank with its 'up-gunned' 75mm main armament, which could tear through frontal armour and finish up in the petrol tank. Again, Captain Langham recounts the situation:

> *"For the rest of the day it surged this way and that until nightfall, while the riccochets from the tanks of both sides were bouncing along our ridge with their peculiar whirr, and keeping our heads down!*
>
> *Meanwhile our medium guns and medium bombers were playing havoc with the soft-skinned vehicles in the enemy's rear. There was a medium battery in the 5th Battalion's area, and every twenty minutes, as a sortie of Bostons passed over the gun line, a salvo would be placed right among the enemy's transport. Hardly would the dust of this*

disperse, disclosing a vehicle or two set on fire, than the aircraft would drop a stick of bombs exactly in the same place. These attacks went on during the next day, and, as the day wore on, so the columns of smoke kept rising from the burnt-out lorries, bearing witness to the enemy's discomfiture and the success of this gun and air co-operation."

By day, the 133rd Brigade's positions would be pounded by Stuka raids and artillery action, with the Stukas doing some execution among gun-lines and transport on the ridge; by night, guided by an immense fire from burning vehicles, the bombers went on dropping their loads until morning. No company escaped without casualties, and all night the stretcher-bearers worked, backwards and forwards. Amongst all this, the defenders would send out strong fighting patrols by night, often as far as four or five miles from the position. One of these patrols, composed of carriers from the 5th Battalion and the 1st/5th Queen's, plus anti-tank guns from the latter, was of sufficient importance for Lieutenant Colonel McCully, Commanding Officer of the 5th Battalion, to command it in person.

The 1st of September saw the final repulse of the enemy after costly attacks during the morning and afternoon, while his communications continued to be pounded from the air. Two nights later, the New Zealand Division attacked southward from the El Alamein line, threatening to close the gap by which Rommel had entered the British position. Bitter fighting ensued, which left the battlefield littered with burnt-out and damaged tanks and vehicles, while the enemy drew back, having suffered a signal defeat. In this defensive battle, the initiative passed from Rommel to Montgomery; it exercised a profound effect upon the morale of the Eighth Army and, in doing so, gave the Royal Sussex Brigade, which held the key to the whole defensive position, an important experience in desert fighting. As Montgomery said afterwards:

"This battle has never received the interest or attention it deserves. It was a vital action, because, had we lost it, we might well have lost Egypt. In winning it, we paved the way for success at El Alamein and the subsequent advance to Tunisia."

On 7th September, General Montgomery 'called off' the battle, incurring some criticism for doing so, but he wished to keep the enemy's main force in the south, so as to help the major attack he was planning in the north. With this object in mind, elaborate arrangements were also made, assisted by the deployment of thousands of dummy vehicles and tanks, to deceive the enemy concerning British dispositions.

While these manoeuvres were in progress, Brigadier *Bolo* Whistler was being moved on to other commands; first to that of the 132nd Brigade, and subsequently, as the advance swept forward once more to Benghazi, to that of the 131st (Queens) Brigade, which joined the 7th Armoured Division and continued with them into Italy. During these campaigns he won two more

DSOs. General Montgomery gave him a higher tribute – his verdict was, *"probably the finest fighting Brigadier in the British Army today"*. As *Bolo* would not now be returning to the 4th Battalion, Lieutenant Colonel R.J. Murphy of The Buffs assumed command of the Battalion on 12th October.

The 4th Indian Division did not take an offensive part in the Alam el Halfa battle as such; the only Divisional representative in the decisive encounter was Captain Jephson of 11th Field Regiment RA, whose battery was covering the extreme left flank of the Divisional positions. His words though do give a clear indication of what had been happening across the whole battlefront:

> *"In my borrowed Matilda for three days I fumed over such targets as I am sure no gunners have ever seen before or since. At least 3,000 motor transports visible, 50 panzers wandering along eastward, several batteries of self-propelled guns coming into action and ambling off, chivvied by more fortunate gunners. All alas, out of range to me, and because of our infantry responsibilities, forbidden to move into range."*

Battle of El Alamein

The 1st Battalion, having rested and re-trained in Cyprus, had moved back with the 4th Indian Division in early-September, and took over the Ruweisat Ridge, which was the backbone of the El Alamein position.

For their part in the Battle of El Alamein, the 133rd (Royal Sussex) Brigade had left the 44th Division and joined the 10th Armoured Division, part of the 10th Armoured Corps – '*Le Corps de Chasse*' - as it was nicknamed. The Brigade's rôle had now become one of 'Lorried Infantry', and the training to fit it for this rôle was vastly different from that so far undertaken by the three Battalions. Training in desert formations was also resumed, with much emphasis placed on anti-tank training. On 22nd October, after a bad sandstorm, the Battalions moved to assembly areas between Bir Gaballa and Ruweisat Ridge. However, some elements remained behind, and with the aid of wireless sets, carried out a deceptive role with the object of denying information to the enemy about the Brigade's move.

The Battle of El Alamein opened on 23rd October and at 9.40 pm, the artillery barrage for the Eighth Army's offensive commenced. The bridgehead through the enemy's minefields in the north was to be made by four infantry divisions: 9th Australian, 2nd South African, 2nd New Zealand and the 51st Highland. The 10th Corps were to go in on the second night, with the object of deepening the gap in the enemy minefield made by the assaulting divisions. Later that night, the 133rd Brigade Group were to move up behind the armour to *SPRINGBOK ROAD*, where they waited to be called upon to move forward when the armour had passed through the minefields.

Before the Battle, the now recovered Commander of the 133rd (Royal Sussex) Brigade, Brigadier Alec Lee, addressed all ranks of the Brigade before the attack and the following is an extract:

> *"…. A superiority of weapons and tanks and equipment will avail us nothing, unless the men behind those weapons and in those tanks also possess a superiority of will-power to fight them harder, more ruthlessly, more daringly, and most important, longer than the enemy. Thus the success or failure of this forthcoming battle depends, in the end, upon us, from the Commander-in-Chief down to the individual private, individually and collectively. Let us see to it that the 133rd Royal Sussex Lorried Infantry Brigade provides an extra surprise to Master Rommel in the hardness of its hitting and lasting power. Let us make him say 'Gott strafe – these men from Sussex – do they <u>never</u> tire?'"*

Brigadier Lee, although from the South Staffordshire Regiment, identified himself completely with the Royal Sussex Brigade, concluded his address by saying:

> *"The last time we met the Boche in France in 1940, through no fault of our own, we were harried by him unmercifully and pushed out of the Continent. We have scores to pay off, so let us see to it that we harry him unmercifully and unceasingly and square accounts with him.*
>
> *To each and everyone I would say,*
> *God guard you,*
> *Good luck and good hunting. Hit first, hit hard, and keep on hitting.*
> *To sit still and rest is to help the enemy.*
> *Victory will go to the side that can last longest."*

At 5.20 pm on 24th October, the 2nd Battalion moved forward to occupy an area on Miteiriya Ridge. At the same time, two companies of the 5th Battalion reported to 8th and 24th Armoured Brigades to provide protection to the Royal Engineers clearing the mine-field. During that night, the 2nd Battalion and the two companies of the 5th were dive-bombed and shelled heavily throughout the night and suffered some casualties. At 3 am on the 25th, 133rd Brigade Headquarters and the 5th Battalion, less the two companies, also moved onto the Miteiriya Ridge. At the same time, the 4th Battalion moved through the minefields and took up positions protecting the right flank of the 2nd Battalion. The Brigade Headquarters followed on through the minefield at 8 am.

Throughout the day, the British armour made numerous attempts to cross the Ridge but enemy anti-tank and artillery fire was such that no advance was achieved. The attack itself, in support of the 2nd New Zealand Division on the Miteiriya Ridge, made no headway; there was considerable congestion between minefields, and considerable damage was done by enemy shelling and mortar fire. The 2nd and 4th Battalions were pinned to the ground from the fire ensuing from the armoured battles and casualties were suffered. During the day, 200 Italian and 100 German prisoners were passed through the Brigade area from various armoured units on the Ridge. At 8 pm that night, the Brigade was withdrawn from Miteiriya Ridge to a rest area further back, which they reached at 11 pm.

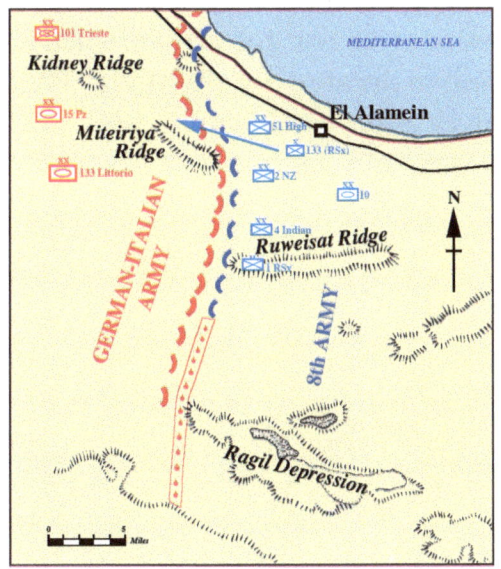

During the period 25th-27th October, while the Brigade was in reserve, 'Butterfly' anti-personnel and HE bombs were dropped on the area by isolated enemy aircraft. No casualties were sustained but three trucks suffered minor damage. However, on the 26th, isolated enemy bombing did cause a few casualties.

In essence, the role of the 133rd (Royal Sussex) Brigade, the Lorried Infantry Brigade of the 10th Armoured Division, was to follow the armoured brigades of the division during the main breakthrough and to mop up pockets of resistance left behind, and then to consolidate the gains. However, as the armoured brigades had failed to break out, the Corps Commander, General Lumsden, in desperation and at very short notice, launched the 133rd Brigade into a badly planned set-piece night attack on the 27th of October, against two enemy strong-points, which had held up the armour for four days. Not only was this an ill-conceived attack but it was not entirely clear, due to the lack of close reconnaissance and the poor quality of the maps, as to the precise locations of the actual objectives. It ended in calamity and the gallant 4th Battalion was practically wiped out.

At 8 am on the 27th, 'O' Groups went forward and the remainder of the Brigade moved up at last light, and then immediately prepared to carry out a night attack to re-capture the areas of *Woodcock* and *Snipe*, from which the 7th Motorised Infantry Brigade had been forced to retire earlier.

The plan of attack was for the 5th Battalion on the left, to capture *Snipe* and the 4th Battalion on the right, to capture *Woodcock*. The 2nd Battalion was to move slightly in rear and was then to occupy a position (*Kidney*) between the other two Battalions' objectives (*at the time this was referred to as Kidney Ridge while in fact it was a depression. The kidney-shaped contour on the map had confused many, until it was eventually occupied*). During the day, reconnoitres had been made as far forward as possible by the Brigade Commander and the Battalion Commanding Officers and their 'O' Groups, but owing to the confusion of the battle still in progress, the topographical difficulties, the darkness and the short preparation time, it was only possible to overlook small isolated parts of the ground across which the Brigade was to attack. Zero hour was fixed for 9.30 pm, but owing to the Battalions being delayed in moving up, it was later put back to 10.30 pm, at which time the 5th Battalion crossed the Start Line, while the 4th Battalion was 20 minutes late in doing the same. Five field artillery regiments supported the attack with concentrations laid down on *Woodcock* and to the rear of *Snipe,* as it was not known for certain whether elements of the 7th Motorised Brigade were still in the area of *Snipe* itself. Poor topography was a severe limitation; indeed Brigade Headquarters itself was unable to determine its own exact location until the position was accurately

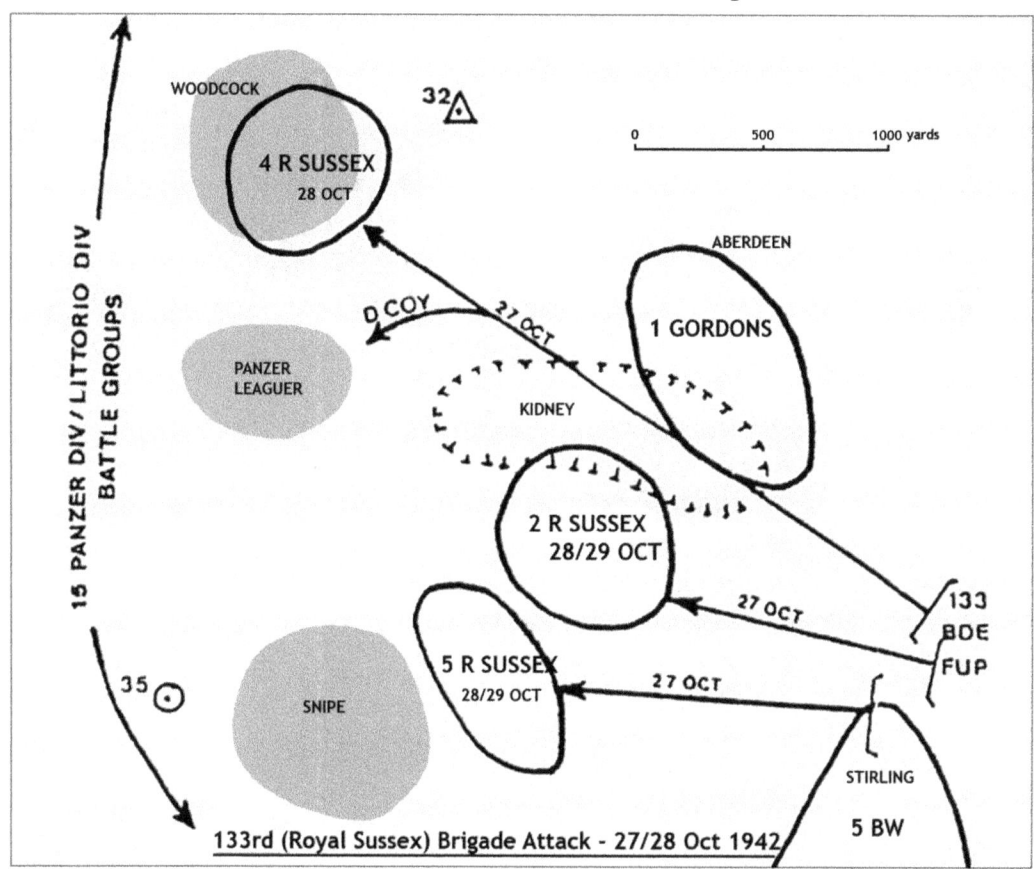

133rd (Royal Sussex) Brigade Attack - 27/28 Oct 1942

surveyed-in three days later. To help overcome the inadequacy of the maps, the Battalions all employed 'pace-counters' to physically pace the distance from the Start Line to the objective; an efficient system of calculating the distance travelled, as long as one could accurately determine beforehand, where the starting point was, and where one was required to finish.

The 5th Battalion's attack on *Snipe* was led by A and C Companies and although A Company reached its objective and started to dig in, C Company met much stiffer opposition, having had the misfortune to run into machine-guns firing on fixed lines. The consequence of this was that it suffered severe casualties, and the majority of the Company failed to reach its objective; it had lost some 80% of its fighting strength, including all its officers. Meanwhile, A and B Companies and Battalion Headquarters had dug in on the forward slope, and the Battalion anti-tank guns were brought up and dug in. However, it was later found that it was 800 yards short of its real objective, owing to the Start Line being further back than thought at the time. A number of enemy prisoners were taken and these were handed over to the 1st Gordon Highlanders, of the

51st Highland Division, who were to be found occupying positions to the east of the *Kidney* feature.

The 4th Battalion had initially encountered no enemy during its advance but after about 3,000 yards, crossfire from the left flank fell on the two leading companies. D Company, in reserve, immediately wheeled to assault the source of fire and, on closing, the enemy was found to be a close leaguer of panzers. The resulting battle decimated the Company, with the Company Commander and many others being killed. Nevertheless, D Company's actions had diverted fire from A and B Companies who had at last found the enemy and captured 200 prisoners and five 88mm guns. The 4th Battalion had advanced 2 miles to find *Woodcock* and started to dig in. However, they were isolated from the rest of the Brigade and, with the ground being so hard, the men were only in shallow scrapes and with their anti-tank guns prominent above ground.

At first light on the 28th, enemy tanks were detected approaching from all around. Only three 6-pdr anti-tank guns, under the command of Major Ormerod, made it to the *Woodcock* objective. These were unable to dig in due to the rocky ground and as dawn broke they were picked off from a distance by the German tanks. The next to be picked off were the radio vehicles of Battalion Headquarters and the Forward Observation Officer from 104th Regiment RHA, followed by the infantry. Meanwhile three further 6-pdrs under Sergeant S.G.J. Davies made their way forward and with a few infantry were all that remained in the very exposed and isolated position. His small detachment held an advanced position just behind a low ridge at Point (Pt.) 32, and later in the day, four enemy tanks appeared over the ridge and brought heavy fire to bear on the detachment. Sergeant Davies ran to one of the guns, and acting as the No. 1, engaged them and knocked out three German Mk. III tanks, and caused an Italian Mk. I3 tank to surrender, but regrettably, the three anti-tank guns were destroyed in the process. His coolness under fire and gallant conduct undoubtedly prevented the enemy from breaking through the position at a spot where its consequences would have jeopardised the safety of the rest of the Brigade. Sergeant Davies was subsequently awarded the Distinguished Conduct Medal for his outstanding actions.

The 4th Battalion was deep in enemy territory and out of contact with everyone, including its reserve company and, of more concern, its artillery support. The panzers closed in on the unprotected infantry, with no assistance coming from the promised support of the flanking armoured brigades, and before they were totally crushed, the survivors were obliged to surrender. Little help was provided by the tanks of 2nd Armoured Brigade, one of the closest armoured brigades who had detected the Battalion in its final throes, but had made no attempt to help extricate those that they could see being led away; such was the abysmal state of infantry/tank co-operation that the armoured brigade commander had considered it unwise to commit his troops so far forward, and nor was any attempt made by anyone in the 2nd Armoured Brigade to advise higher or flanking formations of the 4th Battalion's desperate situation. As a result, no one in 133rd Brigade, seemed to be aware of the 4th Battalion's fate; besides the total breakdown in communications, it was also felt to be impossible, owing to enemy fire, to even look over the intervening ridge. Notwithstanding the content of the respective War Diaries, the Adjutant of the 2nd Royal Sussex, Captain H.B. *'Jasper'* Booty was later to describe[36]:

> *"I remember looking down through my binoculars at the 4th Bn, who were very well forward as your map shows, and were all being rounded up by the enemy. We were powerless to shoot without inflicting casualties on our own men[37]."*

Even so, there was still uncertainty at Brigade level; Lieutenant Norman Craig, an officer from The Welch Regiment who was attached to the 133rd Brigade, and later to the 5th Royal Sussex, made the following observation on Page 61 of his book[38] when he arrived at the Brigade Headquarters on the morning of 28th October:

> *"Just as we arrived a liaison officer drew up in a jeep and called out to the Brigadier, 'There's still no sign of the Fourth, sir'. The brigade had made an attack the previous night: one battalion had overshot its objective and vanished."*

Nevertheless, it was not until darkness fell that it was formally determined whether or not the forward positions had been over-run. After dark, a patrol under Major C.G.M Gould was despatched, and returned with the information that the position was in enemy hands.

By the end, fifteen officers and 327 men of the 4th Battalion were missing, believed captured, and the Commanding Officer, Lieutenant Colonel R.J. Murphy, had been killed.

The morning of the 28th of October found the 5th Battalion on the left, securely dug in on a forward slope, but unable to move due to hostile artillery and sniper fire. Due to C Company's losses, the Battalion was echeloned back on the left. The 2nd Battalion was therefore brought up on their right, thus extending the line. It was during the reconnaissance, which preceded this move, that Lieutenant Colonel Hooper, Commanding Officer of the 2nd Battalion, was shot dead by a sniper as he viewed the ground, and Major C.F. Nix of the 4th Battalion took over command of 2nd Royal Sussex. Later that day, Capt D.R.C Hayes, the Adjutant of the 5th Battalion, was killed by an anti-tank shell, while trying to speak on the wireless. All three Battalions were under continuous fire from small arms, mortars and artillery throughout the day and confined to their

---

[36] *Roussillon Gazette.* Edition No. 16 - Winter 1993, Page 8.

[37] Personal letter to Colonel R.R. McNish of The Royal Sussex Regiment dated 29th April 1993.

[38] *The Broken Plume.* Norman Craig, Imperial War Museum, London 1982.

slit trenches, and thus any communications between them was almost impossible.

On the extreme right, the survivors and rear details of the 4th Battalion were taken under command of the 2nd Battalion and formed a defensive flank. In spite of the intense shell and machine-gun fire on the position, Private E. Eaton of the 4th Battalion drove his 15-cwt truck backwards and forwards between the Regimental Aid Post and the Advanced Dressing Station as it was not possible for ambulances to approach. He helped to both evacuate casualties and bring forward valuable medical supplies, food and water. For his most commendable gallantry and devotion to duty, without any thought for his own personal safety, Private Eaton was subsequently awarded the Military Medal. The 133rd Brigade now occupied a salient some 1500 yards deep to the south of the *Kidney* feature. Among the 5th Battalion on the forward slope, casualties rose from the constant shelling and sniping, and it was often not possible to get water and rations up to the forward companies except by carrier. Appreciating the dire situation, Captain G.M. Jelley, commanding the 5th Battalion's Carrier Platoon, although occupying a very exposed position, organised his carriers and led them forward to each company with the necessary supplies. He was continually under small-arms fire and anti-personnel shells from anti-tank guns, which could detect his movements in the moonlight, and although one carrier was destroyed under him, he transferred to another and carried on until the task was complete. He was subsequently awarded the Military Cross for his gallantry and determination, and many of his carriers were destroyed as they made gallant forays for resupply and casualty evacuation.

During the night of the 28th-29th of October, an artillery barrage was commenced in the Northern Sector, in preparation for an attack by the 9th Australian Division. The 2nd and 24th Armoured Brigades were withdrawn and the 8th Armoured Brigade was moved into a position on 133rd Brigade's right flank; the left flank being covered by anti-tank guns of the 84th Anti-Tank Regiment RA. Though a little easier during the hours of darkness, movement in forward areas was still restricted to a minimum. One company of the 2nd Battalion was, however, able to move to the area held by the reserve company of the 4th Battalion in order to reinforce that position.

On the 29th, sniping of the Brigade's forward areas continued throughout the day and movement was thereby rendered well-nigh impossible. However, it was not all one-sided as the 2nd Battalion mounted a series of raids to destroy sniper positions, and to locate others for treatment by British guns and mortars. It also took forty-one German prisoners, mainly from the 115th Panzer Grenadier Regiment. These were mostly snipers and anti-tank gunners who had been operating from derelict tanks in front of the Brigade's lines, and who had been driven out by anti-tank and mortar fire. As an example of such aggressive defence, Captain R.H. Langham, commanding C Company, which was holding a key position at Pt. 33, was awarded a Military Cross for his skill and determination in the way that he handled his Company, silencing many of these snipers and taking many of them prisoner. By a happy coincidence, the gunners that provided the close support fire were from the 98th (Surrey and Sussex Yeomanry) Field Regiment RA.

On the night 29th – 30th, the forward troops were ordered to withdraw some 500 yards to a reverse slope; the 2nd Battalion and the 5th Battalion took up these reverse slope positions but still under constant shellfire; the positions were in fact only just in front of the original front line. Private Daniel Syphas was attached as a stretcher-bearer to one of the Companies in this very exposed position, and with complete disregard for his own safety, he continually moved about this exposed area during the whole period tending wounded and bringing many in to the Regimental Aid Post, including rescuing a wounded sergeant from a particularly dangerous zone on which any movement was fired upon. For his consistent bravery and devotion to duty, Private Syphas was subsequently awarded the Military Medal.

On the 31st of October, the 133rd Brigade, though sadly depleted, was placed under command of the 51st Highland Division for Operation SUPERCHARGE; the attack that commenced on the night of 1st – 2nd November, in conjunction with the 2nd New Zealand Division. Thus it fell to the Royal Sussex Brigade to attack again and assist the final breakthrough, but under very different conditions of command and control to those pertaining on the 27th of October. Operation SUPERCHARGE was to strike the enemy with the Highland Division on the left and the New Zealand Division on the right. The 133rd Brigade, under command of the 51st Highland Division, was to advance and form a hard shoulder protecting the left flank. The 2nd and 5th Battalions were, respectively, given the task of re-capturing *Woodcock* and *Snipe* on the nights of 1st and 2nd November. As Captain Langham said at the time:

> *"Woodcock and Snipe had held up the whole of the 8th Army for over a week and it was therefore an honour for the Battalion to be allotted one of these objectives."*

These operations contrasted sharply with those of the 27th of October. Each move was carefully controlled and operated from a firm base, with Highland and Royal Sussex battalions mutually supporting each other. The operation was covered by massive close artillery fire, with Bofors firing tracer overhead to guide units to their objectives. Thus, although in the darkness, with thick smoke and choking dust, and against heavy machine-gun fire, sub-units sometimes lost direction, but errors did not multiply. An artillery barrage commenced at 1 am (continuing until dawn) for the night attack, while the 151st and the 152nd Brigades attacked the enemy further west, their objective being an advance of 4,000 yards. The 2nd Battalion took *Woodcock* on the night of 1st November with the 5th Battalion swinging south to take *Snipe* the following night. Again, there was close-quarter fighting, mainly with Italians as the Germans appeared to have abandoned their positions under the artillery barrage, while their allies had stuck to their posts before surrendering. During this attack, Private Walter King, when his platoon was held up by intense machine-gun fire, went forward and although badly wounded in the leg, spotted the machine-gun post and ran forward, hopping on his good leg and led a

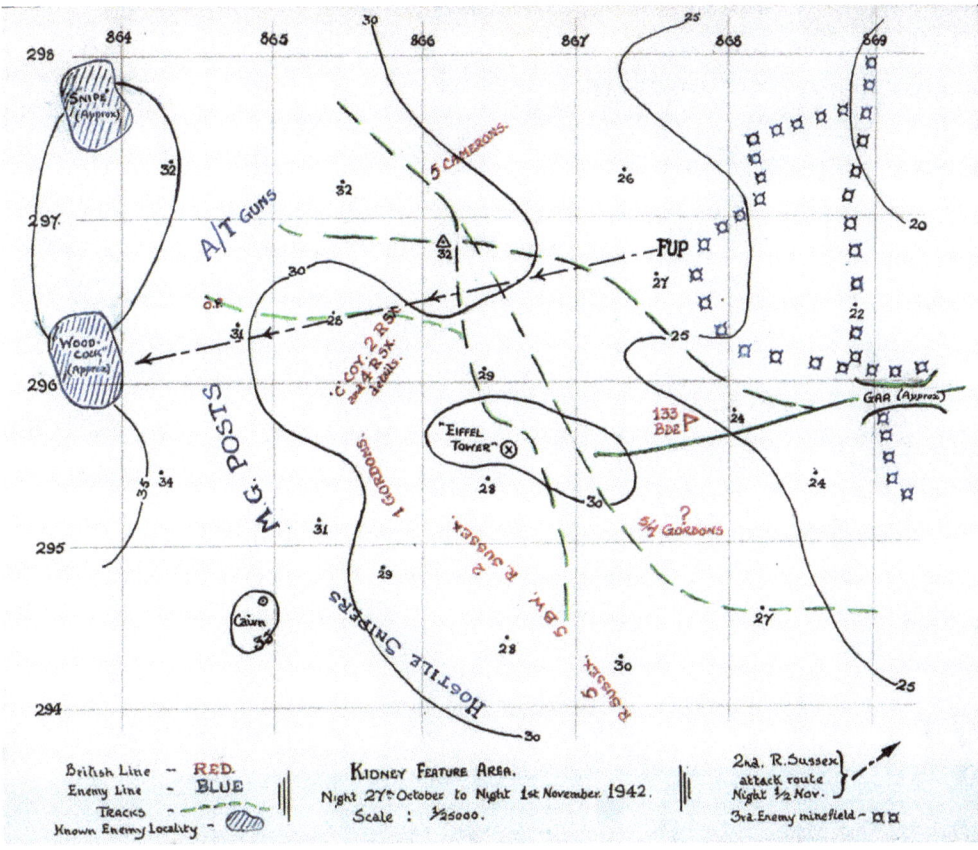

bayonet charge, which completely wiped out the post and enabled his platoon to continue the advance without further casualties. For his gallant and determined action, Private King was subsequently awarded the Military Medal.

At 6 pm on the 2nd, the 2nd Seaforth's, with 40th RTR in support, attacked the area of *Skinflint* (to the west of *Woodcock*), with artillery support and smoke. The attack was from the left flank and the tanks passed so near to the area of *Snipe* itself, that the occupants of that area were seen to be giving themselves up. In consequence, the 5th Battalion, who were to have attacked *Snipe* later at 8 pm under an artillery barrage, were ordered to advance and occupy it straight away. However, scattered Italian box mines held up the advance until the 3rd (Cheshire) Field Squadron RE arrived to clear a passage through the minefield. The area was finally occupied in the early hours of the 3rd of November.

The number of prisoners taken by both of the Royal Sussex Battalions was estimated at over 500, and most of them Italians from the Trieste Division. A Colonel and a Major of the Italian Libyan Army, who had only been at the front for a few hours, merely as observers, were also taken prisoner by the 2nd Battalion! In another part of the line, near Galal, a patrol of the 2nd Battalion captured General Frattini, commander of the Italian Parachute Division, and his staff. The officer commanding the Carrier Platoon, which helped engage and round up these prisoners, was Captain Lionel Queripel – later to win fame at

Arnhem and the award of a Victoria Cross, but regrettably losing his life in doing so. Lieutenant Colonel C.F.A. Nix, now the 2nd Battalion's Commanding Officer, was also gratified to later find four burnt-out mortar carriers of the 4th Battalion on the *Woodcock* position, thus proving that not only had the 4th Battalion been on their objective on the 28th October, but that their fate had now been revenged.

The precision, planning and command of this attack was excellent; an infantry attack planned and executed by infantrymen. This was particularly so, bearing in mind that the Royal Sussex Brigade had already suffered heavily on 27th – 28th October and had defended the salient for four days, its achievement, with only two battalions, in re-capturing *Woodcock* and *Snipe* is more than noteworthy; the Brigade's success allowed armour to break out to the southwest, which persuaded Rommel that the battle was lost.

Before dawn on the 3rd, the 1st Black Watch, of the 154th Brigade, relieved the 2nd and 5th Battalions. By 7 am, the 133rd Brigade had completed the hand-over of areas *Woodcock* and *Snipe* and immediately moved back to a former rest area, and thereby reverting to command of 10th Armoured Division. The rest of the day was spent in rest, cleaning up and reorganisation.

At 9.30 am on the 4th of November, the 133rd (Royal Sussex) Lorried Infantry Brigade, composed now of the 2nd and 5th Battalions, moved forward up behind the 8th Armoured Brigade and the Tactical Headquarters of the 10th Armoured Division, and where they later leaguered up for the night. The 133rd Brigade War Diary makes only one further entry on the Battle of El Alamein: *"The night of 4th-5th November was quiet."*

As at midnight on 2nd November 1942, the casualties suffered by the 133rd (Royal Sussex) Brigade during the Battle of El Alamein were:

	Killed		Wounded		Missing		Total
	Offrs	Men	Offrs	Men	Offrs	Men	
2nd Bn	3	22	7	102	2	20	156
4th Bn	2	16	3	26	15	327	389
5th Bn	3	27	3	81	3	50	167
Bde HQ	-	2	-	3	-	-	5
Total:	**8**	**67**	**13**	**212**	**20**	**397**	**717**

To put these figures into perspective, the number of casualties sustained during the ill-fated attack on the 27th – 28th November were:

7	39	4	112	19	373	554

The *Egyptian Gazette* of 8th November 1942, gave the following account of the 133rd (Royal Sussex) Brigade's last battle on this front:

> *"The Sussex had captured two vital features, driving a wedge into the enemy line. It was certain that the Germans would try to win back the ground. At first light, they attacked with tanks and overran some of the forward troops. They shelled the Sussex line and raked it with machine-gun fire. Every weapon they could bring to bear opened up at the slightest hint of movement. But the Sussex held on grimly. They remained out there in their lonely salient for a whole week. Then the crisis passed."*

Elsewhere, the 1st Battalion's part in the Battle of El Alamein started in a defensive position in the Ruweisat Ridge sector with the 4th Indian Division; it held the main Ruweisat Ridge, as well as a smaller ridge running parallel to it and some 1,500 yards to the south. On the ridge itself, the opposing main positions were only 900 yards apart, with the minefields and wire being a good deal closer. On each side of the ridge, minefields and wire were echeloned back, making a large No-Man's Land, studded with derelict vehicles and burnt-out tanks, grim reminders of previous battles, and which could be used at the time as observation and snipers' posts. The Germans had also placed their wire and anti-personnel mines with great cunning, so that the first patrols were expensive in casualties. The 1st Battalion's principal task was to dominate No-Man's Land and, with their offensive patrolling, to both confuse and to persuade the enemy that the main attack would be launched in the centre.

Every night, patrols went out into No-Man's Land and returned with useful information, but attempts to capture prisoners proved more difficult. One patrol, led by 2nd/Lieutenant Harrington, succeeded in penetrating the enemy's position but was seen by a sentry, who gave the alarm. During the withdrawal, members of the patrol touched off two 'S' mines, and they caused heavy casualties. It was the first time this type of mine had been encountered, and 2nd/Lieutenant Harrington and six of his men were killed. Shortly afterwards, Captain B.B. Clegg was successful in capturing two German prisoners on Pt. 62, on the Ruweisat Ridge itself. The main enemy position here consisted of a group of sangars, one of which was used as an observation post by night. This position formed a salient, which was strongly wired and mined, and artillery could make little impression on the defences. One night, when Captain Clegg had been on a reconnaissance along the edge of the salient, he noticed there was a gap in the wire close to Pt. 62. Just before dawn, he got through this gap, captured the two Germans in the observation post, and brought them back safely to the Battalion lines. In consequence of the information obtained from these prisoners, orders were given for a raid to be carried out on Pt. 62.

A piece of ground was chosen which resembled it, and wire and defences prepared to correspond with the enemy position. B Company, commanded by Major King, was selected for the task and withdrawn into reserve in the B Echelon area to rehearse the details of the raid. These rehearsals were carried out by day and by night, until every man knew his job. In the meantime,

Captain Clegg had carried out more patrols in the vicinity of Pt. 62, and had established that a party of some forty Germans, from positions in rear, came up after nightfall every evening to defend it. Captain Clegg was accordingly placed in command of the actual assaulting force.

B Company Headquarters based itself between Pt. 62 and the Battalion lines, and after dark, Captain Clegg took his raiding party of three platoons to the flank of Pt. 62, and lay up as close as they could to the nearest occupied sangar. His plan was to go straight for the top sangar with ten men and capture what maps and codes he could, whilst the main body mopped up as many Germans as possible. Officers were armed with pistols and grenades, the men with rifles and bayonets.

From their 'laying-up position,' the raiders could see the enemy force making their way to the post over the skyline. As they reached the area, they formed single file and went slowly forward to occupy the various sangars. Almost immediately the raiding party charged and they soon learnt the reason for the enemy's move in single file; an anti-personnel minefield protected the position. Captain Clegg's party was moving fast enough to get through unscathed, but those in rear suffered casualties. The top sangar was quickly reached, but as Clegg was climbing into it, a shot struck his pistol hand, wounding him and shattering his weapon. Withdrawing his small party, he silenced the enemy in the sangar with two grenades. As they were trying to prevent some Germans from escaping, two came up from the front of the position, and were promptly despatched by Clegg with an Italian pistol he was carrying in his other hand. The main assault party had now entered the sangars below the peak and were busy with the bayonet, so that the raid was relatively quiet, and the men were not shouting.

It had been arranged that, as the area was overrun, platoon commanders would return independently to the Battalion lines, to which they would be guided by tracer fire. Sergeant Thorne stayed out and returned the following night, having watched the Germans recovering both their own wounded and B Company's more severe casualties. The Company suffered fifteen wounded, who got back, and about ten missing, of whom most were killed. It was reckoned that twenty to thirty Germans were killed, and about nine had got away unhurt. It was a brilliantly executed night action, which succeeded in making the Germans very nervous in that sector. Captain Clegg was subsequently awarded the Military Cross for his leadership, bravery and devotion to duty throughout this action.

Two other members of the raiding party also deserve to be mentioned for their gallantry. First, Private A.J. Paterson, who was in the 'top-sangar' party, bayoneted two of the enemy, one of whom was about to open fire with a sub-machine-gun. When his section commander was seriously wounded by fire from an automatic weapon, Paterson also bayoneted the firer. He then attempted to assist his section commander to safety, but was fired on by a light machine-gun from another sangar. He immediately left the NCO and charged the sangar with the intention of silencing the gun, when it was put out of action by another soldier. His bravery and devotion to duty was instrumental in overcoming the opposition in the main sangar, thus reducing casualties to the raiding party. For his actions, Alec Paterson was subsequently awarded the Military Medal. The second was Corporal J. Bungard, when, on advancing to the attack, all his section except one man became casualties through anti-personnel mines. He however went forward alone and attacked a sangar from which a light machine-gun was firing on men of another section who were attempting to negotiate another wire obstacle. He threw a grenade through a slit in the sangar and killed the garrison of three. For his bravery and devotion to duty, James Bungard was also awarded the Military Medal.

German Prisoners Captured at El Alamein by Six Royal Sussex Soldiers

This raid even attracted the attention of Winston Churchill, who we know had paid an earlier visit to the 5th Battalion on his way back from Moscow. Now, reading of the 1st Battalion's exploit, he made special reference to it in the course of a message to General Montgomery. It was conveyed in the following letter from the Army Commander to General Sir Oliver Leese, commanding the 30th Corps:

"8th Army
11.10.42.

My dear Oliver,
The Prime Minister has been reading with interest about the raid carried out by the R. Sussex the other night. In a recent cable from England he mentioned, among other things, that he would like to send his congratulations and compliments to the Company concerned.
Will you pass this on and see that the message reaches Firth and his Bn.

Yrs ever
B.L. Montgomery"

As part of its principal task of dominating No Man's Land, the 1st Battalion was ordered to prepare an advanced bastion on the nights of 19th - 22nd October, which stretched some 700 yards into No-Man's Land, with the forward position being only 500 yards from the enemy's wire. It was to be ready by 23rd October and its purpose was not only to draw the enemy's attention to the area but so that it might also be used to assist attacks in the vicinity of the Ridge itself. This involved the digging and camouflage of the defences, and the preparation of 1,900 yards of wire obstacles and minefields, all in bright moonlight. Yet the enemy was not aware of these preparations until the morning of the 23rd, when the bastion was complete. After a description of the patrolling and raiding activities in the Ruweisat Ridge sector, which was held from mid-September until 2nd November, Captain L.W. Weeks quotes the words of a German captured at Tunis a few months later:

> *"Yes, I remember your Division, you were opposite us on the Ruweisat Ridge, and when you were there, we used to stand-to all night!"*

During the final stages of the Battle of El Alamein, the 1st Battalion marched by night from the Ruweisat Ridge to take over part of the Miteiriya Ridge from the 1st/4th Essex of the 5th Indian Brigade, to allow that Brigade to take part in the SUPERCHARGE operation, upon which the 133rd (Royal Sussex) Brigade had also embarked, and which broke through the last Axis defences.

Characteristically, Montgomery was to attribute the victory at El Alamein to his own military genius. Though he invariably claimed the credit for the transformation of the Eighth Army, he owed a great debt to the commanding officers over whom he presided, and who, between them, ironed out the flaws in the conception of his plan for the opening phase of the battle, and translated his intentions into practical and detailed plans of attack. It is not intended to detract from a memorable achievement to observe that the truth is perhaps somewhat more prosaic than Montgomery's version. Field Marshall Sir Michael Carver, a young officer in the Royal Tank Regiment, who survived the battle (later to become the Chief of Defence Staff), offered one of the most judicious appraisals of the 'slogging match' at El Alamein:

> *"It was a battle of attrition,"* he said. *"It may have been expensive and unromantic but it made certain of victory, and the certainty of victory at that time was all important. Eighth Army had the resources to stand such a battle while the Panzerarmee had not and Montgomery had the determination, willpower and ruthlessness to see such a battle through."*

In terms of providing a tribute to The Regiment's bravery and conduct at El Alamein, nothing could be more fulfilling than that made by a fellow brother-in-arms. Sergeant Beaney, also of the Royal Tank Regiment, and supporting the 133rd Brigade, wrote the following letter, which was read out at the annual meeting of the Regimental Association in February 1943:

> *"Sir,*
>
> *I hope like yourself and members serving in England and other parts of the Empire to know what a great show the officers, N.C.O's and men of the Royal Sussex regiment put up at Alamein, as I witnessed their splendid and courageous part. I felt I must write to say I have read of the courage and fighting qualities of the Royal Sussex regiment in the last world war and in past generations before that, but to see it and witness it as I have done is very inspiring. I assure you sir the fighting qualities of the members taking part is something to be envied. Their courage, loyalty, guts and devotion to duty under hellish conditions, is something they and the people of Sussex can be proud of. If guts has anything to do with it, that explains the meaning of the 'Men of the bulldog breed' – ask the Jerry! No praise is too good for them. Their example is a good ideal for the future Sussex Regiments, and I know they will not be let down. In closing, sir, I wish you and them the best of luck and success in the future.*
>
> *From a Sussex man and proud of it.*
> *SERGT. BEANEY*
> *Royal Tank Regiment"*

For its gallant actions in the North African campaigns of 1942, The Royal Sussex Regiment was awarded the Battle Honours of **Alam el Halfa** and **El Alamein,** both of which Honours are emblazoned on the Colours.

Gallantry Awards for North Africa in 1942

Bar to Distinguished Service Order:

Lieutenant Colonel L.G. Whistler DSO	Commanding 131st Brigade

Distinguished Service Order:

Lieutenant Colonel C.E.A. Firth (Glosters)	1st Battalion
Lieutenant Colonel J.J. McCully	5th Battalion

Distinguished Conduct Medal:

Sergeant S.G.J. Davies	4th Battalion

Military Cross:

Captain B.B. Clegg	1st Battalion
Captain G.M. Jelley	5th Battalion
Captain R.H. Langham	2nd Battalion

Lieutenant H.V. Holden-White   No. 2 SBS[39] Unit

Military Medal:

Sergeant D.G. Wells	5th Battalion
Sergeant H.G. White	5th Battalion
Corporal J. Bungard	1st Battalion
Private E. Eaton	4th Battalion
Private W. King	2nd Battalion
Private A.J. Paterson	1st Battalion
Private D. Syphas	2nd Battalion
Private R.R.J. Weller	Att. 3rd Battalion Parachute Regiment

Mentioned-in-Despatches:

Eight officers and five men of the Regiment's Battalions were Mentioned-in-Despatches.

The Aftermath of El Alamein

During November and December 1942, the 4th Indian Division was used to clear up the battlefield and then to follow in rear of the advancing army. The readiness of many of the enemy troops to become prisoners is illustrated by the Reuter's article[40] about an Italian Captain captured east of Matruh, who said there were 150 German and Italian soldiers waiting a few miles away. As the 1st Battalion operating in the region had no vehicles for transporting prisoners, the Italian Captain offered to solve the problem, *"I can easily get you 15 of our lorries in working order,"* he said. *"I will get you the vehicles and the drivers. All you have to do then is collect the prisoners."* In charge of a solitary officer, a convoy of 15 Italian lorries, driven by Italians, went out to pick up the prisoners and take them to the British camps!

The 1st Battalion's Christmas in 1942 was spent at El Adem, near Tobruk, where the Division remained until March 1943. This was because a storm at Benghazi had resulted in the blocking of the harbour, and only one Corps could be maintained in contact with the enemy; the transport of the remainder of the Army being used to ferry petrol and stores forward.

In early November 1942, the 133rd (Royal Sussex) Brigade had been reduced to the 2nd and 5th Battalions. Those elements of the 4th Battalion, which had not been absorbed into either of the other two Battalions, were despatched to the

---

[39] Special Boat Service (Oran)

[40] Italian Offer to Royal Sussex Regiment, *From Reuter's Special Correspondent*, Cairo, Monday (Published on Tuesday 17th November 1942)

Base area to reform the Battalion. However, before long, the whole Brigade went back to the Canal Zone as well, but the Brigade itself was disbanded.

Although the 2nd Battalion had been scheduled for conversion to a parachute battalion, the War Office ruled that it could not be transferred to the Army Air Corps,[41] while retaining its 2nd Royal Sussex title; consequently, the 2nd Battalion remained in the Regiment. Nevertheless, two hundred officers and men from the 2nd Battalion volunteered to parachute[42] and were accepted as fit, forming at Kabrit as the nucleus of the 10th Battalion The Parachute Regiment. Lt Colonel Smyth, who had only recently taken over command of the 2nd Battalion, was appointed to command the 10th Parachute Battalion, although for a short period he was also acting as the Commander of the new Parachute Brigade.

Company-Sergeant-Major T.C. Bentley DCM, one of the original Royal Sussex volunteers who transferred as a Sergeant, later recorded:

> *"Nearly all the Warrant Officers[43] and Sergeants who were fit for that kind of activity volunteered, and the junior ranks followed suit. Colonel Smyth did his best to keep the men in their original sections, platoons and companies."*

On the 29th of December, an important conference took place at General Headquarters in Cairo to decide the future of the 2nd, 4th and 5th Battalions. The conference was composed of Colonel T.F.V. Foster CBE MC, Colonel of The Royal Sussex Regiment, Lieutenant Colonel J.J. McCully DSO, Lieutenant Colonel C.F.A. Nix TD, and Major D. Richards MC, under the chairmanship of Brigadier J.E.C. McCandish CB CBE of the General Headquarters. As a result of the conference, the remaining members of the 4th Battalion were transferred to the newly reconstituted 2nd Battalion, under the command of Lieutenant Colonel Nix, formerly of the 4th Battalion. In order to preserve the Territorial Army element of the Regiment intact, the 5th Battalion assumed the title of the 4th/5th (Cinque Ports) Battalion with effect from 1st January 1943, and under the command of Lieutenant Colonel McCully DSO; Colonel McCully had been awarded the Distinguished Service Order for his outstanding leadership, devotion to duty and calmness under fire for his actions in both the attacks on 27th-28th November and again on the 1st-2nd November.

The Royal Sussex Brigade, composed of the 2nd and the 4th/5th Battalions, subsequently became part of the Persia and Iraq Force, and where it was then

---

[41] Early in the war, Winston Churchill announced the establishment of a new branch of army aviation, the Army Air Corps, formed in 1942. It comprised the Glider Pilot Regiment, the Parachute Battalions (subsequently the Parachute Regiment), and the Air Observation Post Squadrons. In 1944, the SAS Regiment was added to the Corps.

[42] *The Tenth.* Record of service of the 10th Battalion, The Parachute Regiment 1942-1945, A Study by Ron Brammall. 1965.

[43] The four principle Company-Sergeant-Major posts in the 10th Parachute Battalion were found by Warrant Officers from the 2nd Battalion The Royal Sussex Regiment.

deployed. Those who had joined the 10th Parachute Battalion went on to fight in Italy before going back to England to be ready for a great and all but decisive enterprise.

THE BEGINNING OF THE END IN NORTH AFRICA IN LATE-1942

Having been conditioned, since 1940, for reinforcements to the North African campaign to be diverted elsewhere, the situation changed dramatically in late-1942 when Anglo-American forces launched an amphibious operation against French North Africa, in particular against the French-held territories of Algeria and Morocco. The landing, code-named Operation TORCH, reflected the results of long and contentious arguments between British and American planners about the future course of Allied strategy; in both a direct and an indirect sense, the impact of the operation was enormous on the course of Anglo-American strategy during the remainder of the war. It may have been the most important strategic decision that Allied leaders would make. In fact, this amphibious operation inevitably postponed the Allied landings in France until 1944, but at the same time it allowed the United States to complete mobilization of its immense industrial and manpower resources for the titanic air and ground battles that characterized the Allied campaigns of 1944.

Nevertheless, the final plan for TORCH was an ambitious one as the western Allies would transport 65,000 men, commanded by Lieutenant General Dwight D. Eisenhower, from ports in the United States and England, and invade the French North African possessions at Casablanca, Oran and Algiers. The Allied

Operation TORCH - The Three Task Force Landing Sites

move against French North Africa benefited enormously from the fact that the attention of Axis political and military leaders remained focused elsewhere. The Germans were involved in their struggle for Stalingrad and the Caucasus. Moreover, the situation in Egypt had grown increasingly grim for them throughout September and into October, as the British had built up their forces and attacked the Germans at El Alamein, precipitating the massive battle of attrition that the Axis forces had no hope of winning. Not surprisingly, the Axis leaders were concentrating more on what was happening in the Western Desert, and by early November, Rommel's forces were rapidly retreating back into Libya against Hitler's express orders.

American and British forces landed at several points along the coast of French Morocco and Algeria on 8th November 1942, only a few days after the Eighth Army's breakout in the east following the Battle of El Alamein. Coming ashore in Algeria, as part of the Eastern Task Force, was the British First Army, commanded by Lieutenant General Sir Kenneth Anderson, and which was composed of both British and American forces. Understanding the danger of a two-front war, German and Italian troops were ferried in from Sicily to occupy Tunisia, one of the few easily defended areas of North Africa, and only one night's sail from their bases in Sicily. An immediate attempt was made by First Army to cut off Tunis in November and December, before the German troops could arrive in strength. However, because of the poor road and rail communications, only a small divisional size force could be supported logistically, while the excellent defensive terrain permitted the small numbers of German and Italian troops landed there to hold them off. This resulted in the disastrous battles at Faïd and the Kasserine Pass, where the untested and poorly-led American troops suffered heavy casualties, with the US 1st Armoured Division bearing the brunt of the punishment. This allowed most of Tunisia to fall into German hands, with the entrances into the coastal lowlands all being blocked. After these failures, a period of consolidation was forced upon the First Army, particularly in respect of the US tactical doctrine, as well as the need to ensure the better provision of logistic and air support. However, by the time the Eighth Army approached the Tunisian border from the east, following its long pursuit of Rommel's forces after El Alamein, the First Army was in a much better state and able to strike again more effectively.

Hitler, infuriated by Rommel's pessimism that North Africa could not be held, refused to allow him to return from Germany to Tunisia, and on 9th March 1943, appointed General Jürgen Freiherr von Arnim as the new commander of the Axis Forces in Tunisia. The new commander was a prim and unctuous product of the German General Staff, who had refused to cooperate with Rommel in defending Tunisia, and was someone that, before too long, the Royal Sussex Regiment would get to know a great deal better.

Advance to the Mareth Line

The Eighth Army had taken Tripoli in Libya on 23rd January 1943, thereby cutting off the Axis Forces' main supply base. Rommel had planned for this eventuality, and intended to block the southern approach to Tunisia from Tripoli by occupying an extensive set of defensive works known as the Mareth Line, a line of forts and fortifications built by the French in the 1930s. He had concluded that with their lines steadied by the Atlas Mountains on the west and the Gulf of Sidra on the east, even small numbers of Axis troops would be able to hold off the Allied forces.

Although the 4th Indian Division had been in reserve throughout all these strategic landings, manoeuvres and deliberations, with the war appearing to have been going very far ahead, the time in the early months of 1943 had not been wasted, as the 1st Battalion had the opportunity to carry out intensive

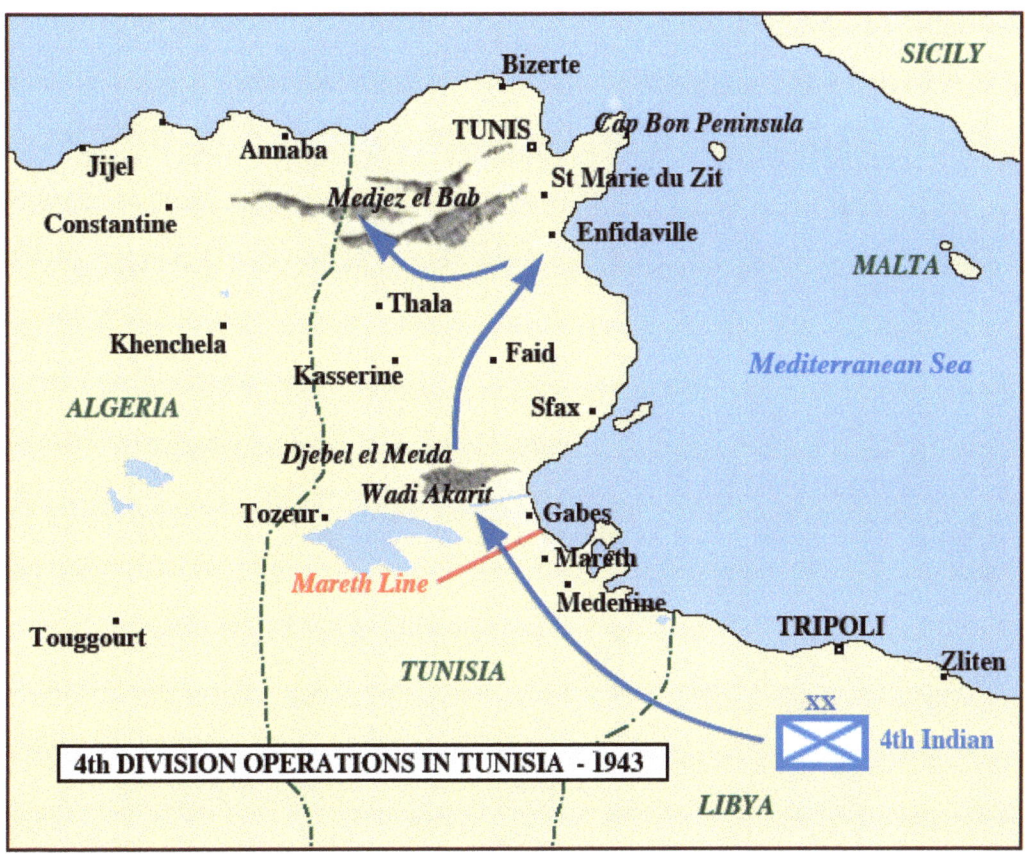

training for the events that were no doubt to follow. Then the portent of the hilly country of the Mareth Line ahead seemed to *'provide a job for the Indians'*, and the Division went forward again, until they were in Tunisia, north-west of Medenine.

Within twenty-four hours of the 1st Battalion's arrival, it had two fighting patrols out and the turning of the Mareth Line was completed *'in true 4th Indian Division style to the tune of Attack and Pursue.'* The pursuing, at all events, went according to plan, until they found themselves in the rear of the Mareth Line, southwest of Gabès. The enemy were then in full retreat, and the Battalion played its first important rôle in the Tunisian campaign on reaching the line of the Wadi Akarit.

Here it was understood that an early conclusion to the campaign might be achieved by the breaking of this line and its westward extension into the Zouai Hills. The latter region was to become the Battalion's chief battleground. Immediately before this operation, the 1st Royal Sussex lay encamped in an open plain covered with yellow flowers and, here and there, a small crop of wavy green barley. Six miles away it was broken by formidable hills. These hills, the Battalion learnt on 5th April, were to be the objective of a silent night attack.

All ammunition and guns were to be carried on their backs – an exercise which was practised throughout the day. Besides these, it would be necessary to carry onto the objectives, the mortars, wireless-sets, batteries, picks, shovels, telephone-cables and other accessories, once they had been secured.

Darkness fell as the Companies marched to their assembly areas – it was a moonless night, and the approach to the hills had to be made stealthily. For several hours no sound was heard but the muffled crunch of feet, the swish of

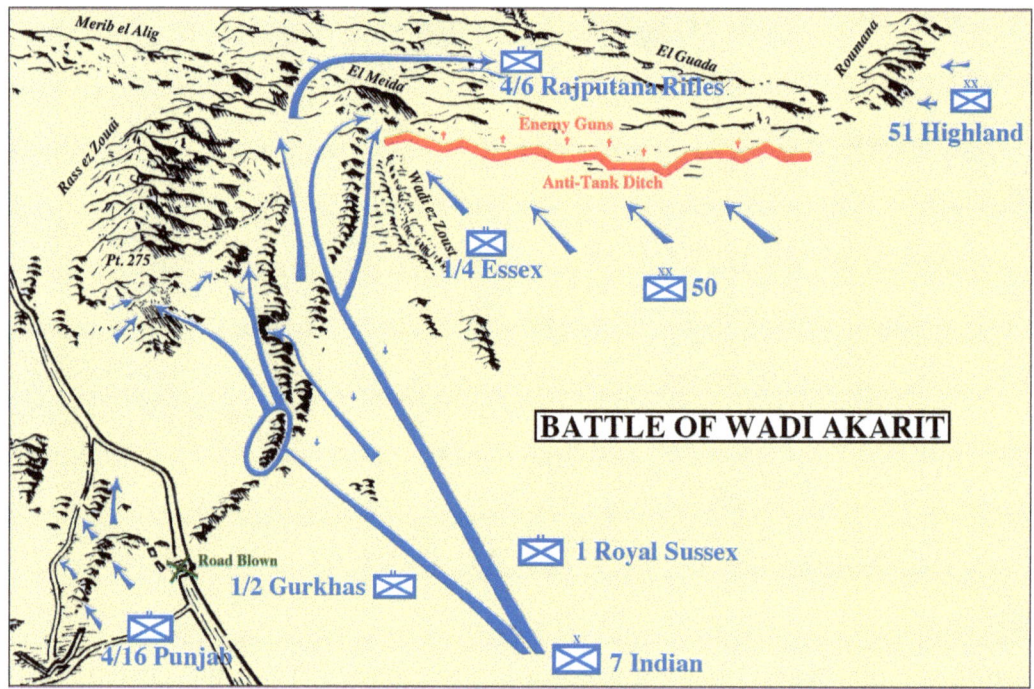

grass, and occasional mutters of martial anathema. Gradually the sinister black shapes of the hills – the Djebel el Meida Hill in particular - loomed up before the advancing force, and towered steeply above their heads as they moved into a small wadi.

When it seemed they must be within easy hearing of the enemy, and the pace-counters were conferring more frequently about their exact position, the leading elements had the misfortune to trample through some 'plane-wreckage. In the dark, it was impossible to avoid it or stop those in rear from walking on to it, and they could only push on, praying that they had not been heard. Captain Weeks (*the Battalion's Patrol Master*) feared that they had, for almost at once there came the swish and bang of a mortar-bomb, followed in quick succession by several more. Intermingled was the chatter of Bredas, and Verey lights and star-shells lighted up the scene.

The 1st Royal Sussex suffered a few casualties but, after a short reorganisation, soon set off again with the two leading companies pushing on towards their different objectives. A carrying-party left behind in the wadi was startled by a blood-curdling yell, *"coming as it seemed from the very bowels of the earth"*. It was the war cry of the Punjabis as they went into the attack on the left.

General Firth, the 1st Battalion's Commanding Officer at the time, when recalling the Wadi Akarit battle, stated that the enemy's defensive fire was not actually provoked by the troops trampling on the 'plane wreckage. The 7th Indian Brigade had advanced to the attack with the 1st/2nd Gurkhas leading, followed by the 1st Royal Sussex, with the 4th/16th Punjabis bringing up the rear. The Gurkhas were to attack the Fatnassa feature directly to their front, and the 1st Royal Sussex, on reaching a position close to the enemy's line, were to change direction half right and advance due north to seize the El Meida hill at the end of the enemy's anti-tank ditch. The Punjabis were then to attack southward after 1st Royal Sussex had made its northward move. Unfortunately, the Gurkhas' silent attack was followed immediately by the enemy's defensive fire, which fell directly on the Royal Sussex and also cut off the taping party from the main body. This intense mortar and shellfire caused many casualties, with many heroic deeds being enacted by both officers and men, especially those concerned with the recovery and care of the wounded.

Despite some confusion, Major Gaylard led D Company forward, its objective being captured just before dawn, although its gallant commander, already mentioned for his heroism at the Battle of the Omars, was killed early on in the assault. Captain Weeks had immediately taken over the Company and led it forward, capturing the objective in the face of stubborn resistance, and then holding it under continuous fire until the rest of the Battalion arrived. Captain Weeks was subsequently awarded the Military Cross for his initiative, leadership and bravery. The rest of the Battalion, guided by the North Star and some helpful artillery shoots by 31st Field Regiment RA on the objective, requested by the Commanding Officer, soon cleared the remainder of the position; some parties even reached a ridge overlooking the line of the enemy's retreat, a thousand yards below.

Meanwhile, the 50th Division's frontal assault on the anti-tank ditch was in full swing, although its infantry on the left flank had been pinned down. Quickly appreciating the situation, Sergeant James Bungard MM led his platoon with great dash into the rear of the anti-tank obstacle, and charging with the bayonet, captured four 65mm field guns and a number of prisoners. These weapons were immediately turned on nearby enemy batteries and mortars, which were shelling the flanking Northumbrian Infantry Brigade. For his gallantry, leadership and determination, Sergeant Bungard was subsequently awarded a Bar to the Military Medal, which he had earlier been awarded at El Alamein.

Dawn found the 1st Battalion busily consolidating its gain, having gouged a hole in the enemy's defensive system, taking 300 prisoners from the Spezia

Division, at a cost of eight killed and fifty-nine wounded. The Italians had now begun to surrender in large numbers, the more so as they realised that the 1st Royal Sussex were behind them. When the filling-in of the anti-tank ditch and the removal of the mines had begun, it became clear that this phase of the battle was successfully over. The tanks then rumbled through the resulting gap to pursue the retreating German columns, though some heavy guns continued to give trouble till the late afternoon. The battle of the Zouai Hills was a triumph but a costly one; even Brigadier Lovett, the Commander of 7th Indian Brigade was thrice wounded, and the Enfidaville Line still remained to be overcome.

In the Enfidaville area, to which the 4th Indian Division next moved, the 1st Battalion took up a position in the olive groves, where intermittent enemy shelling and mortar-fire caused a number of casualties and imposed a strain on the men, for they were already depleted after the Wadi Akarit operations.

The 7th Indian Brigade had been selected to begin the main attack on the Eighth Army front, with the Tebaga Ridge as its objective. It was to be carried out at night, and the 1st Royal Sussex had, as usual, a prominent part to play. The enemy were reacting strongly at this time, and the attack was postponed on three nights running. Eventually it was cancelled when the 4th Indian Division was moved to the First Army front at the beginning of May, to take part in the battle for Tunis. After the campaign it was found that the Tebaga feature had been strongly defended and was the key position of the Axis Forces facing the Eighth Army.

Operations in Tunisia

On 9th April 1943, the command of the 1st Royal Sussex passed from Lieutenant Colonel Firth to Lieutenant Colonel Jack Glennie, who was then twenty-eight years old. This courageous young officer led the Battalion during the concluding operations in North Africa and through the bitterest fighting in Italy. Colonel Firth was appointed to command the 7th Indian Brigade until Brigadier Lovett recovered from his wounds.

The First Army's new equipment contrasted strangely with the battered yellow trucks of the desert veterans, whose sunburnt tan distinguished them as sharply as their vehicles. They now moved down into the Mejerda Valley, west of Medjez el Bab, where it became clear that the concentration of forces was being made for a final break through to Tunis. Expecting a stiff fight, they prepared their attack side-by-side with units of the First Army, feeling a *'trifle uneasy',* since they had come to regard night assaults as the most successful way to defeat the enemy; the situation now was that after another Brigade's dawn attack, it was to be followed by their own Brigade's advance and attack in broad daylight. However, it was preceded by a heavy artillery and air bombardment, and, contrary to expectations, the opposition was light. After some sharp fighting in the foothills, the resistance crumbled.

The attack on Medjez el Bab, launched on 6th May, broke the enemy's resistance in front of Tunis, which was entered on the following day. The 4th Indian Division then had to execute a turning movement to the south, for a very special task lay ahead of them. A large proportion of the German Afrika Korps had escaped into the hilly regions of Cap Bon, and together with considerable Italian forces, seemed likely to put up a strong resistance before North Africa could be cleared of the Axis forces.

As the 7th Indian Brigade moved up in columns of transport towards the

foothills, they could see the outskirts of Tunis away to the left, but their own task was to be one of systematic clearing-up of the hilly country in the St. Marie du Zit zone, 28 miles south of Tunis, which was known to favour the defenders. The countryside, after months of desert warfare, seemed refreshingly like home – redbrick farmhouses perched on grassy slopes, fields of grain, and a general air of peace. The population looked to be generally untouched by war, though the Germans had undoubtedly been through, leaving a tale of wine and food seized and still unpaid for.

A high range of hills was to be the 'first bound', Gurkhas, Punjabis and Royal Sussex each had their objectives to clear and secure. Here they encountered the first German rearguard, firmly dug in and protecting the only road up to the hills. A sharp battle developed in the afternoon of 11th May, with the enemy laying a 'veritable carpet of mortar-bombs' along a wadi that had to be crossed. Eventually the carriers and tanks gained the day, and with their supporting fire, one company advanced, taking many prisoners in the captured positions.

White flags now appeared, *"very fine large ones too,"* says Captain Weeks, *"prepared as if especially for an occasion such as this."*

All that evening, while the Battalion consolidated its positions, prisoners were streaming back to improvised cages, and still more appeared willing to give themselves up. One deputation intimated that a whole battalion was willing to surrender at dawn, if it could be to the British, and even asked to use the field-telephone to discuss the matter with the commander. Others did not stand on formalities, and when morning came, the carrier screen reported several thousand coming down from the hills, many of them driving their own trucks. The majority were Italians, however, and it was still suspected that the Germans might attempt some form of 'Dunkirk' withdrawal from Cap Bon. With this in mind, the advance continued with due caution and reconnaissance, anticipating rearguard actions. It was the forward elements of this reconnaissance, which had the honour of receiving the surrender deputation from von Arnim.

General von Arnim

Carriers were nosing their way cautiously along the winding road leading to the high hills, rounding up small parties of prisoners, and always watchful for mines, road-blocks and ambushes. That these precautions were still necessary became evident when, on nearing the summit, they came under fire from an anti-tank gun, which forced the advancing troops to deploy off the road as several more shots followed and burst a few hundred yards behind. Suddenly, however, a car was seen coming down the road, flying a large white flag and conveying the impression that someone really important wished to surrender. The vehicles brought Oberst (*Colonel*) Nolte, Arnim's Chief of Staff, with other officers and interpreters. The party, conducted back through the British lines, intimated that the Nazi General and his officers were quite prepared to surrender to the Eighth Army, and especially to the 4th Indian Division. Nolte said that he had been authorized by Arnim to seek terms of surrender for the supreme commander of the Axis Forces in Tunisia, as well as for Gen. Krause, the German Panzer general, and for both their Staffs. At the 4th Division's Headquarters, near Ainel Asker, Nolte was shown a typewritten note setting out terms for the unconditional surrender of the Axis forces and the immediate cessation of hostilities. He reiterated that Arnim was surrendering only himself, Krause and their Staffs, and that they had no power to accept other terms. The Axis commander declared that his forces were too widely scattered for him to order them to cease-fire even if he wanted to and so Arnim's surrender was accepted.

Slowly the thousands of prisoners were disposed of, being either marched or driven back into captivity. As the Germans came down from the summit, they were both smart and cheerful, singing their usual marching-songs, rendered familiar by the wireless, and bearing themselves in a manner, which might have won congratulations from their captors – if other things could have been forgotten. Lieutenant Roy Rees commented at the time:

> *"We proceeded up the road a little further and then came across a sight I shall never forget. Masses of Germans and Italians were lined up by their transport and they were having a roll call! After giving 'Heil Hitler' salutes, they were ready to be marched away! Meanwhile, General von Arnim and his staff were located and surrendered to our CO Jack Glennie."*

When von Arnim surrendered to Jack Glennie at St Marie du Zit on 12th May 1943, he apparently said, *"I fought against the Iron Regiment during the last World War. Now I surrender myself to them in this World War."* Dressed in immaculate uniforms, looking thoroughly spick and span, von Armin's staff lined up, while the General himself, entered an open car and stood holding the windscreen with his left hand in Hitler fashion while he gave the final salute to his Staff, and drove off with a Gurkha officer and a guard of The Royal Sussex. Arnim stood up in his car practically all the way acknowledging the salutes and cheers of his defeated soldiers!

General von Arnim's Staff Car

In his diary, Lieutenant Rees concludes the battle for Tunis with the following:

> *"When evening came all organised resistance ceased. Thousands of prisoners had been caged on Tunis Racecourse. It was now dark as light-machine guns fired victory bursts of tracer shots into the night sky. I joined our CO in the caravan of General von Arnim and we toasted the Allied victory with German brandy. However, it was a sobering thought that the German prisoners would possibly be sent by sea to Canada, whereas we would be thinking of battles ahead in Italy."*

The Axis Forces in North Africa finally surrendered on 13th May 1943 and Captain Weeks concluded:

> *"For some, Tunis was the culminating glory of the North African campaign, but for the men of the 1st Battalion The Royal Sussex*

Regiment the names Hallouf Pass and von Armin's Wadi will bring back immortal memories."

Two years and 336 days after Italy had declared war on Great Britain, final and complete victory had crowned allied arms in Africa.

General von Arnim's staff car was used for some time by Lieutenant Colonel Glennie, and was finally sent home to the Depôt at Chichester. The car now has pride of place in The Royal Sussex Museum in the Fortress Redoubt at Eastbourne.

For its gallant actions in the North African campaigns of 1943, The Royal Sussex Regiment was awarded the Battle Honours of **Akarit,** *Djebel el Meida* and *Tunis*, of which the first Honour is emblazoned on the Colours.

At the conclusion of all the North African campaigns, The Regiment was awarded the Battle Honour of **North Africa 1940-43,** which is also emblazoned on the Colours.

Gallantry Awards for North Africa in 1943

Bar to Distinguished Service Order

Brigadier L.G. Whistler DSO   131st Brigade

Military Cross:

Captain G.W. Hawkes	1st Battalion (7 Inf Bde LO)
Captain S.J.F Upton	1st Battalion
Captain L.W. Weeks	1st Battalion
Rev F.W. Phillips RAChD	1st Battalion (Padre)
Captain T. Reilly RAMC	1st Battalion (RMO)

Bar to Military Medal:

Corporal J. Bungard MM   1st Battalion

Military Medal:

CSM J. Greenfield	1st Battalion
Corporal D.R.G. Coppard	1st Battalion
L/Corporal J.H. Hickman	1st Battalion
Private B. Ives	1st Battalion
Private N.W. Mackinlay	1st Battalion
Private E.G. Peacock	1st Battalion
Private E. Rossiter	1st Battalion

Mentioned-in-Despatches:

Six officers and men of the 1st Battalion were Mentioned-in-Despatches.

PERSIA AND IRAQ

During the Second World War, Persia and Iraq did not figure too much in The Royal Sussex Regiment's long list of Battle Honours, but the Regiment's service in the Persia and Iraq Command (PAIFORCE) did fill an honoured chapter in its long annuls. Following their courageous and determined exploits at Alam el Halfa and El Alamein, the 2nd Battalion and the newly formed 4th/5th Battalion of the Regiment came straight from the Western Desert, where they had played their part in breaking Rommel's last assault against Alexandria.

When they came to PAIFORCE in January 1943, the two Battalions not only found themselves as a key element of the organisation, but expected that those highly acquired qualities which they had developed and used to break Rommel's drive in North Africa, would continue to be required to meet and defeat a fresh German swing southwards through the Caucasus. This was not to be as the Germans had been routed before Stalingrad, and thus the principal threat had rescinded. In consequence, the whole purpose and *raison d'être* for PAIFORCE became one more concerned with garrison duties rather than being committed to operational exploits.

Nevertheless, the rôle of PAIFORCE was to keep the lines of communication clear and through which the vital arms and supplies were able to flow through the Persian Gulf to Russia. It was a vital strategic and essential logistic commitment, and over five million tons of materiel – a quarter of all the Allied supplies, delivered through one route or another - was successfully passed through the Persian lines to the Russian forces engaged against the Germans on the Eastern Front. The two Battalions of The Royal Sussex Regiment played a key part in the protection of these lines and, while often unspectacular, it was work by no means done without its incidents, and its value cannot be denied.

PAIFORCE, as a new command, had few amenities at the start. The country was not fully mapped, information on local conditions had to be acquired by experience and the Royal Sussex, during their first months, learned many lessons about a climate that ranged from the extremes of both heat and cold. The men of Sussex had many stories to tell of how, during their first winter in Persia, their tents night after night were flooded out, and of how, in their first summer in the Southern Iraq Desert, in the harsh desert conditions, they were scorched day after day by in the harsh desert conditions and the blazing heat, with temperatures up to 121 degrees.

Although coming within the PAIFORCE organisation in March-April 1943, both Battalions formed part of the 6th Indian Division but in different Brigades. The 2nd Battalion, commanded by Lieutenant Colonel C.F.A. Nix TD, left Quassasin in the Canal Zone on 10th March 1943 and arrived at the outskirts of Baghdad on the 17th after a 1,000-mile journey by road, almost entirely across the desert, with only the occasional sign of man or beast. On 30th March the 2nd

Battalion joined the 24th Indian Infantry Brigade at Khanaqin. The 4th/5th Battalion, commanded by Lieutenant Colonel J.J. McCully DSO, had already moved to Khanaqin in February 1943. Here it commenced training for mountain warfare, before moving to Teheran on 24th May, where it joined the

27th Indian Infantry Brigade, and was brigaded with Battalions of the Guides Infantry and the 10th Baluch Regiment. Much of the work of both Battalions was monotonous, but it had been no less strenuous on that account for they had to keep themselves fully fit and trained as fighting Battalions for the day when they could be required for active service in another front or theatre.

In addition to the day-to-day duties such as the protection of the convoy routes and oil wells, guarding base installations, countering Kurdish offensives, and searching for enemy saboteurs, both Battalions undertook periods of intense training in desert fighting and mountain warfare. It was often the case that some officers and men were inclined to be contemptuous of their garrison duties and were impatient to take part in operations of a more aggressive character, and would volunteer for more active jobs whenever possible.

In February 1944, the 4th/5th Battalion moved to the Lebanon for training at the Mountain Warfare School near Tripoli and obtaining a good report, all ranks hoped that a move to the Italian Front might now take place. But this was not to be, and the Battalion was further disappointed when Lieutenant Colonel McCully left on 30th April on his appointment to command the 24th Indian Infantry Brigade, although still within the 6th Indian Division. Major W.R. Allen assumed command of the Battalion and soon, an added complication became apparent with the political situation in Greece becoming more acute; a Greek armoured unit had refused to move from Tripoli to Damascus and the Battalion had to help to disarm it.

At the end of May 1944, the 4th/5th Battalion moved to Teheran where it took over guard duties from the 2nd Battalion, and where it had the privilege of providing a Guard of Honour for the Shahinshah and Shareen of Persia. Still hoping for an operational tour, the Battalion moved to Khanaqin for jungle warfare training in expectation of service in the Far East. However, by February 1945, the Battalion was back in Baghdad and a month later it moved to Mosul. On 12th July 1945 Lieutenant Colonel Allen was posted to the UK on compassionate grounds and Major D.T. Davis assumed command, although six months later, he in turn handed over to Major G.M. Jelley MC, whereupon, following the end of the war in the Far East, the Battalion moved to Palestine for guard duties at Halfa. And two months later, in November 1945, Lieutenant Colonel J.B. Ashworth DSO arrived to take over command – three changes of command in eight months!

THE ITALIAN EPIC

Soon after the middle of May 1943, the 4th Indian Division began to move back from the scene of its Tunisian triumph into Libya. A fortnight's rest at Misurata was allowed them before training recommenced in June.

During that month, King George VI, the King-Emperor in those days of gathering victory, came to review the 4th Indian Division in Libya, the troops whose exploits were already a legend in the fighting forces of the world. Later, in August, a special representative party from the Division was detailed for a tour of Great Britain. A total of thirty-four all ranks was selected, representing every Indian race and creed, as well as British members from the 1st Royal Sussex and 1st/4th Essex, and the Division's gunners and signallers. It was perhaps that aspect of an Indian division – that Indians and British fight together – which left the deepest impression wherever the contingent went on its tour. For a crowded fortnight, the United Kingdom paid whole-hearted tribute to these straight fine soldiers whose deeds had won such accolades. The representatives of the 1st Battalion of The Royal Sussex Regiment were Company-Sergeant-Major J. Downes and Private N. Mackinlay MM.

For the rest of the year, the 4th Indian Division passed under the command of General Headquarters Middle East and, while Sicily was falling to the Eighth Army and a front was being established in Calabria, the Division trekked back through Egypt to Palestine.

The German Lines of Defence

In late 1943, Allied armies under General Harold Alexander were fighting their way northward in Italy against determined German opposition commanded by Field Marshal Kesselring, whose forces had prepared a succession of defensive lines on the Italian peninsula from the area south of Rome, to the northern lands beyond Florence. The most southerly defensive line was the Winter Line, which was a series of military fortifications, the primary one being the Gustav Line, which ran across Italy from just north of where the Garigliano River flows into the Tyrrhenian Sea in the west, through the Appenine Mountains to the mouth of the Sangro River on the Adriatic coast in the east. The centre of the line, where it crossed the main route north to Rome (Route 6) which followed the Liri Valley, was anchored around the mountains behind the town of Cassino, including Monte Cassino, which dominated the entrance to the Liri Valley, and Monte Cairo which gave the defenders clear observation of potential attackers advancing

towards the mouth of the Liri valley.

On the western side of the Appennines, the Gustav line had two subsidiary

The Defence Lines Showing the Depth of the German Winter Line

lines: the Bernhardt Line in front of the main Gustav positions around Cassino and the Adolf Hitler Line some 5 miles to the rear. The Winter Line was fortified with gun pits, concrete bunkers, turreted machine-gun emplacements, barbed-wire and minefields. It was the strongest of the German defensive lines south of Rome, and some fifteen German divisions were deployed in its defence. It took the Allies from mid-November 1943 to late May 1944 to fight through all the various elements of the Winter Line, including the forthcoming battles at Monte Cassino and Anzio.

By the 9th of November forward elements of the British Eighth Army were in contact with the forward defences of the German Winter Line, which had been set on the high ground north of the Sangro River. The main attack across the Sangro by V Corps, comprising the British 78th Infantry Division and the 8th

Indian Infantry Division, with supporting and diversionary attacks further inland by the 2nd New Zealand Division and XIII Corps, was delayed by bad weather until late-November. After several days of hard fighting, the Germans had withdrawn to the defences they had prepared on the high ground to the north of the Moro River.

The Moro River runs from the central mountain spine of Italy to the Adriatic coast, south of Ortona, and along which the Gustav Line was sited. Organized along the Garigliano and Rapido rivers this Line had Monte Cassino as its lynchpin, and sited on which was the soon-to-be famous sixth-century Benedictine monastery. The taking of Monte Cassino would become one of the most important battles of the Second World War as it effectively blocked the Allies route north to Rome, and it had to be taken despite the difficulties of doing so from a military point of view.

The move to assault Monte Cassino started in December 1943. The US Fifth Army (under General Clark) advanced to Cassino while the British Eighth Army (General Leese) continued its advance up the Adriatic side of Italy. The French Expeditionary Corps commanded by General Juin achieved the first success. Within his command were men from Morocco and Algeria and both were skilled in mountain warfare. The Moroccan 2nd Division quickly overwhelmed German forces at Mount Santa Croce, about 10 miles to the northeast of Monte Cassino. The Algerian 3rd Division attacked German forces at Colle Belvedere and Mount Abate, both about 5 miles to the north of Monte Cassino. The success of these attacks meant that Monte Cassino was surrounded to the north, west and south.

On the Eighth Army's front, the intention had been to punch through the Winter Line and then advance to Rome. The 78th Infantry Division, which had been spearheading V Corps since the Volturno Line actions, and had sustained over 7,000 casualties in less than six months, was relieved by the fresh 1st Canadian Infantry Division, and was ready to renew the offensive on 5th December 1943. The plan was for the Canadian Division to attack across the Moro in the coastal lowlands to take Ortona first and then Pescara. Inland, in the jagged hills above the headwaters of the Moro, the relatively fresh 2nd New Zealand Division would attack toward Orsogna, while between these two the 8th Indian Infantry Division would hold the centre of the

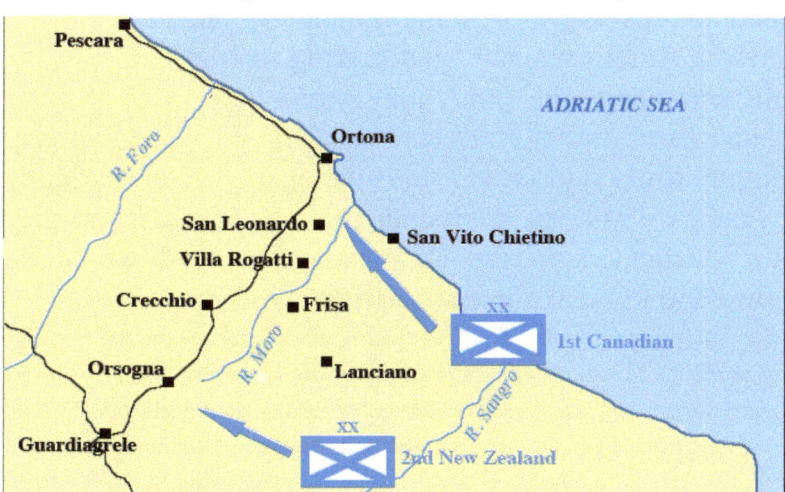

front in a relatively static role.

On 6th December the Canadian forces began a series of large-scale assaults on major crossing points along the Moro River with the objective of securing a large bridgehead along the defensive line. Three primary points of attack were chosen: Villa Rogatti, along the western edge of the Canadian sector; San Leonardo, some 3 miles south of Ortona; and San Donato, a small town near the Italian coast. The Germans fought desperately to hold the line of the Ortona-Orsogna highway, since the town of Orsogna, 18 miles inland, represented a key bastion of the Gustav system. Here, on 7th December, the newly arrived 2nd New Zealand Division attacked with two brigades and fought their way into the centre of the town. A heavy counter-attack flung them back, and after a battle of rising intensity, a raging blizzard with intense cold, ended the general offensive against the Gustav position for the time being.

The 4th Indian Division Moves to the Italian Front

In December 1943, the 4th Indian Division mustered again at Suez, and with all their vehicles, ammunition and equipment, sailed from Port Said in LSTs (Landing Ship Tanks – the original roll-on - roll-off ferry)[44]. The Division subsequently disembarked on 8th December in raw blustery weather at Taranto in Italy, a major port, which had been severely damaged by bombing and shelling, with few useable quays, and thus had to be ferried ashore in smaller landing craft. The 1st Royal Sussex then marched to improvised camps among the olive groves outside Taranto. In the main, they were billeted in farm buildings, but to keep off the rain and sleet they found it necessary to erect tarpaulins to replace the tin roofs, which had already been blown away with the wind. Cold and bronchitis lengthened the sick parades but in a remarkably short time the troops became acclimatised. Aware that they would be in action again before too long, serious field training began in earnest to integrate the new Drafts with the seasoned desert veterans.

The military background to this move was the expanding situation on the Italian battlefront, where the Americans had been making their attack over the Rapido River against the entrance to the Liri Valley, while in a series of bitter battles between 27th November and 30th December, British, Canadian and Indian troops of the Eighth Army had broken into the enemy defences along the Adriatic. On 13th January 1944, the 4th Indian Division learned that they would relieve the New Zealanders in the Orsogna sector, and would be expected to storm the town and to break the enemy front.

---

[44] Landing Ship, Tank (*LST*) was the military designation for naval vessels created during the Second World War to support amphibious operations by carrying significant quantities of vehicles, cargo and troops, and for landing them directly onto an unimproved shore. The first tank landing ships were built to British requirements by conversion of existing ships but, thereafter, the British and the Americans collaborated on a joint design, with the majority of construction carried out in the USA and supplied under lend-lease arrangements.

On 14th January the 7th Indian Brigade moved forward in drenching rain and relieved the 5th New Zealand Brigade on the right of Orsogna. The line followed the reverse slopes of narrow hills and consisted of linked-up strong points. As long as groups moving in the open kept below the crests of the knife-backed ridges, they were moderately safe, although behind the front, the roads for a considerable distance were under intimate observation by the enemy and any extensive movement drew fire. There was intermittent shelling and mortaring in both directions and Colonel Buckeridge recalls that below them in no-man's land was a small two-storied building, which was used by the Germans as a forward observation post. As he recorded at the time,

> *"I remember watching it one morning through a slit in the wall and noticed what appeared to be a sheep standing on its hind legs at a window and looking at us through binoculars. I called for our sniper, Private Francis, who fired one round at which the sheep reared up, discarded its skin and the occupant disappeared in haste."*

The battle for Orsogna was expected to open on 7th February and no one was happy at the prospect as the plan of attack represented an attempt to break the enemy at his strongest point. However, on 21st January, General Tuker was told that the assault on Orsogna had been abandoned and that the 4th Indian Division would move to join the US Fifth Army at once. General Tuker was devoutly thankful and wrote:

> *"I must say that I think Providence has been kind to this Division. Each time when we were about to be cast at some awful fortress something has intervened to help me fight the battle of stopping a needless sacrifice of life. I hope it is not Fifth Army's intention to use us against some impregnable place."*

The Divisional Commander's fears were not without foundation – the 4th Indian Division had been ordered to Cassino.

In mid-January, US Fifth Army Intelligence had informed General Clark:

> *"German strength was ebbing due to casualties, exhaustion, and possibly lowering of morale. It would appear doubtful if the enemy can hold the organised defensive line through Cassino against a co-ordinated attack. Since this attack is to be launched before Operation SHINGLE (the attack on Anzio) it is considered likely that this additional threat will cause him to withdraw from his defensive position once he has appreciated the magnitude of that operation."*

However, such optimism did not take into account the geography of Monte Cassino. The very nature of the ground gave the German defenders at Cassino a very good view as to what the Allies were doing. This height advantage was

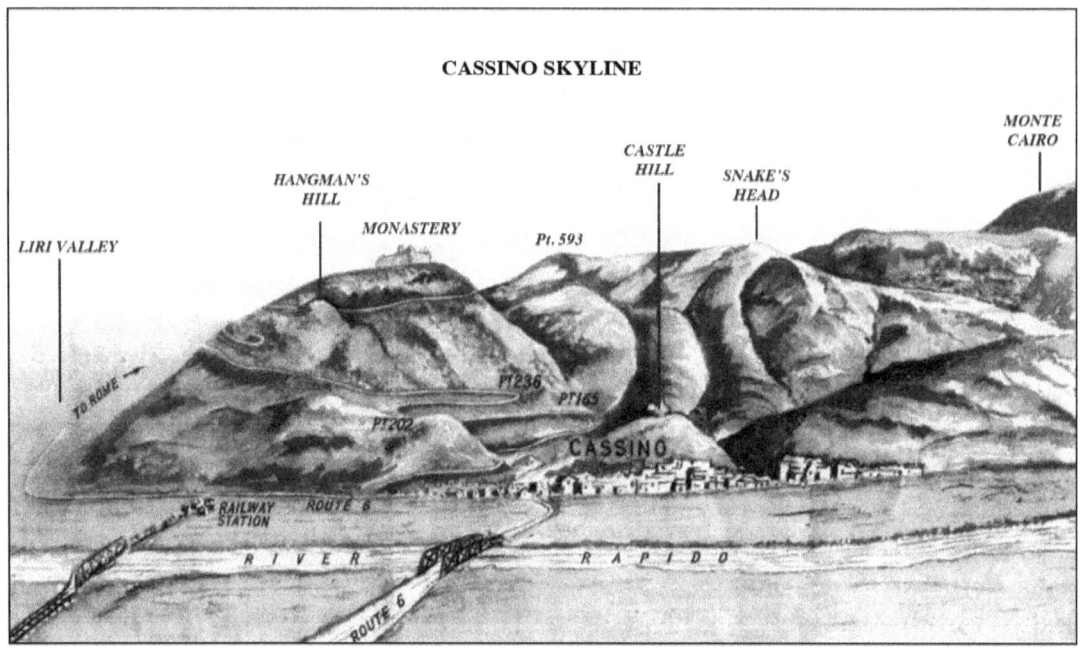

to be very important. The Germans had positioned their mortars with skill and they were to prove a major thorn to the Allies as they advanced. Equally as dangerous were German minefields that lay in the path of the advancing Allies. Despite the earlier Free-French successes, the US Army suffered heavy losses while trying to capture the German positions in December 1943 and January 1944.

The 'main door' into the Liri Valley was easy for the enemy to hold and correspondingly difficult to force. The valley's inner wall, consisting of a series of steep-sided mountains, was dominated by Monte Cairo (5,000 feet high), and these mountains came down to the headland of Monte Cassino and Monastery Hill. From the Benedictine Abbey on this eminence, the enemy enjoyed an uninterrupted view over all the approaches to the Rapido Valley. Well-hidden emplacements for automatic weapons on their forward slopes, and mortars tactically sited on the reverse slopes, had reinforced the natural strength of the mountains. The town of Cassino was very strongly fortified, and its narrow streets and massive architecture were well suited for defence. Self-propelled guns guarded every approach to the town, and its defenders were closely supported from numerous machine-gun emplacements blasted out of the rock on the peaks and ridges of the steep slopes beyond. The approaches to the river were heavily mined. South of Cassino the approaches were also guarded by mines and wire, and covered by fire from the pill-boxes and machine-gun emplacements on the west bank, and by artillery and Nebelwerfers[45] higher up the valley, as well as enfilading fire from the high

---

[45] The 21cm Nebelwerfer 42 (*literally 'fog-thrower'*) was a German multiple (5 tubes) rocket launcher with a range of 8,500 yards. Originally designed for poison gas and smoke weapons, it was used

ground on either side. The Italian General Staff, which had often used this area for its training exercises, believed its defences to be impregnable to any army advancing against Rome from the south – and the Germans had made thorough preparations to substantiate that belief. The Americans, fighting against these powerful defences, were halted by German counter-attacks. The enemy, having lost ground in the highlands above Cassino, reinforced their lines, and by mid-February, the four battalions of the 90th Panzer Grenadier Division were in position, with the original defenders having been reinforced by a battalion of the Fallschirmjäger-Regiment 3[46].

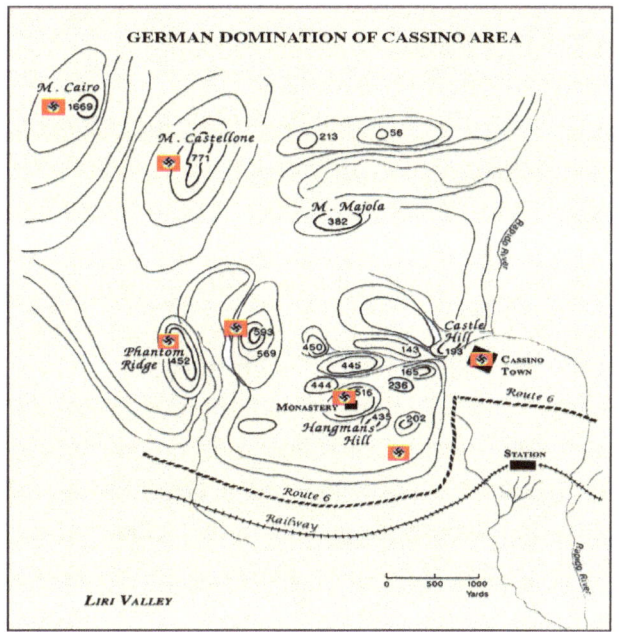

It was in these circumstances that General Sir Harold Alexander, Supreme Allied Commander in Italy, brought the 2nd New Zealand Division and the 4th Indian Division under command of the American Fifth Army as the New Zealand Corps, commanded by Lieutenant General Sir Bernard Freyberg VC. General Alexander ordered a new Cassino offensive combined with an amphibious operation at Anzio, a small port on the west coast of Italy. The main objective of the operation was to cut the communication lines of the German 10th Army and force a withdrawal from the Gustav Line.

Battle of Cassino

The 1st Royal Sussex, having come up into the line with the 7th Indian Brigade on the Orsogna sector early in 1944, were thus transferred to the scene of conflict which, of all battlefields in the Second World War, most resembled the Ypres of 1915, although the terrain could hardly have been more different.

On the 2nd of February, the 1st Battalion arrived in the US Fifth Army area and was concentrated 20 miles behind the front at Latina, some 30 miles northwest of Naples. Over the next eight days, various reconnoitres were carried out on the Cassino front but the future rôle of the 4th Indian Division seemed to change daily, varying between the mobile follow-through rôle in the Liri valley, to an outflanking move through the mountains to cut off Cassino. General Tuker made it quite clear that the old Italian fortress towns, like the Monastery at

---

instead for high explosives. The thin walls of the rockets had the great advantage of allowing much larger quantities of high explosive to be delivered than artillery or even mortar shells of the same weight.
[46] 3rd Parachute Regiment.

Cassino, dominated the landscape and controlled the roads, which offered the only lines of approach. He emphasised that the most satisfactory way of dealing with them was by obliteration from the air. In his concluding views to the Corps Commander he had said:

> *"To go direct for the Monastery Hill now without 'softening' it properly is only to hit one's head straight against the hardest part of the whole enemy position and to risk the failure of the whole operation."*

When the Divisional Commander penned this appreciation, he was a sick man and bedded down in his caravan, and a long-standing ailment would force him into hospital. On 4th February, he temporarily handed over command to Brigadier Dimoline; this change of command on the eve of a critical operation was a severe blow to the Division. At a time when, as never in its history, the 4th Indian Division needed a commander of sufficiently wide experience and standing to insist on the acceptance of his findings on the conduct of the forthcoming operation, it was bereft of its leader.

The continually changing rôle of the Division produced a great deal of planning and counter-planning at all levels in the 1st Battalion, and training ranged from infantry/tank co-operation one day to mule loading the next. It made it very difficult for the Battalion to settle down for the next big operation, especially as two large Drafts, totalling 120 men in all, had just arrived in the Battalion. However, orders eventually arrived for a quick move to take over from the Americans in the mountains north and west of Cassino.

On the night of 10th-11th February, the 1st Battalion moved in American transport to a new concentration area at a village called San Michele, which lies in the foothills of the Rapido Valley to the northeast of Cassino Town and the Monastery. The area was approached up the old Route Six, which ran from Naples to Rome. American six-wheeler transport had to be used because the tracks were so primitive and muddy that the British two-wheel drive vehicles could not cope. Even so conditions were too much even for some of the American vehicles and two lorries, notably the trucks carrying the Mortar Ammunition and the Battalion Reserve Ammunition, went right off the track and were lost; this loss was to be felt more than could have been possibly bargained for at the time. Three further lorries carrying blankets and greatcoats were also lost. As Colonel John Buckeridge commented at the time:

> *"About two miles short of the town, we turned off right and as we did so, I could see the Monastery looming up in the distance above the town. From that moment on we got the impression that the Germans could observe all movement in the Rapido Valley and in the surrounding foothills. Indeed, from the accuracy of their shelling and mortaring, we knew they must have OPs up in the Monastery."*

Brigadier Glennie would later write:

> *"Went half-way up Mt Cairo in 1966 and looked back on our positions. German OPs could see in detail our assembly areas – mule track and all positions on Snake Head Ridge."*

The Battalion was dumped at San Michele, the location where the Battalion's administrative area and echelons would become based. Arrangements were made for a move over the Rapido River to the Cairo area, and although the Battalion had also asked for mules, and in spite of the desperate efforts made by the 7th Brigade Staff, it got less than a third of its minimum requirements. On the night of the 10th, the whole Battalion moved on foot in single file for 7 miles, and in filthy weather along winding cart tracks on raised banks, just above the fields, which the Germans had flooded deliberately. The tracks were peppered with shell and mortar holes and often knee-deep in mud, and led them to the lower slopes of Monte Castellone, just beyond Cairo village, where they arrived at 3 o'clock in the morning. During the move forward, the Battalion had been shelled continuously for 5 hours, including at times by British guns, and were then shelled intermittently for the rest of the day. This galling experience was to be repeated all too often during the following days. After reaching Cairo village before daylight, the Battalion rested in the open with no cover for the rest of the day, while the rain poured down incessantly.

The confusion over the front at the time is illustrated by a perilous uncertainty as to who held what position. At 2 pm that same day, the 1st Battalion was ordered to attack the Belvedere feature that night, which was a slight surprise as Belvedere was behind them and was supposed to be held by the Free French. Accordingly, reconnoitres were carried out and orders for the attack were given out down to platoon commander level. However, a strong protest was made to 7th Brigade Headquarters as to the lack of mules and, because of the earlier mishap, the Battalion had less than half of its ammunition supply with it, and no mortar ammunition at all. At 6 pm the attack was called off by Brigade as they thought the French might still be there after all!

At 2 am on 13th February, 1st Royal Sussex were ordered to take over from the Americans that night but owing to the uncertainty of the American positions, the Point 593 – Snakes Head area allotted to the Battalion was selected from the map. The American guide leading the Commanding Officer up to the sector led him instead towards the German lines. Having beaten a hasty retreat after being fired upon, they eventually entered the American position from the enemy side! On arrival, Lieutenant Colonel Glennie[47] found that the sector was held by four American battalions, each of them only about 100 strong, and found from three different Regiments (Brigades), and from two separate Divisions.

---

[47] Commanding Officer of the 1st Battalion The Royal Sussex Regiment at Cassino.

The 1st Battalion, after a two-hour climb up a narrow rocky mountain track, relieved the Americans on the Pt. 593 - Snakes Head feature. The Americans were completely exhausted but it was found that the US battalions were not actually holding Pt. 593 as originally supposed but were just below the crest, which was to have significant repercussions. Although the relief was completed without incident, it was extremely complicated owing to the different organisation and the relief of four American battalions from assorted US formations by a single British battalion. The one consolation observed by the Commanding Officer was that the Staff Colleges of both nations obviously taught the same battle procedures for *Relief in the Line*.

The battered Point 593 from Snakes Head Ridge

Colonel Buckeridge, who was commanding No. 13 Platoon in C Company at the time, gives a very clear account of the actual handover:

"C Company was ordered to be in the vanguard of the relief of the Americans on Snakes Head Ridge, with 13 Platoon at the very sharp end. The goat track up which we were guided ran along a steep rocky slope strewn with boulders. It was pitch black and the going was tough as we climbed ever upwards. It was clear that all the foliage, trees and bushes had been blasted away and there was no cover from the rain, when we made the odd stop to draw breath. When we arrived at our designated position, I was told by a very tired American that we were on Point 593 (the height in metres), and that the Germans were a 'short' distance away in front of us along a ridge which had been christened 'Snakeshead'. It was, of course, pitch black and pouring with rain so we could not see anything but it was clear that the Americans were occupying a series of what we called 'sangars', which were two-man shelters built up with rocks and stones. The Americans were totally exhausted, dead on their feet, or just dead. No sooner had we arrived than they just 'bugged out' as quickly as they could without us having any time to quiz them on the situation. It was simply a case of us

> *occupying their sangars, posting sentries and OPs and waiting for dawn, which could not be far off.*
>
> *I was soon to realise that the Americans did not really know where they or the Germans were. They, the Americans, were certainly not on Point 593 but about 70 yards short of it. The point was occupied by the Germans and was slightly higher than the narrow plateau where we were. Snakeshead Ridge was a razor-back feature hardly wide enough for a platoon to deploy."*

The feature that the 1st Battalion found itself on at first light on 13th February consisted of this long narrow ridge stretching from Snakes Head for 400 yards to the fatal crest at Pt. 593, which was not only held by the enemy but also dominated the whole area. B and C Companies were in positions just under the crest, with the Germans being some 70 yards away on the other side. Facing west, A Company held the length of the ridge while D Company was in reserve behind Snakes Head. Battalion Headquarters was located in a small ruined cottage only 200 yards from the enemy, and there it stayed for over three weeks. As Lieutenant Colonel Glennie said at the time:

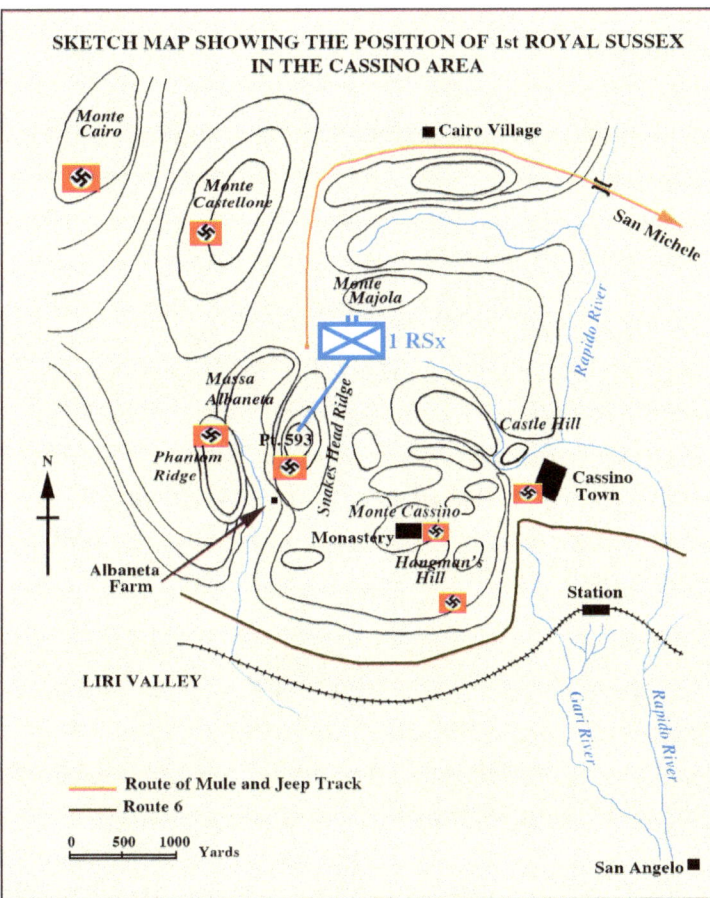

> *"It may sound silly to have been so far up but there was nowhere else from which I could control the situation."*

A thousand yards eastward stood the Monastery, from which the enemy overlooked all positions on the ridge. Behind Pt. 593, they held two other Points and Massa Albaneta, and also Phantom Ridge, some 500 yards to the west. Furthermore, Monte Cairo looked down from the northwest, so that the enemy could hardly have a better view of the British lines and the approaches to them. In relation to the Allied line as a whole, the Battalion was actually behind the enemy, and this no doubt accounts for the fact that it suffered from its own artillery fire as well as that of the Germans.

Furthermore, the Battalion's Administrative situation was deplorable as it had only the minimum ammunition, with very few grenades and no reserve for the 2-inch mortars. As all the main mortar ammunition had earlier been lost down the side of the mountain, the 3-inch Mortar Platoon relied initially on the stocks of ammunition left behind by the Americans. In addition, there were no reserve rations and barely one blanket per man, a major concern as it was mid-winter and freezing most of the time. Despite the considerable efforts made by the rear echelons to rectify the situation, the shortage of mules, the length of the 7-mile supply journey each way, and the heavy shelling of mule tracks, all combined to degrade the resupply requirements[48].

Lieutenant Rees, who was commanding the Carrier Platoon, made a comment in his diary at the time:

> *". . and I could not envisage the Carriers being of much help in these mountains. In fact when the Battalion trekked up the mountains to relieve the Americans, the Carriers had to be left behind, but the personnel, including myself, took up positions on the lower slopes of Mount Cairo and Mount Castellone to render support as necessary to the rifle companies. The same situation applied to the Anti-Tank Platoon. The Battalion, when in the line, could only be reached by mules, and supplies had to be taken up every night by mules under the control of Carrier Platoon personnel.*
>
> *Thus, the Carrier Platoon personnel were to help with the servicing and supply to the rifle companies. Being based on the lower slopes of Mount Cairo and Mount Castellone, there was constant shelling of these positions, and then under cover of darkness the personnel had to get the food supplies up the mountain every night."*

It seemed quite clear to all ranks, and in common with the other units of the 7th Indian Brigade, that the Brigade had been bounced into taking over from the Americans before it was ready to do so. There is no doubt that the Americans had fought very gallantly but in the last few days had become completely exhausted, and had only just managed to hold on to the ground they had won - but the Germans definitely held the initiative in the mountain sector. The whole of the landscape had been blasted bare by shelling and mortaring; movement by day on the ridge was confined to the cautious belly-crawling of individuals as anything more invariably drew fire from the enemy, thus making attempts at serious reconnaissance virtually impossible. Digging in was almost impossible owing to the rocky nature of the ground and, therefore, defensive positions

---

[48] Some 30% of the mules slipped over the mountainside on each journey with the consequent large losses of equipment.

tended to be fairly primitive and generally consisted of very shallow sangars. Attempts were made to raise the height of the sangar walls but this was hindered by the amount of stones and rocks that could be collected while crawling around in the prone position.

Silent patrol-movement on the rocky slopes at night was also virtually impossible, although attempts were often made. It was not only extremely hazardous to patrol in the pitch-black, but the noise from wearing hob-nailed ammunition boots while moving across a terrain of solid-rock, was not always conducive to the expected thoroughness of night patrolling. On the night of 14th-15th February, a patrol from A Company tried to find a way round the right of Pt. 593, but the No-Man's Land of only 70 yards gave very little room for manoeuvre, and the patrol immediately bumped opposition without really gaining any new information. The following night, a patrol from B Company reconnoitring Massa Albaneta immediately drew fire from the feature, but it did, if nothing else, confirm that the position was still held by the enemy.

Sangars on Snakes Head Ridge

Despite claims by troops on the front-line that no fire had come from the Monastery, at 9.30 am on the 15th of February, the Monastery was heavily bombed by Allied aircraft. Although the enemy were warned beforehand, the Battalion was not; indeed even the Brigade Commander had no notice of the bombing until the first bombs fell. Lieutenant-Colonel Jack Glennie is said to have remarked, *"They told the monks, and they told the enemy but they didn't tell us"*. The bombing was an awe-inspiring sight and the Battalion felt as though they were in the front row for it, although it did suffer some casualties caused by the rocks and splinters from misplaced munitions.

Once the monastery had been bombed, the German Army moved into the ruins. As Basil Liddell Hart pointed out later in his book *The Other Side of the Hill*, the bombing:

> *". . . . turned out entirely to the tactical benefit of the Germans. For after that they felt free to occupy the ruins, and the rubble provided much better defensive cover than the Monastery would have been before its destruction. As anyone with experience of street-fighting knows, it is only when buildings are demolished that they are converted from mousetraps into bastions of defence."*

Notwithstanding this, Colonel Buckeridge would later write:

> *"From my Platoon position on Snakes Head Ridge, just below Point 593, I actually saw small groups of men in German Army uniform going into and leaving the Monastery in daylight on several occasions before the bombing, through a large door with 'PAX' over the lintel. I was interested to note that Feldwebel Wilhelm Weier[49] confirms my observations, which have tended to be denied by various academics and historians over the years. I believe that, even today, the official line taken by the tour guides in the Monastery denies this fact."*

Nevertheless, it was generally felt in the 7th Indian Brigade that an opportunity had been lost, as, with some notice and with the necessary ammunition, the Brigade could have captured the Monastery by attacking as soon as the last bombs fell. Brigadier Lovett also expressed the view that it was impossible to persevere with the main attack until Pt. 593 had been neutralised. He said that the capture of this latter position should be regarded as a separate operation, and in the light of this recommendation the main attack was postponed for 24 hours.

Later that day, at 12 o'clock mid-day, the 1st Royal Sussex was ordered to clear Pt. 593 in the preliminary assault and establish itself on top, while still being required to hold its present positions. At that stage no patrol information had yet been built up and no reconnaissance was possible by day. This meant that very little was known about the ground or the enemy's positions and strengths. In particular, as there was very limited room for deployment, it meant that it was only feasible to deploy one company in the clearing operation, and C Company under Major B. Dalton was given the task.

---

[49] An account described in Annex A.

At 10 pm that night, C Company attacked the summit of Pt. 593, while B Company tried to work its way round the left flank of the feature. It was a hazardous operation in the extreme, and stiff and very confused fighting ensued in the dark, in very rocky and steeply sloping ground, only 50 yards from the Start Line. So valiantly was the attack pressed home by C Company that it might have succeeded if it had not been for the shortage of grenades. The Germans were strongly entrenched in good positions, and had apparently inexhaustible supplies. The 1st Royal Sussex had not, and this was the deciding factor, resulting in C Company sustaining heavy casualties. It was less than 70 yards to Pt. 593 and it soon became clear that the Germans had standing patrols out in No-Man's Land, with the approach routes to their positions all covered by Spandaus[50] firing on fixed lines from several directions. In addition, their main and reserve defences were dug-in down a sheer slope on the northwest face, with well-prepared routes up the slope to mount counter-attacks.

The enemy, from their very strong positions, rained grenades down on the attacking troops. Despite this, Corporal Osman, under a hail of rifle fire and stick grenades, led the remnants of his section onto the objective and destroyed an enemy machine-gun post, and for his outstanding courage and leadership was awarded the Military Medal. C Company countered the enemy with all their grenades, including the reserve grenades brought up from the other Companies. Major Dalton, although wounded and under heavy fire, and regardless of his own safety, organised this further supply of grenades and led his men again to the attack but heavy enemy fire stopped them again from penetrating the enemy position. Just before first light the Company found itself in a thoroughly precarious position – in the open and continuing to be grenaded by the Germans from their formidable positions – and was therefore ordered to withdraw 50 yards back to its own positions. On being given the order, Major Dalton, ably assisted by Corporal Osman, personally supervised the evacuation of the wounded and carried out a search of No Man's Land, under heavy fire, to find out if any of his men were lying wounded, and he was the last to leave the position.

German Spandau Team in Action at Cassino

---

[50] The 'Spandau' MG 42 (*Machinengewehr 42*), a 7.92mm machine-gun, entered service in 1942. It had one of the highest average rates of fire of any single-barrelled man-portable machine-gun, of between 1,200 and 1,500 rpm, resulting in a distinctive muzzle report.

Almost half the Company had become casualties; two officers and thirty-two men were killed or wounded, out of the three officers and sixty-three men who went into the attack. Major Dalton was subsequently awarded the Distinguished Service Order for his magnificent leadership and gallantry, and for his inspiration to the whole Company.

On the morning of 16th February, the Monastery was bombed once again by the Americans, and once more the Battalion had no prior warning, although this time the bombers were more accurate, using light bombers from a lower altitude. What had been a vast solid building had huge chunks of its walls and masonry blown into the air, with the resultant debris being reduced to a shambolic and impenetrable mess.

At 11 am on the 16th, the 1st Royal Sussex was again ordered to capture Pt. 593 that night. While the rest of that day was spent in planning and orders, with the very limited information it had available, the difficulty of the terrain, and the shortage of essential ammunition such as grenades, the Battalion was not really ready to attack such a strong position that night. Lieutenant Colonel Glennie believed the Battalion needed another 48 hours to carry out the necessary reconnoitres and subsequent planning, and to build up sufficient stocks of ammunition and other essential supplies. He also felt that oblique air photographs of the objective were a real necessity but these were not available. Despite all these limitations, the Battalion got on with it as not only was it repeatedly being emphasised that something must be done at once to take the pressure off the Anzio beach-head, which was in imminent danger of collapse, but also because it had the 'superiority complex'[51] common to the rest of 4th Indian Division that so far they had always been successful. Notwithstanding this, the Commanding Officer felt, as did the Company Commanders, that the attack was being undertaken in far too much of a rush. He was particularly concerned about the shortage of grenades, essential for close-quarter fighting, and which was now aggravated by the fact that it had been necessary for C Company to use up nearly all the Battalion's limited supply the night before. A similar worry was that the 2-inch mortars had only twelve bombs each, and the reserves of small-arms ammunition were not sufficient for such an operation

From the experience of the previous night's attack, it was not difficult to appreciate the challenge that the Battalion was up against. It would not be possible to deploy for a daylight attack as the enemy overlooked the whole area, while a night attack would have to cope with the extremely difficult and rocky nature of the ground, particularly as the objective was on the top of a rocky outcrop with very large boulders, many of them over six feet high. In

---

[51] Without doubt, the 4th Indian Division had a superiority complex in that they had never been beaten – through Eritrea, the Western Desert and Wadi Akarit – they had never known defeat. But Italy was different – the terrain, the conditions and the enemy were much greater and more debilitating than anything they had experienced before. They had yet to learn how to lose.

such conditions, control would be extremely difficult. Coupled with this was the fact that as the objective was only 70 yards from the forward positions, direct artillery support would be impossible, although artillery support on other positions such as the Monastery and Points 574 and 505 was possible, albeit that it would not materially help the actual assault. It was also already clear that the area involved was too small for the deployment of more than one company for the main attack, and once captured, the objective was likely to be extremely exposed after first light, which meant that a strong fresh company with plenty of reserve ammunition would probably be needed to hold it. The other key factor was that unless someone could work miracles on the supply route, the Battalion was likely to be very short of grenades and small-arms ammunition.

It was obvious that the operation was rather more than the ordinary scheme of things and would be influenced by significant tactical and administrative limitations. The plan decided upon, therefore, was that D Company, reinforced by one platoon of A Company, was to be specially equipped as an Assault Company with as many grenades as possible, and were to be given all available patrol boots. It was to capture Pt. 593 in a left flanking attack, with C Company, consisting of only two weak platoons, would be in reserve. Once D Company was firmly established on Pt. 593, B Company, heavy laden with reserve small-arms ammunition and wearing greatcoats, was to move onto the position and consolidate. Having done so, D Company was then to withdraw into reserve as the objective did not have sufficient room for more than one company; the Verey light signal for D Company to withdraw, once B Company had relieved them, was to be Red – Green – Red. Battalion Headquarters was to be set up on the Start Line in C Company's forward positions, and artillery support would be used to neutralise the Monastery and Points 575 and 505.

Taking account of the difficulties, this plan was considered to give a reasonable chance of success. The attack was due to start at 11 pm in order to allow time for more grenades to be brought up after dark. In the event, due to conditions on the supply route and the heavy shelling, less than half the required grenades arrived. The attack was postponed twice, by half-an-hour each time, to wait for the grenades to come up but still they did not arrive. D Company was therefore seriously handicapped as the Assault Company, and hurriedly had to collect a few more grenades from the other Companies before the attack started.

As was inevitable from the conditions and the broken, rocky ground, the operation was confused from the outset, and a malign fate seemed to dog the whole operation. The artillery, in trying to hit Pt. 575 and Pt. 505, swept the Start Line with a number of 'shorts', which were just failing to clear the crest of the Battalion's positions. These caused casualties in A, B and C Companies, and Battalion Tactical Headquarters, and disorganised the start of the attack. However, D Company escaped this and pressed home its assault with great gallantry, and the forward platoons worked round a barricade of boulders and gained a foothold on the slopes of Pt. 593. But the Germans were still there as well; the enemy were very well protected in good sangars and there they remained. They also had a very good supply of grenades, which they literally rained down onto D Company who were in the open. The enemy also did considerable execution with their large number of excellently sited Spandaus (it later transpired that they had two Spandaus per section). Against this, Lieutenant David Cox showed great gallantry - with Tommy-gun and grenades - he personally destroyed two Spandau posts, and though badly wounded, crawled forward and established himself in an enemy sangar on the objective. Lying among three dead Germans, two of whom he had killed, his Company Commander gave orders for him to be evacuated but Cox said he would fight on. Some time later he was hit again by two German grenades bursting close to him but at last, a Corporal lifted him on his shoulder and took him down the hill. For Lieutenant Cox's most courageous action and for the fine example, which he set, he was subsequently awarded the Distinguished Service Order, although it is understood that he had been recommended for the Victoria Cross.

In the confusion several small parties of D Company went right beyond the objective and some fell over a large perpendicular drop of 40 feet and were injured and taken prisoner; others, beyond the objective ran into enemy reserves, which were now appearing on the scene. At this stage, Major G.W. Hawkes commanding D Company was wounded while trying to reorganise his Company, which by now was scattered in small parties fighting it out bravely with a dwindling supply of ammunition, their grenades practically used up, against a very brave, hard fighting and well protected enemy.

Under Major John Gratton, a brave and efficient officer of the Hampshire Regiment, A Company had staged its attack on the right but was unaware that about fifty yards from the Start Line was the 40-foot drop, which limited the Company's room for deployment. Accordingly, A Company shifted over towards the centre of the position, but here they came unexpectedly on a perfect natural obstacle, from the enemy's point of view, in the shape of a large cleft in the feature about 15 feet deep and about 20 feet across. The enemy, on the other side in sangars and in the ruins of an old fort, hurled unlimited grenades and swept the crest with Spandau fire. All the officers of A Company were hit, with Captain B. Gain, a very brave officer, being killed outright.

The two platoons of C Company, under Major Dalton, came up to assist A Company but all attempts to get forward under intense grenade and Spandau fire failed. There ensued a grenade and Tommy-gun fight at close range but gradually the Companies' ammunition ran out, and the last of the Battalion's reserve of grenades had been used up. By now, D Company was practically out of ammunition and all its officers were wounded. Unfortunately, at a critical point in the attack, the enemy sent up three Green Verey lights, which was confused by some elements of D Company for their pre-arranged signal to withdraw through B Company, and some relinquished their hold on the crest and fell back; the remainder of the Company gradually filtered back with Lieutenant Cox being carried by one of his men.

It was now very nearly first light and a final effort was made by B Company who attempted to attack between the elements of A and C Companies and the remainder of D Company, and for a short time it looked as though 1st Royal Sussex would carry the day. However, B Company also came up against the natural obstacle and incurred heavy casualties. As the battle now consisted of elements of the 1st Battalion practically out of ammunition and being grenaded in the open by Germans in sangars, while also being silhouetted on the crest for the German Spandaus, which were doing great damage, the attack was called off and the Battalion was forced to retire the 50 yards to its original start point.

Out of the 12 officers and 250 men who took part in the attack 10 officers and 130 men were casualties.

The magnitude of the task that 1st Royal Sussex had undertaken may be gauged from the fact that, following other failures, the Pt. 593 position was not finally captured until three months later when a full-scale attack by the Eighth Army in the Liri Valley had isolated the mountain positions. In attacking Pt. 593, a Polish Battalion was wiped out except for a few dozen survivors. A further attack was carried out four days later by two Polish battalions with tank support, when the position itself was practically untenable due to the Eighth Army's advance. After severe fighting all day, and with very heavy losses to the Poles, the capture of Pt. 593 was finally successful.

This account gives as clearly as possible what happened in the 1st Royal Sussex attack on Pt. 593. It was pieced together long after the event when it was fairly clear as to what had actually happened. On the night in question it was by no means clear; the battle was very confused and control was practically impossible. However, one or two facts clearly emerged; the officers and men who took part in the attack fought really hard and very bravely against a very strong and determined enemy fighting at night on his own ground in ideal defensive positions. There was a tendency at the time for some to comment unfavourably on the failure of the 1st Battalion to capture the objective. As mentioned earlier, the 4th Indian Division was not used to failure and this was the first failure to capture an objective for a long time. Nevertheless, it was NOT the last. The ensuing fighting at Cassino and through the rest of Italy showed what a really tough proposition German Paratroops and Panzer Grenadiers were when fighting on ideal defensive terrain. The 4th Indian Division never maintained its 100% record of success; later, when the critics understood the magnitude of the task, and then had seen the terrain, and then realised that a completely fresh Battalion the next night, the 4th/6th Rajput Rifles, had still made no impression on the enemy position, they tended to revise their views.

There have been several inaccurate statements made about the attack, in various histories, *e.g.* The 4th Indian Division History. Too much stress has been laid on the effect of the three Green lights fired by the Germans – some have even suggested that this was a deliberate ruse. It has also been called loosely "the signal for withdrawal". It was no such thing. D Company was to be relieved on the objective by B Company, which was specially equipped to hold the position. When B Company was in position, and only then, D Company was to withdraw through them. This method had been successfully employed, on various occasions, by another Division during its operations in mountainous country in Italy. All too often it had proved too difficult for an assaulting company to hold its objective once captured, and a fresh company, fully loaded up with ammunition, seemed to have been the answer to the problem.

On 17th February, the Battalion was reorganised into three companies, with D Company being temporarily disbanded, having provided one platoon complete for C Company. Following a conference at 7th Brigade Headquarters, the 4th/16th Punjab Rifles were ordered to attack Pt. 593 that night. As part of this, 1st Royal Sussex, less one company, was to come under command of 4th/16th Punjabis to exploit through Pt. 593 to Pt. 444 towards the Monastery.

The 4th/6th Punjab Rifles attack on the night of 17th-18th February followed the same course as that of the 1st Royal Sussex on the previous night, and although some of them swept across the top of Pt. 593, the enemy, after hard fighting, remained in possession. The 1st Battalion was not called upon to take part in any exploitation that night.

On the following night, after a very gallant but unsuccessful night attack against the Monastery by the 1st/2nd and 1st/9th Gurkhas, the two battalions were withdrawn and 1st Royal Sussex was left holding the mountain salient of Snakes Head Ridge with 2nd/7th Gurkhas on its left. Shelling by Allied artillery was very troublesome during the day, and at least one regimental artillery concentration landed on the 1st Battalion's forward companies. The Battalion was left in its positions until the next big attack, which was due to be undertaken by the New Zealand Division and the 5th Indian Brigade. Plans for this were ready within a week but, for various reasons, the attack was repeatedly postponed for a month. In the meantime, 1st Royal Sussex remained in position on the Pt. 593 – Snakes Head Ridge – a long spell of twenty-two days, continually under enemy shellfire, and all within 70 yards of the enemy positions. The weather meanwhile was indescribable except in the unprintable terms of the gallant British soldier!

On 5th March the 1st Royal Sussex became the Brigade Reserve in the 'Bowl', only 500 yards behind the front line and there it remained until 19th March, being mortared and shelled incessantly. The Battalion then moved back to its original sector where it took over from the 5th Buffs, and where it remained for a further seven days.

If this history seems to labour the Cassino picture over much, it is because the conditions were unique and little known today; it is without doubt that the sector held by the 1st Battalion could only be described as unique - a long thin salient in the heart of the enemy defences, with the forward troops only 70 yards from the enemy and Battalion Headquarters only 200 yards behind. It had inadequate cover from mortars, shelling and rifle grenades, and no cover whatsoever against the elements, with the same troops holding it for twenty-two days on end, followed by a further seven days after a spell in reserve.

The enemy systematically searched the mule tracks with his guns and mortars as well as harassing the Battalion positions. It took a steady toll of casualties and throughout the period the Brigade averaged sixty casualties per day. The Battalion's Regimental Aid Post was in the same cottage as Battalion Headquarters, as it was the only possible place for it. Stretcher parties going to it invariably carried a large Red Cross Flag and moved in full view of the Germans. They were never fired on. The German stretcher parties were observed doing the same in the Monastery area. The evacuation of casualties from the Regimental Aid Post was carried out by relays of stretcher-bearers stationed and living in slit trenches every 400 yards along the supply route. It often took as long as five hours to get down to the Advanced Dressing Station, after which there was a bumpy Jeep journey further to the rear. There is no doubt that in spite of the efforts of the Medical Services, several casualties died because of the appalling journey down the mountains.

Stretcher Bearers Passing RAP at Cassino

Colonel Buckeridge recalls the evacuation system, after he was wounded during the Battalion night attack on 16th February:

> *"Tim Riley (the RMO) said I should not walk and arranged for me to be strapped to a stretcher on the side of a mule; I know not what was on the other side of the mule to counter-balance my weight. . . .. About every 100 yards there were so-called resting places manned by a couple of soldiers detailed off as stretcher bearers or coolies. The start of my journey was hair-raising to say the least. Within a couple of hundred yards the mule had slipped twice and I had rolled off the stretcher each time. That was enough, and I decided to hobble down the*

mountain on foot. A fresh escort accompanied me between each resting place. 'Resting Place' was an apt name for on one occasion a Jock in the Cameron Highlanders was discovered dead in one.

It took me about three hours to stagger down the mountain to an Advanced Dressing Station in the village of Cairo, where they put me on a 'Stretcher Jeep' with another casualty. By now it was daylight and under the protection of the Red Cross flag, we drove across the Rapido Valley like the clappers to another medical station near San Michele."

In the forward companies, deployed just below Pt. 593, there was unceasing vigilance because of the extreme closeness of the enemy. By night half those of any post had to keep awake while the other half slept. The enemy, at first the 15th Panzer Grenadier Division and later the famous 1st Parachute Division, such redoubtable fighters were relieved by other battalions or companies every five days, so the 1st Royal Sussex always faced comparatively fresh troops.

The enemy had a goodly supply of rifle grenades, which they used on the forward companies, with the grenades arriving out of the blue with no warning, and causing a steady trickle of casualties. Retaliation was difficult – the forward positions were too close for artillery support and until the Battalion received grenade discharge cups (requested months before) it failed to silence these weapons. Although designed for the 36 Grenade, with the 7-second fuse, firing the 4-second fused grenades from cup dischargers, when they arrived, produced an excellent airburst and silenced the enemy, but alas they only arrived there in time for the Battalion's last two days in the position.

The Head of the Jeep Track where it met the Mule Track Resupply went Up to Snakes Head Ridge and Casualties came Down, changing the type of Transport at this Point

The part of the routine everyone looked forward to was the arrival of the mules each night with hot food, rations, mail *etc*. Intense enemy shelling forced the mule loading point to be moved back across the Rapido River to the San Michele area. Consequently, the mule train, which could not emerge from its cover until after dark each night, had the long seven mile journey each way, including a stiff climb nightly, before finally arriving back under cover before first light.

The Battalion Second-in-Command Major S.J.F. Upton MC was in overall charge of the supply arrangements assisted by the Headquarters Company Commander, Captain J.A. Day and Major Jones, the Commander of Support Company. Nightly, one of these officers together with the Company-Quartermaster-Sergeants and the Company storemen in charge of the mules, made this long trek, over tracks that were narrow, often icy and the sides precipitous. The mules were under a mixture of French, American, Italian and Indian ownership and one never knew what language they answered to! Mule drivers of various nationalities were also not always totally reliable. Add to these factors the constant enemy shelling and mortaring of the supply lines and one has a picture of the difficulties they all faced every night.

"Guts, heroic endeavour, and devotion to duty," said Colonel Glennie, *"overcame their nightly difficulties and perils as the enemy bombarded the supply lines."*

One of the stalwarts of this gallant resupply system, Private Goodall, the muleteer of A Company, was awarded the Military Medal for gallantry in handling the mules and their cosmopolitan drivers, under continuous and intense shelling.

Food cooked in the A Echelon area was varied as possible, but the best meal was undoubtedly hot Meat Pasties, which were easy to distribute in forward section posts, with the second favourite being doughnuts. However, many members of the forward Companies only recall ever receiving all-in stew!

Advancing Up the Mule Track at Cassino Monastery in the Background

There were altogether over one hundred dead Americans and Germans in the position and it was not till the end of the Battalion's stay that it was able to start collecting these bodies and carrying them down the mountain for burial. They were strapped onto mules returning at night having delivered the rations; a grim procession indeed coming down the mountain.

A regrettable fact about the Pt. 593 position was the frequency with which it was shelled by Allied guns; any new artillery regiment moving into position seemed to think that the Pt. 593 feature (well behind the Monastery) was an excellent one for target practice, with the Battalion Headquarters cottage providing a perfect aiming mark. The Battalion's own Forward Observation Officers and the Battery Commander did their best to stop this habit and towards the end of its stay, there was a distinct improvement in this respect. One night, however, Battalion Headquarters was sniped by one medium high-velocity gun from the direction of the Allied lines; the Headquarters was not protected from this side. One shot was fired at it at exactly five-minute intervals from 7 pm until 11 pm, and while the fire was accurate, no direct hit was scored. In an effort to trace the gun, all artillery pieces in the Army were stopped firing, but this rogue gun persisted. No flash was ever seen and the identity of the gun, and whether it was friend or foe, has ever remained a mystery. For those inside Battalion Headquarters, the three hours were somewhat tense; for B and C Companies watching from near Pt. 593 it was an interesting spectacle, and it was rumoured that a lot of betting took place as to probable hits!

On 5th March, the 1st Battalion was relieved by the 2nd Cameron Highlanders and went back into the Brigade Reserve in the 'Bowl'. During its time in the 'Bowl' the Battalion was constantly shelled and mortared, and enemy gunners were spurred to greater effort during the next big attack, which started on 15th March. This attack started with the bombing of Cassino by the Strategic Air Forces from 8.30 am to 12 noon. It was an awe-inspiring sight indeed and although it destroyed the town completely, it seemed to have no apparent effect on the morale and fighting qualities of the defenders, who gave the attacking New Zealanders a warm welcome. On 19th March an armoured thrust was launched down the valley running between Snakes Head Ridge and Phantom Ridge by a gallant foray of the 7th Indian Brigade Reconnaissance Squadron in 'cut-down Honeys',[52] and some New Zealand and American tanks. C Company secured the firm base and start line at the head of the valley and the tanks moved through completely unopposed, taking the enemy completely by surprise. They shot up Albaneta Farm (Massa) and started to move up the track leading to the door with *'PAX'* over the lintel at the back of the Monastery, and they could see the Liri valley below, when they were stopped by mines and hostile fire. Much consternation was caused amongst the enemy and some prisoners were taken. No infantry were available to accompany the tanks but if there had been an Infantry Brigade so available to exploit this audacious tank action, the outcome could have been decisive and the bitter fighting in Cassino town would have been avoided. C Company, which had been made up to strength by A Company, held the firm base throughout but they suffered many casualties through shelling and mortaring.

---

[52] The M3 Stuart, an American light tank was named by the British after the Confederate General Stuart, while its unofficial nickname of *Honey* came from a US tank driver who remarked, *"She's a honey"!* The turret was removed from some examples to improve speed and range, and many of these were converted to the armoured personnel carrier rôle.

The Battalion's time in the 'Bowl' came to an end and on the night of 20th-21st March, it took over its old position on the Pt. 593 – Snakes Head Ridge from the 2nd Camerons. The sector remained fairly quiet while the 5th Indian Brigade fought their magnificent battle from the Castle Area to Hangman's Hill. Due to extreme weariness and casualties neither 1st Royal Sussex nor the rest of the 7th Indian Brigade were really fit now for offensive operations in the mountains. Altogether during the six weeks it was engaged, the Battalion casualties were 22 officers and over 300 men. As the majority of these came from the Rifle Companies, whose initial strength would have been about 350 at the most, it explained why the Battalion's usefulness in offensive operations was severely restricted. In the 4th Indian Division, more than 4,000 men were killed or wounded during the Cassino operations.

Many fine things have been written about the part played by the 4th Indian Division at this battle and the efforts of the 7th Indian Brigade in holding the heights for so long. Eric Linklater[53] summarised the situation on the mountain as follows:

> *"And still it rained, and snow fell on the mountain heights, where, week after week, the 7th Indian Brigade held their grim sangars, in despite of German mortars, German machine-guns, and all the malignity of nature.*
>
> *Never have troops endured with more patient valour the peril and abomination of war than did these men of the 1st Royal Sussex, the 4th/16th Punjab Regiment, and the 1st/2nd Gurkha Rifles in their vigil on the rocks.*
>
> *It was impossible to relieve them, and their open positions, on narrow ground so closely overlooked, could not be much improved. In their lines and on the supply route they lost an average of sixty men a day, but the remainder held their ground."*

Finally, on 25th March, the 1st Battalion was relieved by the 5th Northamptons, from the 78th Division. The Battalion walked wearily down the mountain track, now covered in snow by a heavy fall on the two nights of the relief, and was just out of sight of the Monastery's observation posts by first light.

One writer describes the ruins of the Monastery as *"an eternal memorial to the humble greatness of the Infantry private soldier."*

Thus ended the 1st Battalion's operations at Cassino. They are worth recording because Cassino was easily comparable with some of the major battles of human attrition in the Great War. In the opinion of members of the 1st Royal Sussex who had also fought in Eritrea, the Western Desert and later in Italy,

---

[53] *The Campaign in Italy*. Eric Linklater, HM Stationery Office. 1951.

Cassino was the toughest phase of all. Many fine things have been written about the part played by the 4th Indian Division at this battle and the efforts of the 7th Indian Brigade in holding the heights for so long. Field Marshall Wavell's description of the 4th Indian Division rather sums up the contribution made by all ranks of the Division:

> *"One of the greatest bands of fighting men who have ever served together in this troubled world of wars and warriors."*

During March 1944, Major General Tuker[54] handed over command of the 4th Indian Division and in his letter to the 1st Royal Sussex, he wrote:

> *"The Division has made the whole of my life worth living. It has shown me what my old battalion showed me but on a huge scale in varied colours – courage, daring, utter endurance until death. May God bless them all in their supreme nobility and selflessness,"*

Everyone had played their part in this great endeavour; the two new Drafts that had reached the Battalion just before the Cassino battles – fine material, but quite raw. They were pitched into the longest and bitterest conflict, without respite, that any soldiers could expect. In the Commanding Officer's estimation, they acquitted themselves nobly and none could have done better. Their magnificent conduct he ascribes partly to the work of a very fine lot of battle-experienced Non-Commissioned-Officers, who welded them together.

In addition to Major Dalton, a veteran of the long African campaigns, from Eritrea to Tunis, and who proved to be one of the mainstays of the Battalion, mention has already been made of Major Gratton and Major Hawkes for their gallant leadership, both wounded in the attack on Pt. 593. There were also Major Brand MC, wounded early in the operation and killed later in the war, the valiant Captain L.W. Weeks MC, described as 'the willing horse' and a patrol expert, Captain T. Reilly MC, the devoted medical officer, and Padre James, who often worked with him at the Regimental Aid Post, and constantly visited the forward companies. Captain Weeks, whose impressions of the North African fighting have been quoted earlier, died of wounds from a rifle-grenade, following the long journey down the mountain.

A prodigious and Herculean figure amongst the men was the already mentioned Sergeant Osman MM. Major Dalton gives a clear indication of his magnificent contribution to C Company:

> *"A real 'swede basher'[55] - in appearance, a powerful figure with a smile for everyone, a personality to which men warmed and the good*

---

[54] As was the practice at the time, General Tuker on being commissioned in the 1st/2nd Gurkhas, carried out his first year's commissioned service with the 1st Royal Sussex in India.

[55] Sussex men – a lot were farmers' boys.

manners of a real yeoman. He was a professional footballer by trade and a gentleman by inclination. In the battle he arrived as a normal L/Cpl of his platoon and after the first attack he commanded the platoon for the next six weeks until he led them off the mountain.

Always full of aggression he almost wore out the Brownings the Yanks gave us. During the second attack on Pt. 593 he was magnificent in assault and in rescuing casualties when we withdrew. He was wounded and no one would have thought ill of him if he went back. How he managed in some cases to stagger back carrying two men is amazing.

After the two hammerings the Company had received and during those weeks of attrition a man of Osman's qualities was an asset beyond value."

The stretcher-bearers, ever answering the call to evacuate casualties, whatever the situation; the small rosy-cheeked Lance Corporal Chapman, and the tall, rather serious Lance Corporal Gould, cool, capable and inspiring, both of who were subsequently awarded the Military Medal. Major Dalton's signallers, Smith and Young, real Sussex men performing 'wonders which would have floored Marconi', emerge memorably from this historic ordeal, along with Private Eather, a Signal Linesman, would also be awarded the Military Medal for continually volunteering to go out and repair broken lines of communication, by day and by night, while under heavy artillery and mortar fire. And Company-Quartermaster-Sergeant Briggs; he made the journey from A Echelon to the Company every night come what may, and almost always with exactly what had been requested on the previous night. Even discounting the hazards of war, the obstacle of terrain alone made it a feat to be proud of.

In Colonel Glennie's judgement, it was the Regimental mixture of Swede, Cockney, and a dash of Irish which produced the cheerful obstinacy demanded by the situation, and he quotes the admirable Brigadier Lovett as admitting that the Regiment was kept so long in the Pt. 593 sector because he felt that no other could have endured it. For the greatest gallantry, tactical ability, devotion to duty, and imbuing in all ranks an offensive spirit of a very high order, while commanding the 1st Battalion The Royal Sussex Regiment, Lieutenant Colonel Glennie, although wounded early in February and refusing to be evacuated, was subsequently awarded the Distinguished Service Order.

The Polish Corps eventually stormed the Cassino Monastery, after the 8th Indian Division and the 4th British Division had broken the Gustav Line along the Liri River. The Poles approached by way of Pt. 593 on the same thrust line as that taken by the 7th Indian Brigade in the first assault by 1st Royal Sussex. Desperate fighting ensued at Piedimonte, four miles west of the Monastery, before the enemy was finally hurled from the high ground. Upwards of 1,000 Polish dead are buried in their cemetery on the slopes of Pt. 444.

Finally on Cassino, we are fortunate in that through our research into the updating of the Regiment's history of the Second World War, we have been given access to the personal recollections of a German ex-Parachute Sergeant (Feldwebel) named Wilhelm Weier. He took part, amongst other campaigns, in the defence of Point 593, the principal objective of 1st Royal Sussex, and he also witnessed the death of Captain Bernard Gain. This research was initiated and undertaken by ex-Sergeant Leslie Deacon, who, like his father before him, served in The Royal Sussex Regiment. We are extremely grateful for Leslie's detailed work and efforts in Germany in locating and interviewing Feldwebel Weier, and Weier's detailed and informative account is shown at Annex B.

The Advance Through Italy – The Lower Adriatic Phase

After the 1st Battalion had been relieved and withdrawn from the battlefield at Cassino, it went back several miles to a rest area where it was reinforced by officers and men from several regiments to help make up for the losses it had suffered during the previous six weeks in battle. This allowed the Battalion to revert to four Rifle Companies and as most of the reinforcements had not seen action before, it embarked on a crash course of training to both integrate the new arrivals into the Battalion and to quickly make it fit for action again. Hardly had the Battalion absorbed the reinforcements when it was sent back into the line in the foothills on the Adriatic front for a couple of weeks in a 'holding rôle'.

On 25th March, Major General A.W.W. Holworthy DSO MC had taken over command of the 4th Indian Division and he would subsequently lead it up to, and through, the Gothic Line. It was deemed good fortune that the Division should retrieve one of its own as its new commander, coming himself from the 3rd Gurkha Rifles, had, amongst other Indian appointments, commanded the 7th Indian Brigade in the Western Desert in 1942.

Lieutenant Colonel Glennie was admitted to hospital in April 1944, and the following month, Lieutenant Colonel Phelps arrived from Egypt to take over command of the 1st Royal Sussex on 11th May. At the same time, the Battalion was relieved of its 'holding rôle', ironically enough, by the Italian Folgare Division – an old foe of desert days! Shortly after, Major Shinkwin MC also rejoined the Battalion on 19th May as Second-in-Command.

After Cassino, the whole of the 4th Indian Division was moved to the Adriatic sector and by 10th April 1944 found itself back in the sectors occupied in its previous tour of this front in January. The 7th Indian Brigade was deployed to hold the line from Orsogna to Guardiagrele and an Indian Army observer furnished a good description of the front:

> *"The bleak-looking farmhouses, which dot the countryside, are the scene of many quick, murderous encounters. Both Indian and*

> *German detachments live in much the same fashion. Downstairs, in the tool-sheds and cattle stalls, the infantry platoons are quartered. The cellar serves as a bolt-hole in emergency. The upper storeys, reached by outside staircases, which give excellent observation, house the machine-gunners, signallers and other specialists. Everyone moves discreetly during the day to avoid unwelcome attention from enemy guns. When darkness falls, the danger mounts. The farmhouses nearly all have blind walls, behind which a raiding party may approach unseen. Throughout the night, therefore, sentries are stationed on all sides in slit trenches. Alarm wires are strung and likely approaches are mined or booby-trapped. The techniques of surprise, like the precautions against it, demand courage and resourcefulness of a high order, as well as skill in battle tactics which are a mixture of gangster and Red Indian practices."*

In the early morning of 11th May, three Allied corps attacked along the line from Monte Cassino to the Arunci Mountains and hurled themselves at the Cassino positions, which fell after a week's bitter fighting. As a result a general German withdrawal on the Adriatic front became a possibility.

In its sector the 4th Indian Division was ordered to maintain intimate contact everywhere in order to intensify pressure if any thinning-out was detected. Deep fighting patrols encountered some resistance and on the early morning of 26th May, D Company 1st Royal Sussex carried out a raid on Le Piane, a small village between Arielli and Crecchio, to test dispositions and to take prisoners to secure enemy identification. The right forward platoon, commanded by Lieutenant M.J.A. Dickson, having passed through the village and found no prisoners, pushed further forward and came under heavy Spandau fire and suffered casualties. With complete disregard for his own personal safety, Lieutenant Dickson went forward to recover two wounded soldiers, one of whom was found to have been killed, and then, under cover of Bren-gun fire, he and a few men rushed the enemy and forced them to retire to a more strongly held depth position. Realising his group was not strong enough to make another assault, they remained in position until their ammunition was almost expended. Although in a weak and exhausted condition, Lieutenant Dickson continued to direct his force until

ordered to retire. He was subsequently awarded the Military Cross for his courage and initiative. Meanwhile, the second platoon was clearing the other side of the village, and Lance-Sergeant Gardner was leading his section forward when it also came under Spandau fire. He immediately rushed the position with his section, driving them out with Tommy-guns and grenades. Rapidly following this up, he and two of his men completely demoralised and routed the enemy. Sergeant Gardner was awarded the Military Medal for his leadership and courage, as was Private Willard for his superb and individual effort in the same fight, for not only silencing two Spandaus but also inflicting casualties and putting the remainder of the enemy force to flight. At the same time, C Company which was holding a firm line on the flank of this attack, were able to cut off and capture two prisoners, who confirmed that the formation in front of the Battalion was very weak and made up of a mixture of very young soldiers, with some older ones who had seen service on the Russian Front. However, despite the 1st Battalion's success, other regiments carrying out similar tasks, suffered serious casualties from what was a still a very determined enemy.

On 30th May a number of Italian formations arrived to take over on the Orsogna – Maielle front: the new allies exhibiting more enthusiasm than common sense; their advance parties arrived with flags flying and bands playing and were surprised when they attracted such a heavy artillery response from their former allies.

By the end of May it was apparent that the battered and retreating forces on Fifth Army's front would not be able to stand in front of Rome, and that a long retreat to the main wall of the Apennines might be anticipated.

Rome fell to the Americans in June, just two days before the Normandy landings, with the latter event tending to obscure the former in the eyes of the waiting world.

On 2nd/3rd June, 7th Indian Brigade led the relief of 10th Indian Division and took over in the centre of the coastal sector, although the 4th Indian Division had no more than established itself in its new positions when the long expected German withdrawal began. Following some successful probing, the Division advanced and by 11th June the 7th Indian Brigade had crossed and were soon well north of the Pescara River.

Despite the fall of Rome the German withdrawal strategy in Italy during the summer of 1944 had been dominated by three intentions: first, the German planners wished to deny ground to the Allied armies until it could be sold at an incommensurate price in blood. Secondly, they wished to make progress more difficult as the nature of the terrain progressively favoured the defenders; and thirdly, they wished to hold back the advancing Allied forces from the High Apennines until the mighty wall of the Gothic Line defences had been completed. Thus the Germans continued to hold firm on their Gustav Line and the ability to wage war in mountainous terrain continued to be a major commitment.

It seemed apparent that the Germans would make a long withdrawal towards their next important barricade across the peninsula; the Gothic Line. This was a formidable defensive system in considerable depth, embracing the entire breadth of the belt of interlocking ranges of the Apennines across Italy. The eastern sector ran along the Foglia River and was anchored at the Adriatic town of Pesaro. While the main mountain ranges stopped short of the coast, high foothills running almost to the sea provided excellent defensive positions. Once an attacking army won past Rimini, 20 miles up the coast from Pesaro, it was thought that the Gothic Line would be turned; it was expected that once the Eighth Army entered the Po Valley it would be able to exploit rapidly across the

The Gothic Line Defences in Northern Italy

plain. Optimism at the ability to force the pace was to be sadly disappointed, particularly as the rivers and the extensive canal system north of Rimini continually hampered progress. Instead of making the expected rapid advance, the Eighth Army entered upon a long and discouraging period of nearly four months fighting, crossing numerous river obstacles in winter weather in operations that can best be described as the *'battles of the rivers'*. The operations did, however, tie down numerous German forces that might otherwise have been used to help oppose the Allied advance in Western Europe.

It was the Allied intention to hasten the enemy's withdrawal as much as possible and to attack the Gothic Line before the Germans had the opportunity to complete its defences. But to do this a series of strongly defended intermediate positions south of Florence had to be overcome.

The Advance Through Italy – the Central Region Phase

After being relieved on the Adriatic coast on 13th June, the 4th Indian Division shifted to the Campobasso training area, near to Benevento, in the mountains east of Naples. Although the 1st Royal Sussex had been introduced to skiing in the Lebanese mountains in November 1943, it now began a period of vigorous training for mountain warfare, including mountain climbing techniques, with the intention of breaking through the mountainous central sector of Italy. However, as the Gustav Line was eventually penetrated by 18th June, the Battalion was never committed to a true mountain warfare rôle. Notwithstanding this, within a fortnight, it was trekking northwards as the Germans had withdrawn so fast that the 4th Indian Division was thrown into hot pursuit in the foothills of the mountains on the right of the Fifth Army.

The 1st Battalion itself made contact once more with the enemy to the northeast of Lake Trasimeno, in the foothills to the north of the River Arno near Arezzo. To the north of Lake Trasimeno, the ridges grew higher and narrower, valleys deeper and more abrupt, and more numerous high vantage points crowned with walled villages or *palazzo*. Patches of woodland decked the hillsides and summits, and each valley carried a powerful and abundant stream, which fed down towards the Arno or Tiber. Almost all the roads were constructed east and west, along the meandering defiles of these tributaries, affording the enemy an admirable system of transverse communications. Such terrain prevented the concentration of forces and lent itself to surprise – two tactical advantages, which might have eased the task of the defenders. Fortunately, the Wehrmacht High Command had nullified these advantages by leaving their own troops in the line for long and exhausting periods. Nevertheless, even enemy forces that were generally thin on the ground would normally counter-attack fiercely to regain lost positions.

From the Arezzo there began a period of thrusts and company actions, which brought the Division alongside their old comrades-in-arms, the New Zealand Division. But sadly, as a sort of *quid pro quo*, the 1st Royal Sussex would lose their close and gallant warriors - the 4th/6th Punjab Regiment - a regiment they had served alongside since they had joined the 7th Indian Brigade in 1940. The Punjabis had been despatched to a well-earned rest in the Middle East and were replaced by the 2nd Royal Sikhs.

The Germans continued their swift withdrawal through this rugged terrain and did their best to hold up the 1st Battalion's advance by blowing craters and destroying the small bridges along the narrow paths and tracks along which it was advancing, and which was not made any easier by the intense heat and dust.

Using two-man Spandau or anti-tank gun positions, the Germans held up the advance continually, with each position having to be winkled out by rifle sections using simple but time-consuming fire and movement battle techniques.

On 8th July, 4th Indian Division took up the running and on 10th July the 7th Indian Brigade crossed the Nestore River and beyond it lay a long ridge, rising steadily towards Monte San Maria di Tiberina, a small fortress village perched on an isolated pinnacle high above the ridge of the same name. This eyrie-like hamlet commanded the ground as far as the Tiber, and was held by the enemy in some strength. The leading Indian battalions of the Brigade had secured entry to San Maria but were forced out by enemy counter-attacks. In the late afternoon of 11th July, B Company of 1st Royal Sussex, under Major Cavalier, passed through the Gurkhas and advanced along the crest of the ridge, with artillery in support. By 10 pm the Company was within one mile of the objective but was encountering stiff opposition. A second Company – A Company - then came forward into the fight although its commander, Major D.H. Brand, a gallant officer with a fine fighting record, was

killed and the advance progressed no further. At first light, a patrol went ahead and discovered that the enemy had withdrawn, which meant that San Maria was quickly occupied by 1st Royal Sussex, and allowed a rifle platoon to be pushed forward some 3,000 yards to the northeast to occupy Mount Cedrone. However, the enemy reacted vigorously to the seizure of Monte Cedrone and counter-attacked in company strength at dusk on 13th July. Although these were repulsed, because of their insecure position, the occupying Royal Sussex platoon was withdrawn that night.

While the San Maria fight was in progress, the 2nd Royal Sikhs had captured Monte Civitella at dawn and its seizure gave 7th Indian Brigade observation over Route 73, one of the principal east-west highways in the mountain block.

After the Brigade had crossed the Arno, the German resistance stiffened until, as the advancing forces approached the mountains once more, it became clear that the Division had arrived before the forward positions of the Gothic Line.

As the main weight of the Fifth and Eighth Armies had been directed up the spine of Italy and on the West Coast, the Germans had massed most of their troops to meet this threat, leaving only light forces to oppose the Italians on the Adriatic. The 4th Indian Division's relentless advance was therefore suspended on 10th August as this weakness in the enemy defences had become more apparent when the New Zealand, Canadian, South African and Indian Divisions had broken through to Florence. It was clear that there was no longer any necessity to battle forward ridge by ridge, pinnacle by pinnacle or river after river; in thirty-two days, the 4th Indian Division had advanced 25 miles as the crow flies, and probably twice as much by march distance, across terrain, which in reality, might have been designed specifically to protect the defenders.

With great secrecy, the 4th Indian Division was withdrawn from the line and moved to the Lake Trasimeno area for a brief period of hard training, before being moved east across the Apennines, and through the Italian Folgore Division screen to the east of Gubbio. The Germans were not aware that the 4th Indian Division, the Canadian Division and other formations had moved to the eastern side of the Allied Front and, although the Gothic Line positions had been prepared, they were not able to man them properly before the Allies struck.

The Advance Through Italy – The Gothic Line Phase

Towards the end of August not only the German High Command but also the rank and file knew that the war could not be won. Month after month of remitting defeats, with the strongest positions wrenched from their grasp, brought home to the Nazi's cannon fodder that they were fighting a lost cause. Notwithstanding this, when the leading formations advanced from Sigillo on 25th August, the enemy had excelled himself in his demolitions along the Flaminian Way. Every bridge had been blown and the roads blocked by craters, with houses and trees demolished to hinder any rapid follow-up. In many places it was simpler for the advancing troops to build a diversion rather than attempt road or bridge repairs.

Having pulled back to Lake Trasimeno, it was then the task of the 4th Indian Division, together with other British and Canadian formations, to break through the covering enemy positions and advance quickly to assault the Gothic Line. The rugged terrain heading north and to the east of Gubbio, meant that the advance had to be made on foot, or by overloaded Jeeps and trailers, along narrow tracks and lanes. Within the 1st Royal Sussex, the advance was undertaken by companies and platoons, often on different routes and in single file, and normally led by the Battalion's Reconnaissance Platoon in their Bren-

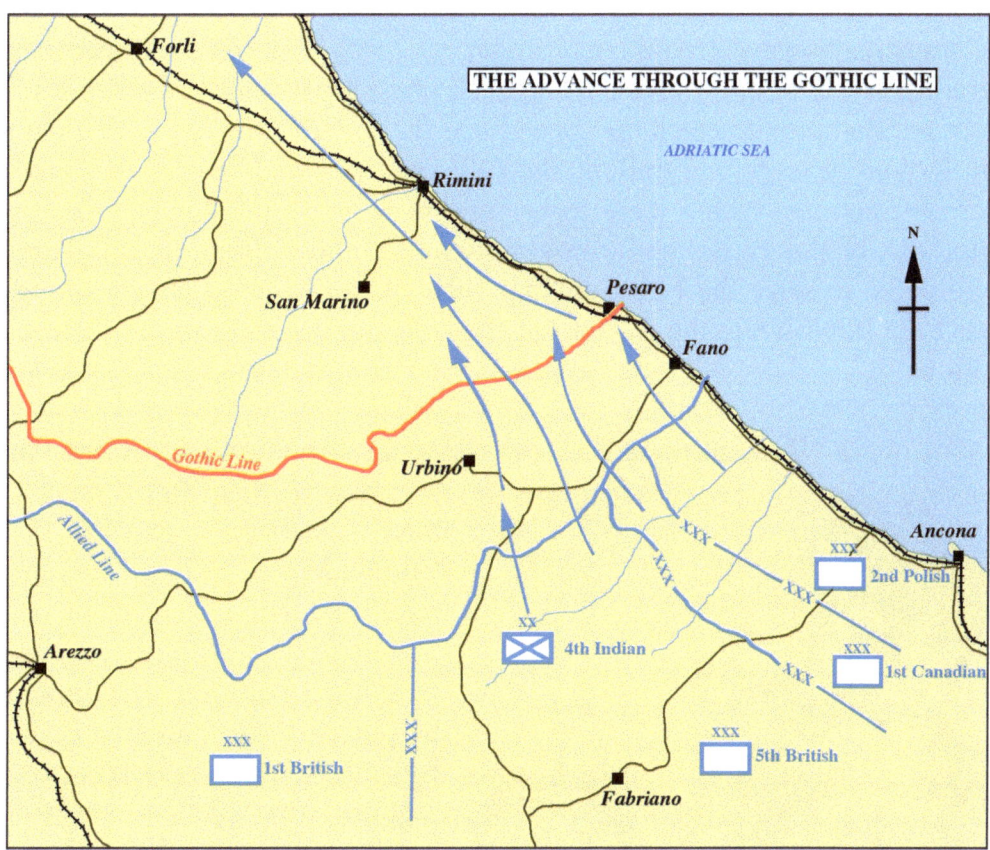

Gun carriers or the small 'Honey' tanks. Artillery Forward Observation Officers and mortar fire controllers also moved with the leading troops so that supporting fire was always on hand. The Germans, taken by surprise, suffered a staggering blow, for the Division carried out its task with such success that the enemy never really recovered until the Gothic Line had been breached. There were a series of swift advances – in one case of 25 miles in thirty-two hours – and the advance was characterised by company and platoon battles, followed by rapid pursuit.

On the night of 26th August the leading elements of 7th Indian Brigade had reached the line of the Metauro River, 4 miles south of Urbino. The following day 1st Royal Sussex passed through the 2nd Royal Sikhs and entered Urbino, the birthplace of the great artist Raphael. When C Company, commanded by Major K.H.S. Wilson, led the way into Urbino, the whole of its 20,000 inhabitants lined the streets and gave voice in a great welcome. Later, as a mark of gratitude, the Mayor presented the Division with an engraving, a copy of which is kept in the Regimental Museum. Colonel Buckeridge, at the time commanding one of the two leading platoons to enter the town, recalls the presentation:

> *"Although fully armed and ready for action, the officers of the Battalion wore their peaked caps with our silver Regimental Badge. And not for the first or last time, I discovered that the Italians could not understand why we had the Red Cross of St George in the middle of the badge. Often they thought we were doctors!!"*

C Company, however, could not linger to enjoy the pleasures accorded to liberating soldiers, and moved off again at first light, without waiting for the rest of the Battalion to catch up. Speed was the order of the day and, moving on from Urbino in jeeps and trailers, the Company met and dealt with craters and other obstructions, which were to become familiar as the advance developed. As the rest of the 1st Battalion moved forward from Urbino on 28th August, it was ordered to seize the Piave di Cagna Ridge and Monte Calende in order to protect the flank while the rest of the Brigade '*squared up*' to the Gothic Line positions.

Seldom in war is infantry-tank co-operation all that it should be, but in this advance it was almost perfect; as the leading battalion, the Commanding Officer had earlier requested that, instead of the normal practice of attaching tanks for each individual battle, a squadron might be placed under battalion command for the entire operation. This request was granted and paid of handsomely over the next few weeks; being part of the Battalion Group, it enabled both elements to get to know each other intimately, and thus made co-operation a lot easier. B Squadron of the 6th Royal Tank Regiment, commanded by Major Ken Fidler, was the squadron that came under command of 1st Royal Sussex, and it was to be a close and rewarding relationship.

Working through the foothills, C Company was leading the advance and had almost reached Piave de Cagna when a major obstacle was encountered. The narrow track ran along the steep hillside and the Germans had blown up a culvert and created a very large crater. It was flanked on the right by a steep hill and on the left by a sheer drop into a valley. The leading carrier commander, Corporal White, jumped out of his vehicle in search of a diversion, as on previous occasions, and ran up the slope to the right. He rounded a haystack and stumbled into a slit trench occupied by two Germans manning a Spandau that covered the line of stationary vehicles. Recovering quickly from the surprise and armed only with a revolver, White, with great presence of mind and bravery, promptly despatched both Germans with his revolver. By his courage and initiative, he greatly assisted the Company in its successful occupation of the feature as the Spandau post covered the only approach to the position. Corporal White was subsequently awarded the Military Medal for his most gallant action. At the same time, from across the valley on the left rear, an enemy anti-tank gun opened accurate fire on the Company's stationary vehicles strung out along the track. Captain N. Maugham-Brown, the artillery Forward Observation Officer from the close support battery, immediately jumped on to one of the turret-less Stuart tanks accompanying the leading company group, and pumped .5-inch Browning machine-gun bullets into the enemy anti-tank gun position, which was quickly '*neutralised*'. These two actions were typical of the small battles that the Companies were constantly fighting, and which were generally over and done with in about thirty minutes, before they began pushing forward again.

It was obvious, however, that C Company had run into a prepared position and, as a diversion round the large crater could not be found, a quick attack by No. 13 Platoon was launched. The village of Piave di Cagna, across the valley, ran along a spur connecting two hill features, both of which turned out to be heavily defended. A troop of four tanks from the 6th Royal Tank Regiment moved up to the Start Line, which overlooked the village and, from hull-down positions, poured shells into suspected enemy positions. Lieutenant Buckeridge's Platoon (No. 13) attacked directly below the line of tank fire, which was continued until the advancing platoon, now climbing up the steep far side of the re-entrant, reached the first walls of the village buildings, with tank shells bursting immediately above their heads. The Platoon Commander's signal for the tank fire to cease was a wave of his handkerchief, which was timed so that it ceased as his Platoon drew level with the line of fire.

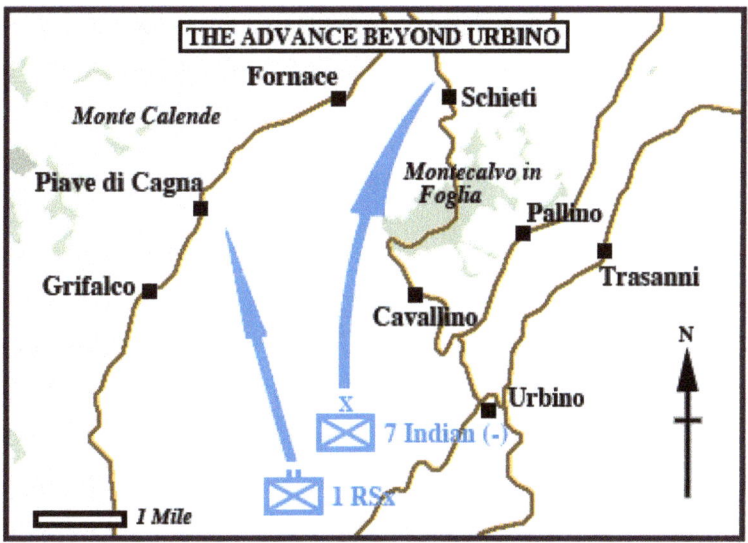

The enemy were overwhelmed before they had time to raise their heads, and the dozen or so still alive were taken prisoner.

In helping to achieve this success, one of No. 13 Platoon's sections, commanded by Corporal J.R. Horwood had to clear houses and consolidate on a hill 50 yards beyond a deep wadi. This was done so quickly that the enemy had no idea where his section was located and when they counter-attacked in strength the following night, they repeatedly came up against the concealed section, which held its fire until the enemy were almost upon them, and then broke up the attacks, inflicting many casualties. The following day, the

Germans shelled and mortared his position constantly but Corporal Horwood maintained complete control over the situation, and by sniping prevented the enemy from consolidating on a feature, which overlooked the whole of the Platoon's position. Corporal Horwood was subsequently awarded the Military Medal for his leadership, courage and initiative.

During the same platoon attack, Corporal C.H. Wilson led his section to attack a heavily defended road junction and they came under withering fire from a Spandau post on the crest of an almost perpendicular slope and he quickly realised that the whole attack might fail if the post was not destroyed. His section was now reduced to four men but dashing forward, he led them up the slope in a most audacious attack. The speed and determination of the assault led to the capture of the enemy post that outnumbered his small party by four to one. For his splendid courage, determination and initiative, Corporal Wilson was also subsequently awarded the Military Medal.

When the sound of fighting had died away, a heavy engine could be heard running, and the Platoon naturally anticipated enemy tanks, but apart from remorseless shelling and mortar fire, nothing developed. As soon as there was a relatively quiet period, the Platoon Commander went to investigate, for the sound of the engine appeared to come from between his own headquarters and one of his section positions. He found a large, brand-new German lorry, laden with anti-tank ammunition and towing an anti-tank gun. He promptly got into the lorry, drove it into the farmyard near one of his sections, and removed the ignition key. Several times that night, while the Platoon remained isolated, Germans attempted to drive the lorry away. However, it appeared that there was only one ignition key, and that was in Lieutenant Buckeridge's pocket! C Company maintained its defensive position at Piave di Cagne for nearly a week and withstood several heavy German counter-attacks, including severe shelling and mortaring.

The advance now continued, punctuated again by quick company and platoon attacks, and, as the Allied formations mustered to attack the Gothic Line (a series of half-prepared but nevertheless strong positions), resistance stiffened. At the same time, anti-Fascist elements began to show themselves to advantage, and recent events had increased the Italian people's hatred of the Germans.

The 4th Indian Division now moved against the primary defences of the Gothic Line, towards the junction of the Adriatic Plain with the foothills of the Apennines. With the stiffening of opposition, shellfire and mines inflicted considerable casualties, but the speed of the advance prevented the enemy from completing or fully occupying prepared positions, despite the assistance of much forced civilian labour.

On the morning of 6th September, while the 5th Indian Brigade was encircling Castelnuovo, the 7th Indian Brigade advanced on the western terminus of the Pian di Castello Ridge, thrusting against the village of the same name, when heavy opposition and shell fire was encountered. This was the start of a series of vigorous and bloody actions by 1st Royal Sussex. In the van, B Company, commanded by Major P.R. Cavalier, was caught on an exposed ridge by enemy self-propelled guns, firing over open sights, and suffered severely, losing three officers and a score of men within five minutes. Having encountered such heavy opposition, Major Cavalier immediately moved his Company with such

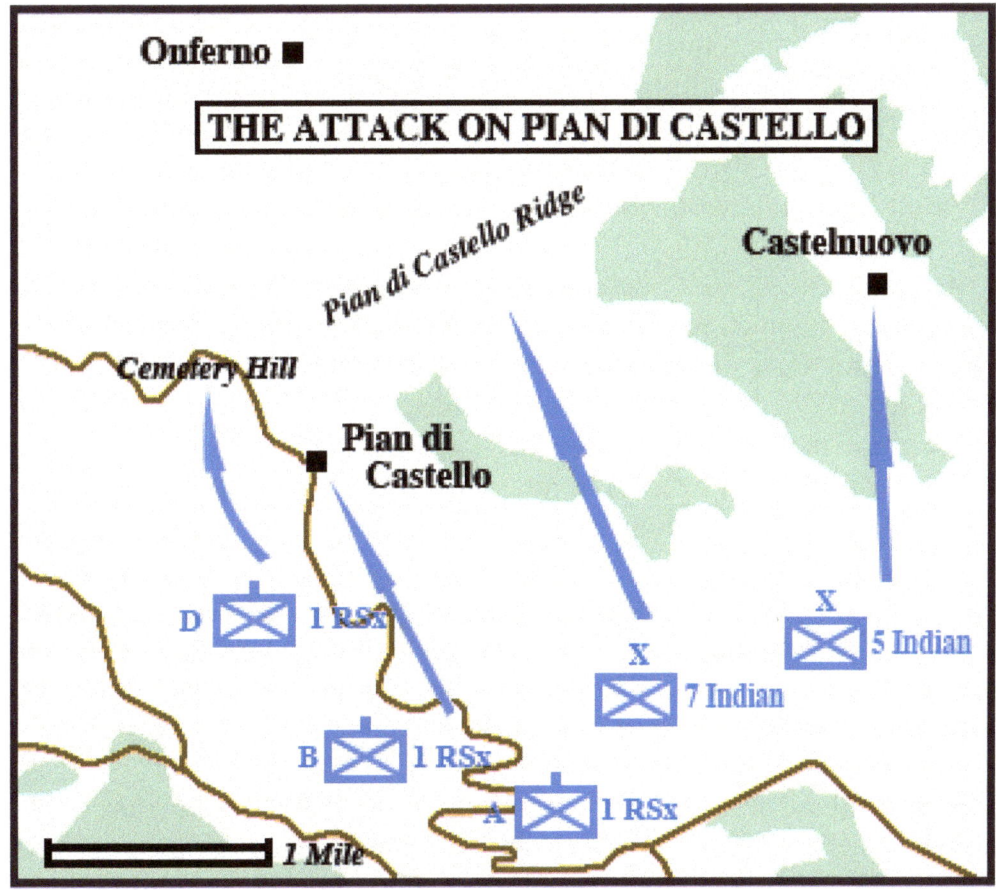

speed and decision through the heavy concentrations of shell and mortar fire that the enemy was completely surprised by this unexpected show of strength. The Germans also suffered in the severe counter-attacks, which they launched and which were repulsed by B Company. Although suffering a head-wound from a mortar bomb, Major Cavalier continued in command of his Company, realising the tenseness of the situation and the vital importance of holding, at all costs, the ground they had occupied. It was here that the Germans laid extensive wooden-box (*Schu-mine*[56]) minefields for the first time, and these

---

[56] The *Schu-mine 42* was a German anti-personnel mine and consisted of a simple wooden box with a hinged lid, containing a 200gr block of TNT; sufficient pressure on the lid triggered the mine. It was cheap to produce and the wooden body made it more difficult to detect with metal detectors.

caused more casualties than any other on that day. A Company then took the lead and managed to reach the outskirts of Piane di Castello. Taking up the remnants of B Company, the combined group went on and managed to negotiate the rugged, mined terrain in the failing light and in the pouring rain.

The next day or so was fairly miserable and, in the main, consisted of mopping-up enemy positions and consolidating the line. Before dawn on 8th September, vicious counter-attacks struck at both 1st/9th Gurkhas and 1st Royal Sussex and a fierce hand-to-hand mêleé ensued before the enemy was ejected. One platoon of the 1st Battalion's C Company was cut off but Lieutenant R.A. Roach had a field day by beating off, in a single-handed grenade battle, all attempts to overrun his isolated sections. Pian di Castello was eventually captured at first light on the 9th of September. Major Cavalier was subsequently awarded the Military Cross for his qualities of leadership, determination and devotion to duty during the heavy fighting in which the Battalion had recently been involved. Private L.J. Bryant, one of the B Company signallers was awarded the Military Medal for frequently going out under heavy shell, mortar and small-arms fire, without orders, to repair and maintain the telephone lines.

On the night of 9th/10th September, D Company 1st Royal Sussex, under command of Major Hugh Sayers, supported by the remnants of A Company advanced from Pian di Castello village to seize Cemetery Hill, some 1,000 yards to the north. The heavy bombardment, which preceded the attack had failed to shake the enemy but fortunately, as soon as dawn broke B Squadron of 6th Royal Tanks moved forward to intervene – it proved an eventful assignment as twenty Germans, including five *Panzerfaust*[57] men were captured. During this engagement one of the tanks was hit and caught fire. At this point, Padre Thornton went forward to assist in recovering casualties - he was carrying a pitchfork when he rounded a haystack and came face to face with fourteen fully armed Germans. Surprise was mutual, but the pitchfork prevailed, and the Padre brought in all fourteen as prisoners.

Before it captured the Cemetery position on the 10th, D Company had also suffered casualties, particularly from the many *Schu-mines*, which they encountered. Before the Company had consolidated on its position, C Company passed through to seize a ridge beyond the Cemetery, which overlooked Onferno below, and from which Gemmiano and San Marino in the distance could also be observed. On the night of 10th/11th September, C Company and two troops of tanks closed up behind a Corps barrage, which marched north towards Onferno, 1,200 yards beyond Cemetery Hill. The tanks followed a track, which led over a steep declivity and in the darkness the leading Sherman, commanded by Sergeant Fraser, executed a complete double somersault and continued on its way undamaged, although its 75mm main armament was out of action! The next three disabled themselves as they tumbled down the slope but the three remaining tanks were able to push on and

---

[57] Hand-held anti-tank weapon.

support the Company. The heavy bombardment of the enemy position only proved half effective for as the leading platoons of C Company advanced uphill in extended order, supported by the three tanks and the Battalion Reconnaissance Platoon, they came under heavy German small-arms fire, including Spandaus, and it was clear that the enemy would not give up this piece of vital ground without a fight. Supported by the tanks, which were battened down, a series of platoon fire and manoeuvre attacks were mounted, with the Germans only being winkled out after vigorous hand-to-hand fighting.

From the newly won position, the ground dropped away steeply to the north and northeast, and all enemy movement could be seen for miles. It was therefore obvious that now the Company was holding the vital ground, the Germans would be determined in their attempts to regain the position as quickly as possible. C Company had two platoons forward (No.13 Platoon commanded by Lieutenant Buckeridge and No. 14 Platoon by Lieutenant R.A. Roach), with No. 15 Platoon being in reserve, but before they had finished consolidating the position, they were met with the first of five major counter-attacks. The attacks appeared first to be in battalion and then company strength, but determined resistance from the mutually supporting Platoon positions and the staunchness of the soldiers, combined with the defensive fire of mortars and artillery, which the Company brought down deliberately on itself, compelled the enemy to draw off, having made no headway. That night, the enemy seemed to concentrate on No. 14 Platoon, which had an uncovered left flank, although No. 13 Platoon on its right was able to give enfiladed covering fire. While the Platoon was besieged, with two of the sections isolated, a counter-attack was mounted from within the position and Lieutenant Roach was observed dashing between his section positions, hurling grenades at the Germans in the open while encouraging his men to stand firm. The Germans became totally disorganised and despite their attempts to overrun the isolated sections, the positions remained intact, and the enemy were driven off yet again. Each time they attacked any part of the position, the enemy could find no counter to the heavy defensive fire, which was brought down on top of C Company, while the defenders, crouching in their slit trenches, once again suffered remarkably few casualties. For the inspiring example that he had set to his men, and for his courage and devotion to duty, Lieutenant Roach was subsequently awarded the Military Cross. Having failed to recapture the ridge, the Germans were soon retreating again.

The advance of the British divisions on the right of 4th Indian Division had ended abruptly against the bastion of Gemmiano; the principal obstacle consisting of a bare ridge 1,300 feet high at the junction of the Ventano and Conca rivers. The high ground extended from east to west for 4,000 yards and constituted a barrier, which could not be bypassed. The position was eventually seized as a result of not only magnificent fighting but also the cumulative effect of ten days of intolerable bombardment and furious assault. There followed a series of advances and major engagements and the Corps Commander announced the general retirement of the enemy on the Adriatic front. Nevertheless, the Germans stood stubbornly along the Apennine foothills and 7th Indian Brigade was brought forward to fill the gap between the 4th Indian and the 46th Divisions. The advance now surged forward nearer the coast and, eventually, after pausing beneath the towering slopes of San Marino, the 1st Royal Sussex went forward once more.

The weather was beginning to deteriorate, with hardly credible effects on harmless-looking riverbeds, as A and B Companies were soon to discover. On the night of 24th/25th September, the two Royal Sussex Companies crossed the dry bed of the River Marecchia and seized Gemmano on the western bank; but then the rain started, and before long, where vehicles had lately crossed on dry shingle, the two Companies found themselves in a hazardous situation having to wade chest-high through water to carry supplies across. On the following night a third company with tank support then pushed through to Cornacchiara,

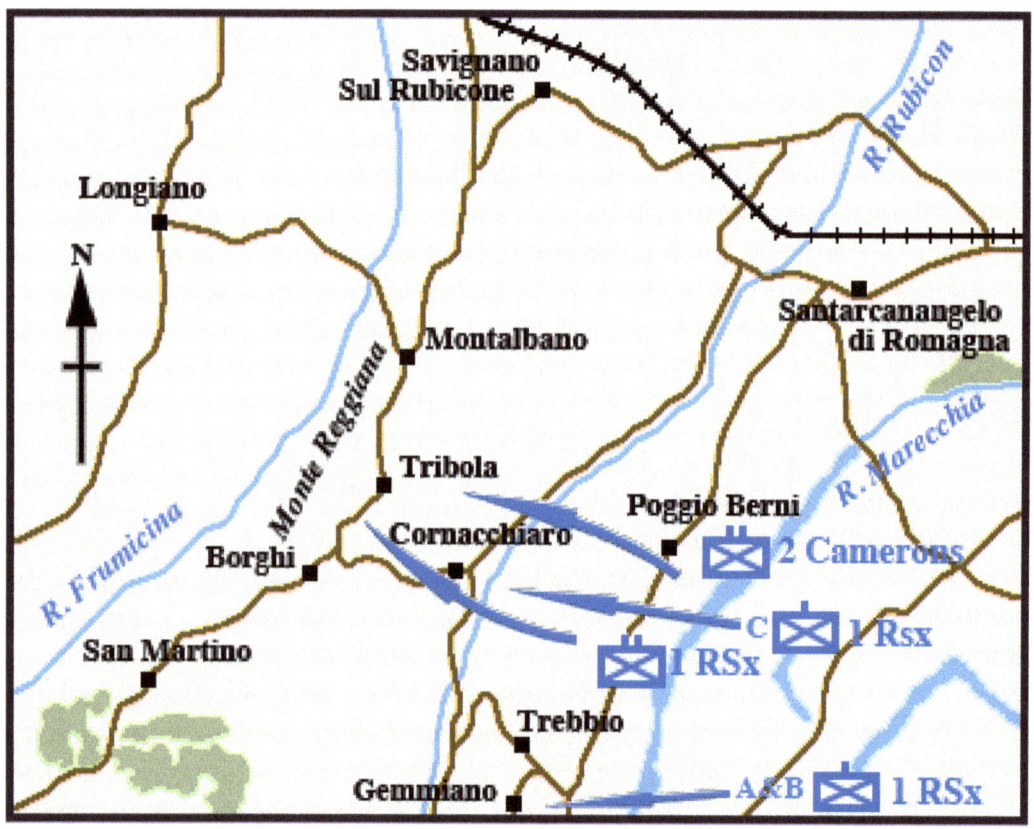

two miles to the west of the river. To relieve pressure on the 46th Division's left flank brigade, the 1st Royal Sussex and the 2nd/7th Gurkhas advanced shortly after midnight on 26th/27th September against intense enemy opposition. The supporting tanks bogged down and although the leading companies drove off repeated counter-attacks, it became necessary for both Battalions to withdraw.

It was on 28th September that the 1st Royal Sussex crossed the River Rubicon, and having secured a firm base on its north side, it took part in its last attack in Italy. On 1st October a fresh attack opened behind a barrage in which 306 guns fired 22,000 shells in three hours. All objective were seized, with 1st Royal Sussex and the 2nd Cameron Highlanders taking Monte Reggiano and Tribola respectively.

The advance through Italy had been unspectacular compared with Cassino, but it had involved continuous engagements and considerable casualties. Few platoons could boast more than a dozen men by the time they were relieved. The situation was now extremely intense, both in terms of operations and the weather, and is summarised quite clearly in the history of the 4th Indian Division:

> *"Like a vehicle that deploys forward, in heavy going, gradually losing speed until it finally bogs down, Fourth Indian Division's drive slowed and came to a halt. For the last ten days of September the hostile elements had excelled themselves. Autumnal gales from the Adriatic brought torrential rains. The watercourses had risen to dangerous levels. On the western flank Central India Horse patrols were marooned on the wrong side of the rivers; men were drowned in endeavouring to rejoin their units. Lieut.-Colonel Peters and his men finally extricated themselves and their mountain guns by means of aerial ropeways. Everywhere the low ground was a sodden morass, ankle-deep in freezing mud. The slopes were greasy and slippery, the crest wind-swept and storm-beaten. For the assault troops life was misery; in the back areas continuous day-and-night labour barely managed to keep minimum supplies moving to the firing line.*
>
> *It was now 37 days since the Fourth Indian Division had moved out of Sigillo and 32 days since it had opened the battle. In this period the three brigades had advanced more than 60 miles of which the last 25 had been in constant contact with a desperately resisting enemy. Casualties had been heavy, amounting to 1,892 all ranks, including a high percentage of junior officers. The average strength of companies was now less than 30 rifles. The battle had been of the most wearing type – no set piece assaults on the grand scale with intimate preparation and subsequent relief, but an unrelenting series of small bitter clashes, with thrust piled on thrust, in which the evenly balanced strengths of assailants and defenders exacted a substantial toll of casualties for each acre of gained or lost ground. Companies seized limited objectives; other companies passed through to register gains or to be flung back; the enemy fought with frenzy throughout the hours of darkness to be gone at dawn – but only as far as the next crest behind. Always a dominating ridge barred the way; when won, a swollen stream curtained by mortar fire lay behind it. To advance up a fire-swept hillside, surge over the crest, descend the reverse slopes in full view of the enemy, pick paths across deadly mined ground along the river banks, splash through icy torrents scarcely colder than the pelting rains, work up another slope against another crest stiff with enemies; with supporting arms, sappers, medicals and supply services following up; battling by night and day against abominable terrain and foul winter*

weather – such was the recurrent log of Fourth Indian Division's five weeks' drive along the Apennine foothills."

The 1st Royal Sussex had been singularly fortunate throughout its advance through Italy in the support it received from the 31st Field Regiment RA, and the 116th Battery in particular; indeed these gunners had been with the Battalion since the Western Desert. The untiring energy of Captain Maugham-Brown is remembered with gratitude.

No less valuable was the co-operation of 6th Royal Tank Regiment, some of whose tanks performed astounding feats. There was the incredible occasion when one of them plunged down a sheer escarpment of fifteen to twenty feet, turned somersaults, and went on without pausing! Major Dalton described them as *"Virtual Gazelles"*.

On 20th October, the 4th Indian Division received orders to proceed to Greece.

At the conclusion of all the Italian campaigns The Regiment was awarded the Battle Honours of **Cassino I,** Monastery Hill, Gothic Line, Pian di Castello, Monte Reggiano **and Italy 1944-45.** The Honours for **Cassino I** and **Italy 1944-45** are also emblazoned on the Colours.

Gallantry Awards for Italy in 1944-45

Bar to Distinguished Service Order:

Brigadier L.G. Whistler DSO	131st Brigade

Distinguished Service Order:

Lieutenant Colonel J.B.A. Glennie	1st Battalion
Lieutenant Colonel G.A. Phelps	1st Battalion
Major B. Dalton	1st Battalion
Lieutenant D.H. Cox	1st Battalion

Military Cross:

Major P.R. Cavalier	1st Battalion
Captain R.A. Alston-Roberts-West	1st Battalion (Bde LO)
Captain E.J. Bowmer RAMC	1st Battalion (RMO)
Lieutenant M.J.A. Dickson	1st Battalion
Lieutenant R.A. Roach	1st Battalion

Military Medal:

Sergeant T.S. Andrews	1st Battalion
Sergeant H. Luxford	1st Battalion
Sergeant G.A.P. Martin	1st Battalion
Lance-Sergeant T.A Gardner	1st Battalion
Lance-Sergeant W.E. Osman	1st Battalion
Corporal W.G. Gould	1st Battalion
Corporal J.R. Horwood	1st Battalion
Corporal L.F. White	1st Battalion
Corporal C.H. Wilson	1st Battalion
Lance-Corporal E.E. Brockhurst	1st Battalion
Lance-Corporal W.J. Chapman	1st Battalion
Private S.G. Avey	1st Battalion
Private L.J. Bryant	1st Battalion
Private H.P. Eather	1st Battalion
Private W. G.E. Goodsell	1st Battalion
Private E.P. Moreton	1st Battalion
Private F. Simmons	1st Battalion
Private C.J. Willard	1st Battalion

Mentioned in Despatches:

Thirty-nine officers and forty men of the 1st Battalion were Mentioned-in-Despatches.

Royal Sussex Officers and Men attached to other Units in Italy in 1943-45

Distinguished Service Order:

Lieutenant Colonel R.O.V. Thompson	1/6th East Surreys
Lieutenant Colonel J.B. Ashworth	1/5th Queens

Military Cross:

Major J.N. Crawford	1/5th Mahratta LI
Major T. Dixon	5th Buffs
Major F.W. Firminger	2/5th Queens
Captain P.M. Mourdant	5th Hampshires
Major A.G. Ryshworth-Hill	Yorks & Lancs
Major W.T. Woodruffe	5th East Yorks
Lieutenant G.B. Burnett	9th Royal Fusiliers
Lieutenant R.A Daniels	7th Hampshires

Military Medal:

Sergeant L.S.D. Morley	Long Range Desert Group
Lance-Sergeant E.E.W. Goldsmith	Special Raiding Squadron
Corporal C. Buss	Long Range Desert Group

Mentioned-in-Despatches:

One officer and two men were Mentioned-in-Despatches.

Escapee

Private J.N. Mack of the 1st Royal Sussex was captured after his sub-unit had been surrounded at Benghazi on 2nd February 1942 and was imprisoned at Monturano in Italy. After the Italian Armistice, the prisoners were being transferred to Germany, but Mack hid in a tree and left the camp the same night. After an unsuccessful attempt to penetrate the lines, he worked for the Italians for three months. Apprehended by the Fascists and handed over to the Germans, he bluffed his German guards into thinking he was an Italian workman. He then returned to the Teramo area to form a guerrilla group, which did useful work harassing the Germans and Fascists until Polish troops arrived on 23 June 1944. He was subsequently awarded a Military Medal for his zeal, ability and powers of leadership.

A GRECIAN ODYSSEY

Situation in Greece in 1944

During their occupation of Greece, the Germans had been resisted by two principal Greek guerilla forces: the communist-controlled National Liberation Front with its military element, the National Population Liberation Army (EAM-ELAS)[58]; and the Greek Democratic National Army (EDES)[59], which occasionally co-operated in action with ELAS. After eliminating all of its political and guerilla rivals, except the EDES, in early-1944 EAM-ELAS set up a provisional government in the Greek mountains that by implication, disowned both the Greek king and his government-in-exile. This government-in-exile, led by George Papandreou, had moved to Caserta in Italy in preparation for its return to Greece. Under the Caserta Agreement of September 1944, all resistance forces in Greece were to be placed under command of a British officer, Lieutenant General Ronald Scobie. On the German withdrawal from Greece in October 1944, the communists and the royalist Greek guerillas were accordingly brought under British auspices in an uneasy coalition government in Athens.

On the 13th of October British troops entered Athens, the only area still occupied by the Germans, and Papandreou and his ministers followed them six days later. Some of those in ELAS, however, would not co-operate with the British-supported government and threatened to take control of Greece; at this point there was little to prevent ELAS from taking full control of the country as, on the German withdrawal, ELAS units had taken control not only of the countryside but of most cities as well. At the beginning, the government had only a few policemen and gendarmes, some militia units, and the 3rd Greek Mountain Brigade; a formation which had distinguished itself at the Gothic Line offensive it Italy, although it now lacked any heavy weapons. The British, being outnumbered, brought in the 4th Indian Division from Italy as emergency reinforcements.

1st Royal Sussex had left the Po Valley on 20th October 1944 having been reduced to about half strength through enemy attrition, with rifle platoons only about 12-strong. The Battalion was given little information about the future, and while most naturally hoped for some rest and reinforcements, they received neither. Having spent a couple of days at a staging point near Rome, the Battalion was moved to the Taranto area where they arrived at the end of October. There they were briefed that they were going to Greece, where British troops had landed earlier in the Athens area and had found evidence that the Germans were withdrawing fast to the north. Colonel Buckeridge recalls the background briefings:

> *"Everyone was given a small blue book written in English and entitled 'Greece'. It contained everything a good soldier ought to know*

---

[58] Ethnikón Apeleftherotikón Métopon-Ethnikós Laïkós Apeleftherotikós Strátos.
[59] Ellinikos Dimokratikos Ethnikós Strátos.

about the history, habits and customs of the Greeks, malaria, fleas, women, good behaviour and cruelty to animals. But we should have been on our guard when the first sentence read 'You are lucky to be going to Greece'."

There was quite an array of shipping in Taranto harbour and the Battalion embarked in one of several LSTs, which was manned by a Greek crew. The ship sailed out to join a convoy, including a Hospital Ship, with the size of the convoy increasing the further they went out to sea. The convoy stopped at Piraeus on 3rd November and the Commanding Officer went ashore to receive orders. The 1st Battalion's objective was to be Salonika but no one seemed to know at that time if the Germans had evacuated northern Greece. However, it was understood that the Communists were waiting in the wings to fill the vacuum if they could overcome the Nationalist supporters; the Battalion's rôle once it got to Salonika was to quell any riots between the two factions and to help establish a Nationalist (Royalist) Government.

Operations in Greece

On 7th November 1944, the 1st Royal Sussex, although prepared for an opposed landing, went ashore at Salonika *(Thessaloniki)* and were greeted by a cheering throng of the locals who, at the time, appeared genuine in their welcome, but that was a snare and a delusion as the welcoming party had apparently been organised by the Communists (ELAS), as the Nationalist support was very patchy in this part of northern Greece. Furthermore, the Germans had destroyed as much of the infrastructure and as many of the public utilities as they could, and the Battalion's principal purpose was to put the country back on its feet as quickly as possible. Unfortunately, the Communists did not see it that way and constantly tried to obstruct the Battalion in its efforts, and thus the patience and good humour of the soldiers was to be tested frequently in the coming months. The activities of these various left-wing groups (notably ELAS) laid a heavy burden on those troops who had fought for years over deserts and mountains, and who now found that they were standing between the bitter fires of civil discord. Major H.G. Castle, previously the 1st Battalion's Intelligence Officer and now commanding C Company, gives a clear indication in his article[60] of how most of the Battalion regarded the situation:

"From the time of Wavell's first desert campaign we have always shared a country with the Germans or Italians, always disputing their right to be there, and always – in the end – doing our part to break their hold.

This had become such a habit, such a familiar existence that we had never imagined ourselves going to Greece – or anywhere else – as the conquering heroes – the Battalion had seen too much of the fortunes

---
[60] *Greece-Austria 1944-45*. Captain H. Castle, RHQ The Royal Sussex Regiment.

and misfortunes of war for that – but there were so many rumours of Grecian receptions, of flower-strewn processions, of garlands and wreaths and kisses, that even the oldest campaigners thought there must be something in this hero business.

But if we did not regard ourselves as conquering heroes we were soon to find others with ambitions to be conquerors – if not heroes.

Salonika, shabby and weary after three years of German occupation, if not another Cairo or Alexandria, was at least a welcome change from the hills and valleys, and the mud and flooded rivers of the Gothic Line.

The Greeks were friendly enough, even if the stories of flower-strewn processions, wreaths, garlands and kisses were below expectations. Nevertheless, we were given a great welcome before we settled down to numerous guards on docks, and ration and ammunition dumps. But if they were friendly to us, the Greeks were not at all friendly to each other. The political quarrels in Athens had their counterpart in Salonika, where Royalists, Communists, Republicans, Right-Wing and Left-Wing made demonstrations and came to blows. It was soon apparent that Greece's united front against the Axis had collapsed and that the country was quickly reverting to the ancient custom of having trouble at home."

By the end of November there were sufficient troops in the Salonika area for the 1st Battalion's Companies to be sent out into the Communist controlled areas to try and disarm and convert the locals. It was also clear that the neighbouring country of Bulgaria was firmly in Communist control and any spread of their influence into Western Thrace and Eastern Macedonia would be fatal. Although the Battalion was ordered in late-November to move east through Western Thrace towards Turkey, there was some doubt that the hierarchy in Athens had really appreciated how totally in control of the area the Communists were, or how much damage had been done by the Germans and Bulgarians in destroying road and rail bridges, and so many of the buildings.

During this time, the 1st Battalion was reinforced and on 17th December, it left Salonika for Drama *(Δραμα)*, a town in the centre of the Eastern Macedonian tobacco trade, and some twenty miles from the Bulgarian frontier, and lying at the foot of Mount Phalakra. It took several days to get to Drama, often across flooded rivers and along rugged mountain tracks and when the Battalion arrived at the appropriately named town, it found a minor riot in progress. The situation in Drama, as in the rest of Greece, was confused and complex. As Major Freer-Smith observed in his account at the time:

> *"In Drama, the history of the Drabescus[61] slaughter BC could easily have been repeated."*

The great, almost epic days when Greeks had formed a more or less solid wall

of resistance against German and Bulgar were gone; the wall had cracked wide open to reveal the old, ugly political quarrels. Greek was now going to kill Greek more bitterly, and more savagely than he had killed Germans. The left-wing partisans and their royalist enemies equally demanded the liquidation of one another, and when the Battalion arrived at Drama:

> *"A series of incidents followed which greatly angered the fair-minded men of The Royal Sussex. Ration-cards were only issued to ELAS supporters. Shopkeepers who refused to pay ELAS levies had their goods confiscated, and they were thrown into jail. Parents were ordered to assemble their children for a procession in which each child was given a stone to throw at the Royal Sussex Headquarters."*

The Battalion could only record what it saw and heard, it had neither the time nor inclination to judge who was right and who was wrong; they were not there to take sides but to see fair play done to both parties. Nevertheless, they found the Greek idea of fair play was not, precisely, the same as their own. It also took some time to identify who was who, because all the locals carried weapons, some wore uniform; all were unshaven and dirty, and looked like the less picturesque version of the traditional bandit in a Ruritanian musical comedy.

---

[61] The ancient city of Drabescus, where the Athenian colonisers around 400 BC, venturing too far from their base, had been cut off and slaughtered by Thracian tribesmen.

Eventually the position became untenable; the Battalion was isolated in Drama, out of range of any assistance that might be required, and surrounded by anything up to two divisions of the hostile ELAS. It was, therefore, decided to move the 1st Battalion to Kavála. Among those compelled to leave Drama was a Colonel Procos, the Nationalist Military Governor of Thrace and Eastern Macedonia. He was most reluctant to quit the local bank buildings, in which he had been guarded by a platoon of C Company, commanded by Lieutenant Buckeridge, and he had to be virtually 'shanghaied' into a waiting armoured car in the middle of the night. At the same time, before withdrawing, the Platoon Commander, acting under orders, emptied the vaults into sandbags, which were then placed with the rations in a three-ton lorry and driven at high speed to Kavála. Only his batman knew of the ruse, and the escort had no idea what they were sitting on. When eventually they found out, they vowed they would never forgive their Platoon Commander!

Arriving in Kavála was akin to jumping out of the frying pan and in to the fire - the town being under a complete ELAS dictatorship, which controlled both the only newspaper and the police force. It also dictated which shops could be opened while it closed those that looked as though they might be wavering from the ELAS doctrine. Similarly, most of the processions and demonstrations were engineered by ELAS, rather than developing spontaneously.

As at Drama, so at Kavála, ELAS controlled the dominating and demanding positions. The Battalion seized what vantage points it could, but ELAS were always one tier above in any house or building. It was an annoying and irritating situation, which required tact and patience. Although they controlled the dominating positions, and while they outnumbered the Kavála garrison and were theoretically more strongly armed, ELAS were badly disciplined and badly led. With all their fine array of troops patrolling the town armed with rifles, grenades, Tommy-guns, light machine-guns and revolvers, with bandoliers full of ammunition, there were good reasons to suppose that part of this strength was more apparent than real. Keen eyes had already discovered that some of the bullets in those magnificent bandoliers did not fit the rifles. And others wondered when they looked at the captured German and Italian guns away up in the hills, whether they were as dangerous as they appeared. In the meantime, A and C Companies were despatched to the airfield to the north of the town, where they watched the ELAS troops on the other side of the airfield, and waited for the next move.

A constant twenty-four hour watch had to be maintained as there were numerous reports of impending ELAS attacks. Then one morning when the sun rose and the mist lifted off the seas, the Battalion found that it had been reinforced. Standing out in the bay was *HMS Caledon*, a heavily armed cruiser. If ELAS had been under any misapprehension about British motives, if they had mistaken tolerance for appeasement, the presence of the *Caledon* changed that; ELAS were now under no delusions.

Despite the fire plan arranged with *HMS Cale*don, with all ELAS strong points, gun positions and barracks becoming potential target areas, the Battalion's principal task continued to be no more than that of a 'watching brief'.

On 16th December the 1st Battalion evacuated the airfield at Kavála and moved into Kavála port, where it embarked in the *Caledon* and sailed to reinforce the garrison at Salonika, arriving on 20th December. The situation in Salonika, the second largest city in Greece, was as tense as that at Kavála. However, after numerous alarms and excursions, with constant patrols and guards through a bitter winter, ELAS decided to withdraw. When the Battalion arrived back in Salonika, they found more troops there than when they had left a month earlier, and very soon they were looking across the River Axios at ELAS troops, commanded by General Begajis, who held the Distinguished Service Order. There followed a period of road block duties, bridge guards and arms searches until the end of February, when British forces moved into the interior to become policemen – to hold the fort while the newly-formed National Guard settled-in.

The Battalion's sphere in this new rôle was at Kilkis – to keep the peace – to act as the representatives of the new Greek Government, struggling to produce order out of chaos – and to 'father' the National Guard. The Government, although only a provisional one, had published a series of decrees – or laws – and the British Army was there to uphold the Government's authority. Whatever the faults of the administration, the Government did at least provide an opportunity for Greece to recover from past disasters and a long tragic era of dictatorship.

On 1st March 1945, B and C Companies were to move to Kilkis, the Macedonian Communist stronghold, in an initial attempt to open up the country. Hearing of this impending move to Kilkis, His Beatitude the Archbishop Damaskinos, Regent of Greece, expressed a desire to bless the troops who were to start pacifying this wild region. The parade accordingly formed up in a hollow square, and the unorthodox Major Dalton improved the occasion by giving His Beatitude a Royal Salute from the stand-at-ease, which quite surprised his critical audience. The Companies, however, were infinitely more surprised at being blessed by an Archbishop.

After the massive Regimental Sergeant-Major Phillips MBE, had been presented to him, the equally impressive Archbishop and Regent, himself a former Olympian athlete, was heard to remark in an aside:

"I could have made a wrestler of that man."

A few words about the Battalion's Regimental Sergeant-Major are considerably overdue. Phillips was as remarkable for his service as for his physical proportions. He had been Regimental Sergeant-Major of the 2nd Battalion, from its reconstitution after Dunkirk to the end of the battle of El Alamein. He then became Regimental Sergeant-Major of the 1st Battalion. When one remembers all the events covered by this period of service, the facts speak for themselves.

Kilkis, like the rest of Greece, or the rest of Europe, was a symptom of one of the fatal maladies of modern times; the tragedy of extremes. The days of compromise and liberation were gone. Now there was a clearly marked fence - if you were a Greek you had to be on one side of that fence or the other - you had to be either Left or Right. The truth, of course, lay halfway between. Many people hated ELAS and all it stood for but equally, had no sympathy for the Nationalists; most people were sickened by the brutality and intolerance in which they found themselves.

This was the situation faced by 1st Royal Sussex at Kilkis, as it faced all other regiments in Greece – like a piece of solid, unresisting metal, which had to be hammered into some form of reasonable shape. The Battalion needed to convince everyone that they were not only impartial but that they were determined to remain so. This meant undertaking patrols, often supported by Sherman tanks, working by day and by night to settle every complaint, every report of persecution and ill-treatment, whether it came from an ELAS village or a Nationalist one. The Battalion dispensed justice impartially; if a man broke the law he was suitably dealt with, irrespective of what his political views were. Constant vigilance, patience and fair handedness gradually persuaded the locals that the Battalion meant business and, despite much provocation and obstruction, the good humour and common sense shown by the soldiers had won the day, and by the time the Battalion left in early-April 1945, they had been accepted. It had been a hard and dangerous struggle with frequent visits to remote mountain villages close to the Yugoslav Border, where they did their best to help restore the lives of villagers who were hungry, poorly clothed and often ill from malnutrition.

On Easter Sunday, 1st of April 1945, the 1st Battalion handed over Kilkis to the 2nd/7th Gurkha Rifles and moved back to Drama. However, it was now operating in the Bulgarian border area, rebuilding lives and villages. All this part of Greece, the Eastern Macedonian area, had been occupied by the Bulgarians since 1941, and was part of their reward for having been so helpful to the Germans. The Bulgarian dictatorship had been harsher and crueller than in the German-occupied area, and the conditions in the villages were the worst that the Battalion had seen in Greece, and with the lowest standard of living in Europe. Here there were also many cases of malnutrition - illness and disease flourished - and every village was as damaged as if it had been a battlefield, while many of them were deserted.

Strong Royal Sussex detachments composed of one rifle company, with carriers and armoured cars, lived under canvas near the Bulgarian frontier and undertook day and night patrols in jeeps, armoured cars and on foot. The effect was immediate – villages which had been abandoned since 1941 were reoccupied, while many arrests were made as wide areas were cleared of terrorism, allowing a more normal pattern of life to be introduced, including the delivery of badly needed clothing for both children and adults.

In these circumstances, the British soldier's most valuable weapon is his sense of humour. That this did not fail the Regiment on the present occasion may be inferred from the following report:

> *"The QM and B Echelon found themselves where, in a more tactical layout, a forward rifle company would have been.*
>
> *The QM, assuring us (as usual) of his best attention at all times, promised that B Echelon would provide another Verdun.*
>
> *It would be easier, he said, for anyone to get something from him without a signature than for ELAS to pass through his lines."*

It was this spirit that the difficulties and dangers of a tense situation were faced and overcome.

The War Diary tells alternatively of patrols, strife among civilians, and football matches, but, reading between the lines, we are able to appreciate that those long-suffering soldiers were doubly blessed. Major Freer-Smith would later summarise the situation in Greece very clearly:

> *"Official histories have been written by several participants in the liberation of Greece and in the prevention of that country from being taken over by the Communists, but there has been constant criticism on both sides of the Atlantic, as to the British handling of the situation there in 1944 and 1945."*

Referring to a Channel 4 Television series in the late-1980s called *Greece, The Hidden War*, Freer-Smith considered that it was completely biased in favour of the Communists. He also went on to say:

> *"Only the British servicemen who were there at the time and saw with their own eyes the Communist atrocities against innocent men, women and children, appear to want the truth to be known and the record set straight.*

> *The troops did so despite a campaign of vilification against them by politicians of the Left and the British and American press. The resentment of the British troops and the accusations levelled against them still burn within them."*

In his book, *Scobie, the Hero of Greece,* Henry Maule provides a very pertinent conclusion about the British contribution to the deliverance of Greece:

> *"Had this little British Force been overwhelmed, as indeed it almost was, the whole of post-war history would have been different. If this Communist coup to take over Greece had succeeded, the Iron Curtain would have stretched from the Baltic to the Mediterranean, and Turkey and all the oil-rich Middle East would have been in Russian clutches. The resolution of General Scobie and his men should be remembered with pride."*

Later would come the news of victory in Europe, and on 9th May there was a march-past at Drama before Lieutenant Colonel Phelps, with the Bishop of Drama and other civilian notables also being present on the saluting dais. The Mayor gave a dance the following month, on King George VI's birthday, in honour of The Royal Sussex Regiment.

Gallantry Awards for 1945

Although no British Gallantry Awards were made for the 1st Battalion's service in Greece, Major H.G. Castle and Major P.H. Jones both received the Distinguished Service Medal (Greek) in August 1946.

FAREWELL TO THE 4ᵀᴴ INDIAN DIVISION

In July 1945, the 1ˢᵗ Battalion left the 4ᵗʰ Indian Division in Greece and flew to Austria. It was a very sad farewell, for they had been with the Division longer than any other battalion. Major-General C.H. Boucher CBE DSO, commanding the Division, issued a special Order of the Day, in which he recognised the fact:

> *"After nearly five years of unbroken service in the 4ᵗʰ Indian Division, the 1ˢᵗ Battalion, The Royal Sussex Regiment, is now about to leave us for another part of Europe. This battalion has served with the Division for a longer period than any other battalion, past or present. The 1ˢᵗ Royal Sussex joined the 7ᵗʰ Indian Infantry Brigade in October 1940. From then until now it has taken part in every campaign in which the Division has fought. This alone must constitute a record achieved by few battalions of the British Army in the present war. The battalion was prominent in all the heaviest fighting in North Africa, at Cub-Cub, Keren, Massawa, Sidi Omar, Derna, Benghazi, El Alamein, Mareth Line, Wadi Akarit and Mejerda Valley. The culminating triumph of the Tunisian campaign was the capture by the 1ˢᵗ Royal Sussex of the Headquarters of the German Commander-in-Chief, von Arnim. It was a fitting end to three years of ceaseless battles up and down the Western Desert, in which the battalion had never failed to carry out its appointed task, and had invariably displayed outstanding gallantry and determination. The victory in North Africa, after a short pause, was followed by a year of violent fighting in Italy, far exceeding in intensity all that had been gone before, as the Germans knew that they were now defending Germany itself. Orsogna, Cassino, Mont St. Maria, Arezzo, and the Gothic Line battles followed one another in rapid succession. They are battle honours, which will always live in the history of the Division. They are battle honours with which the name of the 1ˢᵗ Royal Sussex will forever be associated. As in Africa, so in Italy, the steadiness, courage, morale, and discipline of the battalion remained unsurpassed.*
>
> *Recently, in Greece, the battalion has added to its already great reputation by exemplary conduct and bearing during the civil war and the subsequent reoccupation of the country.*
>
> *The departure of the 1ˢᵗ Royal Sussex will be most deeply regretted by all ranks of the Division, both British and Indian. The quiet, unassuming way, in which the officers and men have always borne themselves, and their unfailing bravery and cheerfulness in the face of danger, have won the highest admiration of all ranks of the Division. Their discipline and esprit de corps, as well as their fighting qualities, have been in keeping with the finest traditions of the British Infantry of the line.*

> *So much have we come to depend on them that it will be difficult to imagine the 4th Indian Division without the 1st Royal Sussex? We wish them the best of luck wherever they may go. All of us who have served in this Division will long remember with pride and gratitude the achievements of this most gallant battalion."*

With these stirring words the Division and the 1st Royal Sussex took leave of each other. During the 1st Battalion's service with the 4th Indian Division, 35 officers and 276 men were killed or died of wounds, and 62 officers and 590 men were wounded. A further 12 men were recorded as missing.

THE FAR EAST

The 9th Battalion is Reformed

While the 1st Battalion was fighting its way through Italy in 1944, we should not forget that the 9th Battalion was equally committed to a series of gallant and exhausting trials and tribulations in the Far East.

Following the withdrawal from Dunkirk in 1940, men and equipment were needed with desperate urgency and a total of sixty new infantry battalions were ordered to be raised immediately; one of these was the Regiment's 9th Battalion, which had originally seen service in the Great War. The Battalion was reformed in the breathless days of June 1940 under command of an able and experienced staff officer with fighting experience in the Great War – an officer who was to gain a considerable reputation in the Second World War and after it – Sir Gerald Templer.

Lieutenant Colonel Templer of The Royal Irish Fusiliers was ordered to proceed to Chichester and reform the 9th Battalion of The Royal Sussex Regiment. To quote Templar's own words:

> *"I have not the slightest idea how it happened but I was given a very large field on the outskirts of Ross, with the promise of a few marquees and sufficient bell tents for a thousand men at eight to a tent. That was all. I then went by train to Chichester, the Depot of the Royal Sussex Regt., dressed as a Royal Irish Fusilier, and reported to the Depot Commander ....*
>
> *Someone told me that the gymnasium was full of regular soldiers of the battalion back from Dunkirk[62] and nobody was doing anything about them. Somewhere I picked up a Sergeant Major by the name of Pack and we went to the gymnasium and saw them all – I suppose about a hundred – filthy, tired, covered in oil and lying on the floor. I told Pack to fall them in, which he did with a voice like the Bull of Bashan, and I told them who I was and that I was raising the new 9th Bn. of their Regiment. I wanted non-commissioned officers and if they came to me I would nearly kill them with overwork, but as from that moment I would give each N.C.O. one more stripe than he had already got. I also wanted some good private soldiers to fill the rank of Lance Corporal. I then said, 'Now anybody who is prepared to take this on, and it is going to be a pretty hard stint, take one pace forward'. Every man did so, which posed a bit of a problem. Pack and I then worked out a rough estimate of the number of Warrant Officers and N.C.O.'s required for a battalion*

---

[62] The only regular Royal Sussex soldiers would have been from the 2nd Battalion but the 3 officers and 225 men who had been recovered from Dunkirk had all been formed up at Tidworth by 1st June?

of a thousand strong and being raised under these extraordinary conditions. He, and two or three senior N.C.O.'s whom he knew, picked out those he wanted. We got them cleaned up and properly fed. Arrangements were made for the tentage and for as large a supply of tin plates and buckets (both latrine and food) as possible to be sent to Ross-on-Wye Station with a couple of selected N.C.O.'s in charge. I stole two subaltern officers out of the Officer's Mess and told them to pack their valises, to go to Ross-on-Wye, and get things organised. They asked how and I said, 'God knows, but do it or you are fired'."

A Cadre for the 9th Battalion was formed at Chichester on 28th June 1940 with Major R.E.C. Luxmore-Ball DSO DCM as Second-in-Command, together with 2nd/Lieutenant N.A. Selkirk as Adjutant and Captain C.J. Lewis as Quartermaster. Another seventeen officers also joined during the next few days. The official date for the formation of the new Battalion was 4th July and it was commemorated with a Service in St George's Chapel. On the 5th of July, the 9th Battalion paraded and marched to the Cathedral to receive from the Dean and Chapter the King's Colour[63] of the late 9th Battalion. The Colour was handed back to the Dean and Chapter for safekeeping after the Service. The Battalion left for Ross-on-Wye on 8th July, where it was joined the following day by the inveterate Lieutenant A.M.T. Trubshaw, the well-known military compatriot of the actor David Niven, who had himself recently rejoined the Colours from his eyrie in Hollywood!

Drafts of more officers and some 800 men soon arrived at Ross-on-Wye and somehow, with the limited weaponry and facilities available, Lieutenant Colonel Templar brought the Battalion into shape. However, he was not allowed to stay very long and by November he had gone, promoted to Brigadier, another step in the distinguished career, which would take him to the very top as Field Marshall and Chief of the Imperial General Staff (CIGS)[64].

Lieutenant Colonel H.A. Davis MBE MC, also of The Royal Irish Fusiliers, took over command of the 9th Battalion on 14th November on Brigadier Templar's departure. The Battalion then moved to Mumbles, where its official rôle was that of a so-called Beach Battalion, and it joined the 212th Independent Infantry Brigade, along with the 10th Battalion The Gloucestershire Regiment and the 6th Battalion The South Wales Borderers. The Battalion spent five months at Mumbles on coastal defence and in further training before moving with the Brigade to South Lincolnshire to become part of a Beach Division. Coastal defence meant being in a constant state of readiness, measured in hours or minutes, frequently 'stood-to', and permanently manning observation posts.

---

[63] After the Great War, His Majesty King George V had instigated the award of a King's Colour to every Territorial and Service Battalion, although they were not to be consecrated.

[64] Templar was broken hearted at having to leave but never lost touch with the battalion he had created and, even as a Field Marshall, he often attended the Royal Sussex reunions.

Conversion and Re-conversion

In early-1942, the Battalion received the news that it was to be converted to tanks – the real thing, black berets and all! In three short months, everyone had to become a gunner, a driver, or a wireless operator in what was now called the 160th Regiment (Royal Sussex), and part of the Royal Armoured Corps. Activity was so frenzied and the 'regiment' so scattered on various courses that the Battalion Diary was abandoned. Nevertheless, by August, they were all together again at Southend-on-Sea where the first tanks (Grants) were issued, and orders were then received for them to proceed to India.

Stress was being laid at that time on the overriding importance of armour in modern warfare, and, with this theory carefully impressed on all ranks, the 'regiment' left for India on the *SS Athlone Castle* on 29th October. Because of the U-Boat threat, the convoy was diverted far to the west of the Southern Atlantic and the troops woke up to the sickly smell of the Brazilian coast and soon, the *Athlone Castle* was alongside in the port of Bahia. Although shore leave was not allowed; under International Law all belligerent troops in uniform were liable to internment and thus could not disembark at a neutral port. Sergeant Tom Webber[65], the Battalion's Medical Sergeant, gave some highly coloured impressions of the situation alongside on 15th November 1942:

> *"Rails and lifeboats crammed with troops*
> *Stared at the natives (sic) standing in groups*
> *Yelling, shouting, going mad,*
> *Throwing down the coins they had*
> *Police and firemen down below*
> *started dashing to and fro*
> *Then someone in a khaki suit*
> *Yelled to a native for some fruit.*
>
> *Pineapples were the boys' delight*
> *And eyes aglow at such a sight*
> *To see them in their birthday skin*
> *Not just chopped up in a tin.*
> *Then looking some way from the rail*
> *They found a great big dirty pail*
> *A bob a tome, the price agreed*
> *They lowered the bucket for their need."*

These were the impressions made before the Battalion knew they were going to go ashore. The poem, which is a long one, goes on to describe the excitement of cleaning equipment and dress, the heady march through the streets, and the people thronging to watch the parade. Then, as the sun went down and the lights of Bahia came on, the bugle sounded the 'Fall In' and they marched back

---

[65] Tom Webber would later become the first President of the Pinwe Club.

to the ship. This was an historically unique experience as the 9th Battalion was the only British regiment ever to be accorded such an honour in Brazil. They left Bahia on the 19th, bound for Durban and this time all troops were granted shore leave. From there, the 9th Battalion set forth for India and on arrival in Bombay, they were entrained for Bolarum.

Having reached Bolarum, near Secunderabad, the Battalion was incorporated into the 26th Armoured Brigade of the 43rd Armoured Division. In February 1943, it received fresh instructions, reversing the doctrine of the past few months! The practicalities of life were such that there was a lack of sufficient trained personnel in the recently established REME[66] to maintain the number of Armoured Divisions then formed, or in the process of forming. Consequently, the 9th Royal Sussex, once more became an infantry battalion, and underwent training in combined operations in the salutary and corrective atmosphere of Poona and Bombay, particularly the latter.

At roughly the same time, the 29th Brigade, after conducting a painful but necessary campaign in Madagascar, had arrived in Bombay, and there proceeded to expand itself into a Division – the famous 36th Division – commanded by Major General F.W. Festing.

In March 1943, the 9th Battalion moved to Kharakvasla and was accommodated in a tented camp. The Battalion was now part of the 72nd Brigade, commanded by Brigadier Aslett, who had captained England's rugby side in earlier days, and was reunited with The Gloucestershire Regiment and The South Wales Borderers whom they had last seen in England. The 72nd Brigade now formed part of the 36th Division, and its Commander was quickly on the scene to welcome the Brigade to Combined Operations.

Kharakvasla was not a bad place, with low sandy hills, a large lake and a reasonable climate, except in the immediate pre-monsoon months. It was also reasonably close to Poona where recreational transport was available, thus giving everyone an opportunity after the war to bore listeners with the well-worn cliché, *"When I was in Poona ..."*! The Battalion was still under establishment in officers because there had been a lot of outgoing postings, and officer reinforcements went on arriving in twos and threes for the remaining duration of the war. Other ranks tended to arrive in bigger batches but less frequently.

In September 1943, Lieutenant Colonel D.H. Oliver took over command of the Battalion from Lieutenant Colonel Davis, and under his command, it marched and fought its way to victory, winning new renown for the Regiment in battles that broke the Japanese power.

---

[66] Royal Electrical and Mechanical Engineers.

Training went on unabated, with an endless sequence of courses and exercises right into the New Year. All of them were extremely exhausting and the troops began to wonder whether Combined Operations was such a good thing after all. The 9th Battalion's first casualties were sustained when a shell fell short on a battle training exercise killing a Sergeant and injuring six more men. The last exercise, of which the Brigade received advance notice on 10th January 1944, was to be somewhat different and would take them to Burma.

General Situation In Burma

The situation and conditions that the 9th Battalion would face in Burma were complex and more than difficult - the previous military achievements had not been successful - in early-1942 the Burma Corps had been forced to retreat all the way back to India. The ill-fated first Arakan campaign of 1942-43, designed to clear the Japanese out of the Mayu Peninsular, had been a failure and by the middle of May, the British and Indian forces were back where they had started, with the 15th Corps sustaining 2,500 casualties. By that time, the army was beginning to accept the unpalatable idea that they were inferior to the Japanese. But General Slim, the newly appointed Commander of the 14th Army, had no such feelings. From June to October 1943 he set about the multiple tasks of re-invigorating his fighting forces and injecting some life into the largely moribund supply and back-up organisation – and little needs to be said about Slim's effect on morale. Few generals in the Second World War were as universally liked as Bill Slim – affectionately dubbed "*Uncle Bill*" by all ranks – he told them that they were going to win battles and they believed him. The other tasks he faced were not so straightforward.

Supplying the 14th Army was a colossal undertaking; supplies had to brought in from India by rail, water or air, but even with an effective supply system, there were not always sufficient supplies available to be brought forward. Both British and Indian rations were in short supply, especially meat, except for sweaty bully beef - but neither Hindu nor Moslem would eat tinned meat so the Indians got none in forward areas. Fresh vegetables and milk products were almost non-existent, and even stocks of rice gave cause for concern. Similarly, there was a dearth of arms and ammunition, of all types and calibre.

Health was the other paramount problem. One hundred and twenty men sick were evacuated for every man wounded, and of the forward troops, 84% contracted malaria[67], and had to contend with dysentery, tick typhus, jungle sores, foot rot and dengue fever as well, plus other tropical infections, which were unknown to the medical staff. At the worst period, 12,000 men a day were being hospitalised, a rate at which the entire army would have melted away in weeks. For these 12,000 occupied beds, there were only 400 nurses to look after them. With no fresh nurses available, the decision was made to treat the

---

[67] Mepacrine, sulphur drugs and DDT were only then beginning to reach Southeast Asia Command. Mountbatten brought with him specialised medical officers and research workers to introduce new drugs, treatments and techniques. From early-1944 health steadily improved.

sick in forward areas instead of evacuating them to India, while only serious casualties would be evacuated by air.

The other major setback was that the state of some of the reinforcement and transit camps in the rear areas was a disgrace. Normal accommodation was in decaying tents or fly-infested *bashas*[68] in remote and depressing areas with no amenities. Many of these were run by idle commandants and NCOs, all determined to remain where they were for the duration. This resulted in a big shake-up and in the course of time, all forward divisions were allotted their own camps in India, with their own officers to run them, and displaying their own Divisional signs. It was a hard time for the 'professional' *base-wallahs*!

With the Supreme Commander, Mountbatten, based in New Delhi, General Slim had moved his Headquarters to Comilla, and the 14th Army was in as good a state of readiness as could be expected. A major effort to drive the Japanese out of Burma was obviously called for and plans had already been drawn up in Delhi. The optimism engendered by Mountbatten, combined with the expectation of the limitless amphibious craft he had been promised, led to an ambitious programme being put forward, comprising seaborne invasions, advances from China and elsewhere and airborne operations, including the air-landing of three of Wingate's *Chindit* Brigades. In the event, all amphibious craft were required in Europe for the D-Day landings, and Southeast Asia Command (SEAC) was forced to return much of the assorted fleet it had assembled for its own operations. The resultant consequences of this meant that the overall programme was postponed, although the occupation of the Mayu Peninsula by 15 Corps, under Lieutenant General Christison, would go ahead with the objective of capturing Akyab. The 36th Division would be attached to 15 Corps for the Arakan campaign, with the 72nd Brigade being held in reserve for the landing at Akyab.

Meanwhile, in the latter half of 1943, the 9th Battalion had been undergoing intensive training at Bhiwandi, Juhu and Kharakvasla. This training had been extremely tough, taking in not only seaborne exercises with landing craft, DUKWs[69] and Alligators[70], but cliff climbing, assault courses, field firing with live ammunition and general toughening up. At Bhiwandi an attempt was made to prove that men could live under canvas throughout the monsoon – it proved

---

[68] An Urdu word denoting a building made of natural materials (*i.e.* bamboo, palm *etc*), and taken into general use in the British Army's vocabulary.

[69] The DUKW (colloquially known as a duck) is a six-wheel-drive amphibious truck that was designed by a partnership between Sparkman & Stephens and General Motors Corporation (GMC) and was used for transporting goods and troops over land and water, and for approaching and crossing beaches in amphibious attacks. The designation of DUKW is not a military acronym; the name comes from the model-naming terminology used by GMC: 'D' indicates a vehicle designed in 1942, 'U' means 'utility'; 'K' indicates front-wheel-drive; and 'W' indicates two powered rear-axles.

[70] The *Alligator* or Landing Vehicle Tracked (LVT) was a class of amphibious vehicles introduced by US Forces in the Second World War. Originally intended solely as cargo carriers for ship-to-shore operations, they rapidly evolved into assault troop and support vehicles. The LVT1 could carry 18 fully equipped men or 4,500 lbs (2,041kg) of cargo.

nothing of the sort – with A Company having an average daily sick parade of 50% of its strength. Nothing could be kept dry, equipment went mildewy, and ringworm and prickly heat were rife. At Juhu the heat was terrible and the vicious red ants found it preferable to live in tents rather than outside.

Nevertheless, it was becoming apparent that the 9th Royal Sussex was about to embark on something more serious than an ordinary exercise.

Battle of Arakan

The 9th Battalion journeyed by rail from Bombay to Calcutta, and then embarked on the *SS Medina* for the voyage to Chittagong in Burma, arriving on 25th January. By early March, the Battalion had advanced 50 miles to Teknaf, on the banks of the Naf River, and were patrolling nightly while continuing to move south towards Maungdaw, where, in the Commanding Officer's words:

"they sat about and held platoon positions in the hills."

Meanwhile, major operations were being conducted on the Mayu Mountain Range, and the assault on the Razabil fortress was successful, leading to the capture of Maungdaw. The 7th Division, prior to further advances, and to

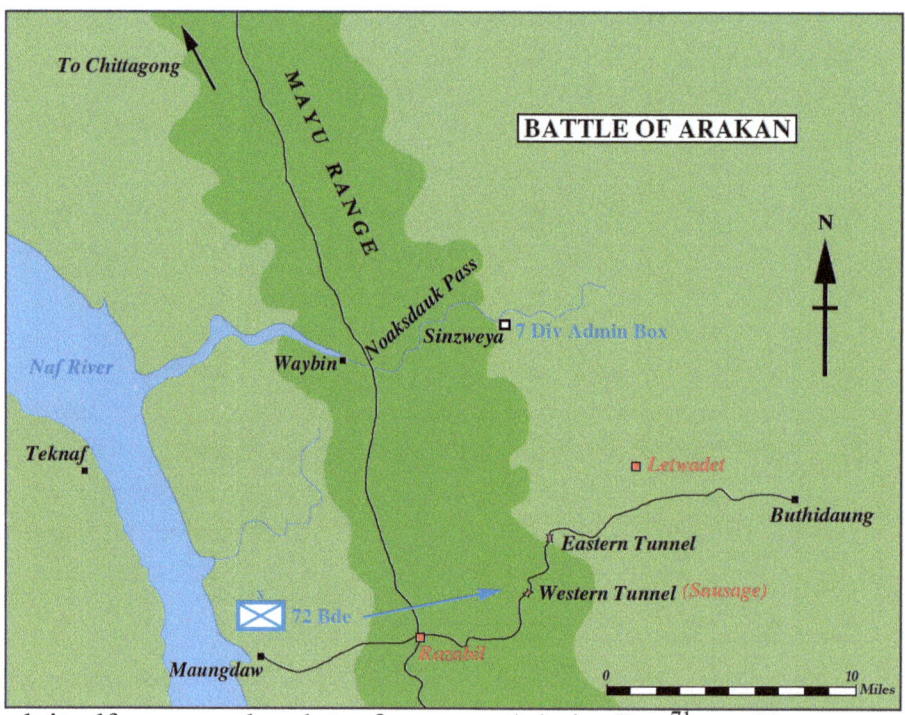

safeguard itself, was ordered to form an Admin Box[71] at Sinzweya. The Japanese offensive was fast and ferocious and while they were able to break in to the Box, very few got out again. Instead of the expected walkover, the

---

[71] The absence of roads, the hilly country and the dense jungle vegetation enabled the enemy to get behind forward positions on many occasions. The counter measures adopted by formations and units were all-round defence and supply by air. These defensive localities were known as 'boxes', and were designed to house a large number of men and equipment.

Japanese found an immovable block of resistance. Supplied by air, the Box held and 5,000 of the enemy's original force of 7,000 were killed. It was now time for the 36th Division to make its contribution to the Arakan campaign.

Two tunnels, halfway along the road from Maungdaw to Buthidaung in the Kalapanzin Valley, had originally been cut through the Mayu Mountains for a light railway but had been dismantled by the river navigation company who owned it, and a road laid over the track. The Mayu Range rises to over 1,000 feet at this point and the Japanese had built three formidable defences dominating the locality, strong enough to be called fortresses, which they were. The first, already mentioned, was Razabil and the second was Letwadet, seven miles to the northwest. The third one of these fortresses was the Twin Tunnels, one of which was to be the objective for the 72nd Brigade.

Before the battle had even begun, Major Neil Selkirk, commanding A Company, had been killed on a patrol. This was unfortunate as he had been one of the original members of the Battalion as well as a first rate company commander. The 72nd Brigade plan was to attack the west tunnel fortress with B Company 9th Royal Sussex, commanded by Major Cash, and B Company 6th South Wales Borderers. The aim of the leading Companies was to advance and capture the western tunnel and surrounding hill area, and then to dig in, appreciating that they would have to deal with the expected counter-attacks, which would inevitably follow a successful assault. The plan included not only the capture of the western tunnel itself, but to destroy the enemy positions that were well dug into the fortified areas to the north, east and south of the tunnel entrance; the immediate fortified area being code-named *'Sausage'*. The task of B Company 9th Royal Sussex was to carry out a two-pronged attack; a full frontal assault on the tunnel entrance itself, and an assault up either side of the entrance onto the heavily fortified high ground above it. An indication of the magnitude and extent of the objective can be seen from the sketch shown below and made by Major Cash[72].

On 26th March, supported by artillery, the 72nd Brigade launched its attack. The Royal Sussex Company moved slowly along the *chaung*[73] and then split into two groups for the main attack – one group from the right and one from the left. The re-entrant in which the *chaung* was situated was very steep at this point and B Company had the unenviable and hazardous task of clambering up hastily constructed scaling ladders to get to the tops of the steep banks, and then, with bayonets fixed, assault the enemy defences, which were camouflaged in thick bamboo in and around the approaches. Although the fortified area above the tunnel had been subjected to artillery bombardment and was now bare of trees and bamboo, the shelling had not broken the Japanese defences.

---

[72] *Green Shadows and Jungle Rain*. David Cash, 1st May 2003.
[73] River-bed.

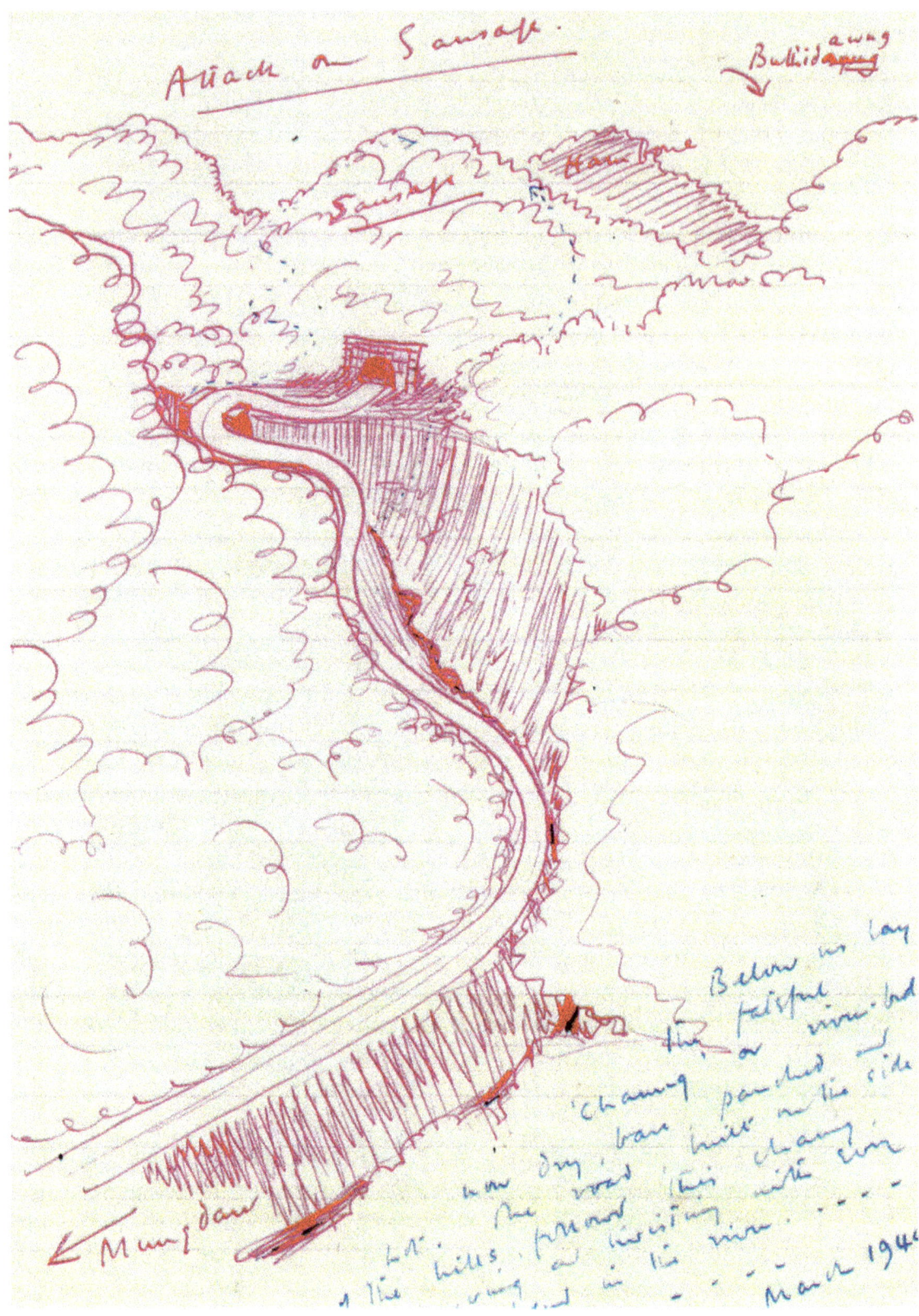

B Company reached its objective without much serious resistance, but having sent the success signal, it was then subjected to sustained mortar and grenade attack, incurring heavy casualties. Lieutenant D.G.F. Pierce had found that his platoon was unable to climb the steep escarpment in front of them and had to cross the tunnel mouth to continue the ascent. Private Simmonds, with tremendous courage and disregard for his own safety, ran across with a Bren-gun and extra magazines and poured rapid fire into the entrance, sacrificing his own life in enabling his platoon to get across. Lieutenant Pierce and seven men were also killed in this attack, an eighth one died of his wounds, while another seven men were wounded. Having taken this precipitous and strongly defended objective, B Company were again attacked in the night but the enemy were repulsed and withdrew in the face of grenades and Bren-gun fire. C Company then took over two features from the 10th Glosters and was shelled, sustaining two casualties.

For his gallant and determined leadership in the capture of this precipitous and strongly defended feature, and then beating off determined enemy counter-attacks, the Company Commander, Major J.M. Cash, was awarded the Military Cross. Corporal G.F. Taylor was awarded the Military Medal for leading his platoon on to the objective in the face of fierce enemy fire and then for personally directing mortar and light-machine-gun fire on to a bunker position that was enfilading his platoon position. Similarly, Lance-Corporal C.E. Davis was also awarded the Military Medal for his great bravery and leadership in the assault and consolidation of his objective in the face of heavy mortar and machine-gun fire, as well as carrying forward badly needed ammunition under continuous enemy fire, thus succeeding in maintaining his section position in very difficult circumstances.

The tunnel was finished off by the South Wales Borderers, supported by the tanks of the 25th Dragoons, one of which fired a round straight up the tunnel, blowing up the ammunition stored inside and causing a certain amount of havoc for the Japanese. On 1st April, the Glosters attacked the eastern tunnel and although they were beaten back, they had another go on the 4th and by the 6th, that too was captured, enabling the 26th Division to pass through and attack Point 551. During that period, the 9th Battalion had no further contact with the enemy and moved into the 1st/2nd Punjab's position guarding the east side of the Admin Box. It was not a pleasant place, with half-buried Japanese, Indians and British in various stages of decomposition, dead mules everywhere, and a shambles of wrecked equipment, medical supplies, parachutes and shattered trees.

Captured Entrance to 'Sausage' Tunnel

The march out of the Box over the Ngakyedauk Pass after a month of inactivity was not easy – the track was dusty, the heat intense and they had to climb up to 1,000 feet over the ridge, with many falling out – but they had undergone their first experience of battle and acquitted themselves well, as had the whole Division. If the 1944 Arakan campaign was not the turning point of the Burma war in a military sense, it certainly was for morale. All at once the dispirited underdog of 1943 realised that he was capable of knocking hell out of any Jap who got within shooting distance. A confident 9th Royal Sussex left for Assam and a rest among the cool pines of Shillong.

Although the Brigade was nominally in Shillong for a rest, it actually spent six weeks carrying out long marches and practice in air-loading. They had, so far, been involved in only one major engagement, while over at Imphal and Kohima on the central front, the 4th Corps was fighting the bloodiest and most decisive battle of the Burma campaign. By now though, the Japanese were on the retreat, which meant that pressure had to be kept up and the enemy denied time to reorganise or regroup. It was at Shillong that the Brigade learnt from General Slim that the 36th Division would shortly be leaving the 14th Army and coming under command of the celebrated American General Joe Stilwell – the one British Division fighting in what was called the Northern Combat Area, alongside the Americans and Chinese.

Northern Combat Area Command[74]

The 9th Battalion accordingly left Shillong for Ledo, and, on 10th July, were flown in from there to Myitkyina – pronounced *Mitchinar*! They arrived with the monsoon roaring down, every man carrying a pack, and 22lb of kit tied up in a ground-sheet. Having landed, they were directed to some scrubland off the strip and ordered to take cover, but from which direction it was never made clear. Suddenly, a leathery face popped up from the path and a voice asked, *"Say, is this the Sussex outfit?"* It was old 'Vinegar Joe' himself!

The Companies had to bivouac in the teeming rain, protected only by ground-sheets. One of the worst aspects of the campaign in the Hukawng Valley was that the troops did not have mosquito-nets, despite operating in one of the worst malarial areas in the world. Mosquito-nets were generally not carried at the height of the monsoon anyway, and nor could they be used in action as they took too long to get out from, especially during any confrontation at night. The only real protection the troops had against malaria was Mepacrine, although many men did acquire mosquito-nets, often making use of discarded jute parachutes as well.

---

[74] The Northern Combat Area Command (NCAC) was a mainly Sino-American formation that held the northern end of the Allied front in Burma. For much of its existence it was commanded by the acerbic General Joseph 'Vinegar Joe' Stilwell and controlled by his staff. The forces initially under the command of NCAC consisted of Chinese units that arrived in India after the long retreat out of Burma in 1942. As the 1944 monsoon ended, NCAC opened an offensive and had been reinforced with the British 36th Infantry Division. The NCAC's main role in the last few months of the war was to support the British main offensive further south.

The Battalion found that, in that region, the supporting arms, which generally characterise modern warfare, were lacking, and the Chinese artillery, though assisted by American liaison-officers, was not highly reliable. Experience of the first 'Air-Drop' is described as *"interesting and exciting,"* for until the pilots acquired accuracy, many packages threatened to land on their heads, and the troops took cover as the 'planes flew over, as though it were a hostile air-raid.

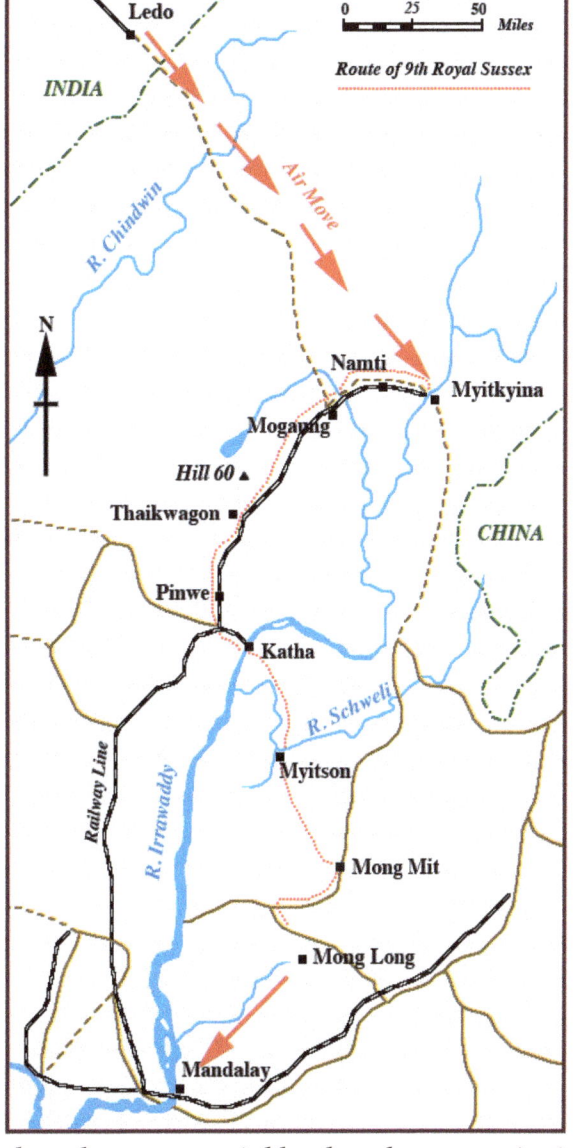

The monsoon rain, however, was in many ways the sorest trial to men unaccustomed to such a deluge. The chronicler in A Company wrote as follows:

> *"After four hours' marching in the drenching rain, breakfast eventually came up in a jeep train at 0900 hours. Breakfast consisted of porridge, bacon and beans, and a slice of bread. None of us will ever forget that breakfast – quite the end! The rain filled the mess-tins of porridge so fast that, however quickly the chaps ate it, it always remained filled, and, by the time one was ready to eat the bacon and beans, one found the former sunk at the bottom and the latter floating on top. A variety of novel expressions were heard as the Coy stabbed at the elusive beans and dredged for the bacon and the bread! We shall leave that, as did most of the Company.*
>
> *This station (Namti) is horrible. Lots of mud and wrecked bashas. Coy. H.Q. is sited under one of them, but, for all the cover it affords, it might as well be in the open. Lt. McArthur of 7 Pl. has been evacuated sick with a swelling under his chin. Possible mumps? Lt. Rutherford-Davidson evacuated with malaria. This leaves the Coy barren of Pl. officers.*
>
> *Coy moved to Mogaung, where we saw our first Jap prisoner. So far the Bn. has not encountered any opposition. 7 Pl. are the only members of the Bn. who have marched the full distance of 40 miles from*

> *Myitkyina. Laagered in an appalling position down a road. During the night, C.S.M. Crosswaite's basha collapsed on top of him and knocked him out. He suffered no ill effects.*
>
> *God! This rain is unending."*

Battles of Hill 60 and Thaikwagon

They had not long to wait for opposition. In August came the battle for Hill 60, a scrub-covered feature, which dominated the entrance to a valley, some 10 miles south of Mogaung. The Japanese had heavily fortified the position and were able to command the approaches, which were in open country, and thus any attack would be in full view of the enemy's defences. The *Chindits* of the 3rd West African Brigade had been attacking Hill 60 for the previous six weeks or so, but despite gaining some ground were unable to hold on due to the lack of air support. The *Chindits* subsequently dug-in some 800 yards from the enemy positions, and awaited the arrival of the British 36th Division.

It was clear that the Japanese occupied part of the feature and had constructed an intricate warren of earthworks, with bottle-shaped fire positions for their mortars, medium machine-guns as well as four 75mm guns. The initial plan of attack was for A and D Companies to make a frontal assault, with C Company securing the left flank and B Company in reserve. In the meantime, it was decided that D Company, commanded by Major Ken Callender, should take up a position on the eastern slope of Hill 60, although it was not known how much of the feature was occupied by the enemy. On the night of 4th-5th August, Major Callender carried out a reconnaissance of the position personally, and finding part of the feature unoccupied, he reconnoitred further until the enemy positions were located. His Company was then brought forward and took over the unoccupied area without opposition. Other reconnaissance patrols were also undertaken to determine the full extent of the enemy defences and reported that there were many more enemy than originally thought, and that they were well dug-in with overhead cover. It was decided, therefore, that the original full frontal night attack would not take place but that there should be an artillery and mortar bombardment of the enemy position, followed by a pre-dawn attack.

In the early hours of 5th August, the Major Callender received orders to clear the enemy from Hill 60 itself and the Company advanced at once. The leading platoon led by Lieutenant F.W.S. Stanbrook, who had been on the earlier reconnaissance, was tasked with taking a patrol forward to ascertain the strength and disposition of the enemy. This was accomplished over very difficult country and in darkness but the information gained was invaluable. Two fighting patrols were then detailed to approach the Japanese position and if no or only slight opposition was encountered, then the patrols were to occupy and hold them. One of these patrols, again led by Lieutenant Stanbrook, got to within 30 yards of the enemy positions without being seen. However, they were soon observed and came under heavy machine-gun fire and the whole

Company was held up. When the patrol was pinned to the ground, Private W.E. Selbourne, on his own initiative, worked his way through the scrub with his Bren-gun and his No. 2, and got into a position, which enfiladed the enemy bunkers. He immediately became the target of enemy fire and his No. 2 was killed almost at once, but by constantly changing his position, despite being wounded, Selbourne succeeded in maintaining a steady and accurate fire on the enemy position.

At one stage during the Company attack, an enemy machine-gun had opened up in the rear of the Company at close range, temporarily halting the advance. Private Gentle, the No. 1 on his section's Bren-gun, moved quickly to a flank across fire-swept ground, stalked the enemy machine-gun and wiped out the post single-handed, killing four Japanese and capturing the gun. By the determination of Gentle and his section in holding its post, they enabled the Company to move forward on to its objective. However, as dawn rose both forward platoons found themselves in exposed positions and pinned down by the fire from enemy machine-guns. The Company Commander worked his way forward under enemy fire and personally organised the withdrawal of these two platoons, as well as supervising the evacuation of the wounded. This phase was greatly assisted by Private Gentle and his Bren-gun, who thwarted several enemy counter-attacks. During the attack six members of D Company were killed and twelve were wounded.

Although D Company was well advanced up the Hill 60 feature, it was pulled back so that artillery could be concentrated on the Japanese-held portion of the ridge, which had a devastating effect on the defending enemy. C Company then came forward and carried out the final assault and as they reached the summit they were greeted with the sight of many of the Japanese soldiers scrambling away down the other side of the hill. While the Japanese did not stand and fight this second assault too fiercely, C Company suffered ten casualties, including Lieutenant Dunford who was killed; some of these casualties, however, were caused through Chinese artillery fire falling short. Twenty-five Japanese dead were found, as well as some grenade-dischargers, swords and important documents. General Festing, the Divisional Commander, came up to inspect and approve, accompanied by General Lentaigne, the *Chindit* leader. The West African *Chindits* then took over Hill 60 thus allowing the 9th Battalion to continue the advance.

Major Callender and Lieutenant Stanbrook were both subsequently awarded the Military Cross for their gallant leadership and devotion to duty. Privates Gentle and Selbourne were both awarded the Military Medal for their gallantry and absolute steadiness under fire, which was an example to all ranks of the Battalion.

The advance was resumed – down the railway-line for the most part – a strange sort of progress, with the Battalion strung out in single file, some 500 strong, supplied from the air but without any other transport. The exception to this was when Jeeps were fitted with railway-wheels, specially made by the Americans, and went trundling down the line, dragging trailers and any old abandoned trucks that could be found. Every now and then they would run into the Japanese, suffer casualties, dive into the jungle, kill some of the enemy, and then renew the advance. This is a typical entry in the Battalion's Intelligence Diary:

> *"Bumped enemy M.M.G. track junction W. of Nampadaung. Killed 5 Japs and captured one prisoner of war. Also captured a sword and machine-gun. Own casualties: Sgt. Everson, Cpl. Bristow, Pte. Pouting killed. We tried to get Sgt. Everson out, but were unsuccessful, as the stretcher was shot up by five enemy, all of whom we subsequently killed. Cpl. Hammond was magnificent with his Bren-gun. He held his fire until the enemy were only two yards away along the jungle track."*

Clearing small airstrips where possible, the 72nd Brigade, taking turns with Brigadier Stockwell's 29th Brigade to supply the advance guards, continued the advance, following a regular routine. Light, sandy soil made it possible to dig in every night, the slit trenches being constructed in 'tight perimeters'. Silence, and no smoking were the orders after dark, which meant twelve hours (roughly from six till six), and anyone moving about was liable to be shot by his own side. Indeed, a number of casualties were incurred in this way. Deaths were also caused by heatstroke, and many men were reduced to a state of complete exhaustion.

The Japanese used comparatively little artillery, but their regimental gun – a 'whizz-bang' recalling the Great War – inflicted casualties from time to time.

Altogether, it was a form of warfare, which took a steady toll. At one stage, D Company had to be disbanded and the remnants attached to B Company, although reinforcements enabled it to be reconstituted sometime afterwards; and still the long march and the occasional engagements went on. At Onbaung, where the Battalion formed a Box, Battalion Headquarters was shelled and mortared on 15th and 16th August and six men were wounded, two of whom died later. Meanwhile, B Company, still reinforced with the remaining elements of D Company, had gone forward through the South Wales Borderers position at Mingon in the worst heat so far encountered, and had been pinned down in open padi by heavy fire from the village of Thaikwagon. Though the mornings are cool in Burma, the sun soon sends the temperature rocketing up and if there is no monsoon rain it gets very hot indeed. On this particular day it chose not to rain and the sun shone down on the heads of B Company without interruption. Those heads were clad in steel helmets; by mid-day they could neither bear to keep them on, nor risk taking them off, for there was no shade to be had and they were under continuous fire. Their ordeal lasted six hours; four men died from heatstroke and Lieutenant Jack Porter was evacuated with heatstroke and delirium and took no further part in the campaign.

Thaikwagon was the scene of another of these 'occasional' engagements. The road, which follows the railway fairly closely down the 'corridor' to Katha, leaves the railway track at Mingon to pass through the village of Thaikwagon and rejoins it further south at Pinbaw. It is not jungle country but is open plain with areas of woodland, with Thaikwagon tucked away in one of the woods. It

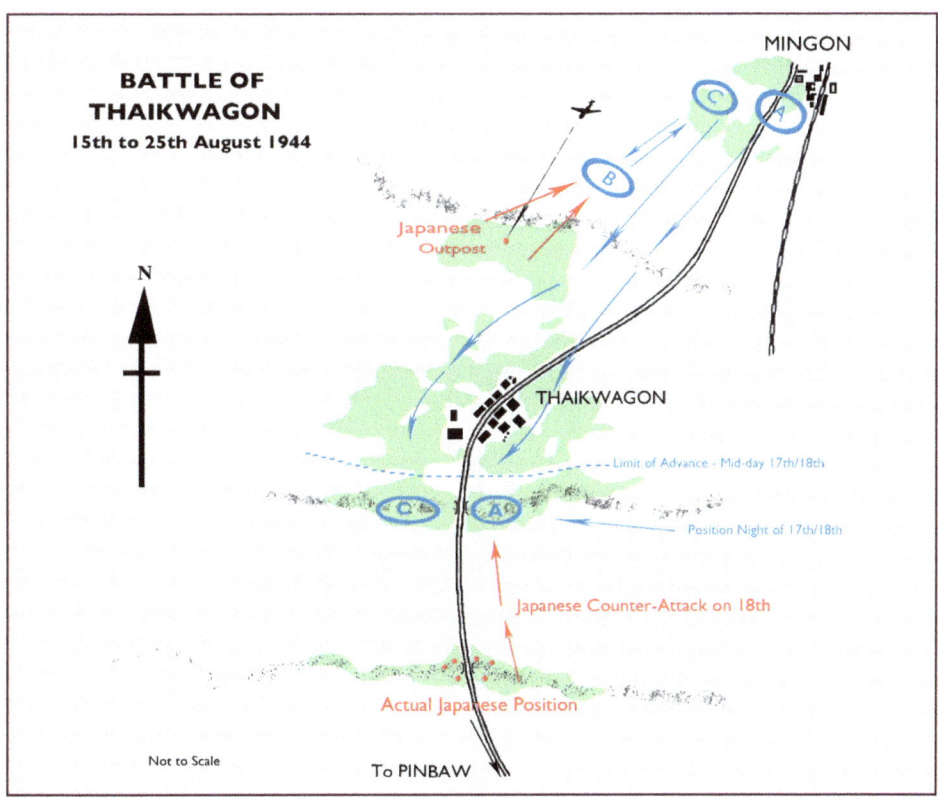

appeared that the Japanese had decided to make their second stand there, and airstrikes and artillery had failed to dislodge them. A and C Companies were ordered to put in an attack; A Company pushed forward across a *chaung* and took the northern edge of the wood, while C Company advanced through the wood on their right-hand side, and cleared Thaikwagon right through to the southern edge, accounting for numerous Japanese as they advanced. The two Companies finally met up on the other side of the forested area to form a perimeter. B Company then came forward and formed a perimeter with HQ Company in the wood itself. Although a few Japanese had been disposed of, there was little sign of the expected resistance. The two Companies went further forward and occupied a copse but the perimeter occupied for the night had been rather elongated owing to the depth of scrub and bamboo. The entry in A Company's Diary[75] records:

> *"That night, about 60 Japs charged the right hand section of 9 Pl. to the accompaniment of shouting and cat-calls. Pte. White made a valiant attempt to stop them with his Bren, but unfortunately a Jap officer charged with such momentum that his dead body fell across the*

---

[75] *Myitkyina to Mandalay – A Diary of the North Burma Campaign 1944-45*. A Company 9th Battalion The Royal Sussex Regiment.

> *gun, effectively blocking it. Pte. White continued to fight ferociously with grenades and anything he could lay his hands on, but sustained four severe bayonet wounds. He was awarded an immediate Military Medal, but unhappily his wounds later proved fatal. Cpl. Evans was also severely wounded before the Japs broke into the perimeter, trundling behind them handcarts. Then an amazing thing happened. The Nips, for reasons best known to themselves, having reached the bridge over the chaung, decided to have a roll call before advancing towards Thaikwagon village.*
>
> *So they conveniently formed up in threes, giving the rear section of 8 Pl. and the rear section of C Coy. across the road a perfect opportunity, of which they were not slow to take advantage, and dealt such fearful punishment to the astounded Japs that, after tossing away a few grenades, they turned and ran back down the road, screaming and shouting, some of them in mortal agony. During this action, Ptes. Butler and Taylor lost their lives, and L/Cpl. Evans, Ptes. Honeysett, Fisher, Ayling, and Craske were wounded[76], but daylight revealed that their sacrifice was revenged, for no fewer than thirteen enemy dead were counted, and, judging by the quantity of blood and bandages left, a larger number was accounted for. Our wireless being 'dis'[77], and the telephone line cut by a grenade, D.F.[78] artillery could not be brought to bear until Cpl. Todd reached B.H.Q. with the required information and took in our own casualties. This last barrage was so effective that the remaining Japs in the area panicked and fled at high speed in the general direction of Tokio."*

The 72nd Brigade was then relieved, having been in almost continuous action for three weeks. The 29th Brigade was then passed through and took up the chase; with the luck that was to remain with them for their whole period of operations, they encountered minimal opposition. They covered 47 miles in a fortnight, roughly three times the distance that the 72nd Brigade had achieved, which was an indication of the difference in the strength of the opposition that they had met. Meanwhile, the Battalion rested at Pinbaw, near Thaikwagon, and duly celebrated Quebec Day, and in October they even received a visit from a mobile cinema. Some reinforcements were also flown in, so that D Company could be reformed under Captain A. Adcock. However, a long rest in one place was not possible for long as they had to maintain contact with the advancing battalions of the 29th Brigade. A series of marches, therefore, took the Battalion towards Mawlu, and on 8th November, orders were received to commence further operations, but without any specific objectives being given.

---

[76] All were A Company casualties.
[77] Not working.
[78] Pre-Registered Defensive Fire tasks.

Battle of Pinwe

Operations began on 9th November with a routine order to resume the advance down the railway line with the 6th South Wales Borderers astride the road to the 9th Battalion's left flank, the objective being to occupy Hpapan and Pinwe, and push on towards the rail junction at Naba. Although fired upon when approaching Hpapan, A Company soon occupied the village with the rest of the Battalion being concentrated just south of Mintha. At 10.30 am, they were dive-bombed by US Thunderbolts, which were supposed to be supporting the South Wales Borderers advance, and inflicted sixteen casualties, two of whom were killed. *"This type of air support"*, signalled the Colonel, *"is not appreciated."* – a model of restraint under the circumstances.

D Company, reinforced by B Company, then went forward but were held up by heavy fire from a *chaung* – code-named Stourbridge – 1,000 yards south of Hpapan, and both Companies were withdrawn. The next day, C Company tried again to do what D and B Companies had unsuccessfully tried to do the day

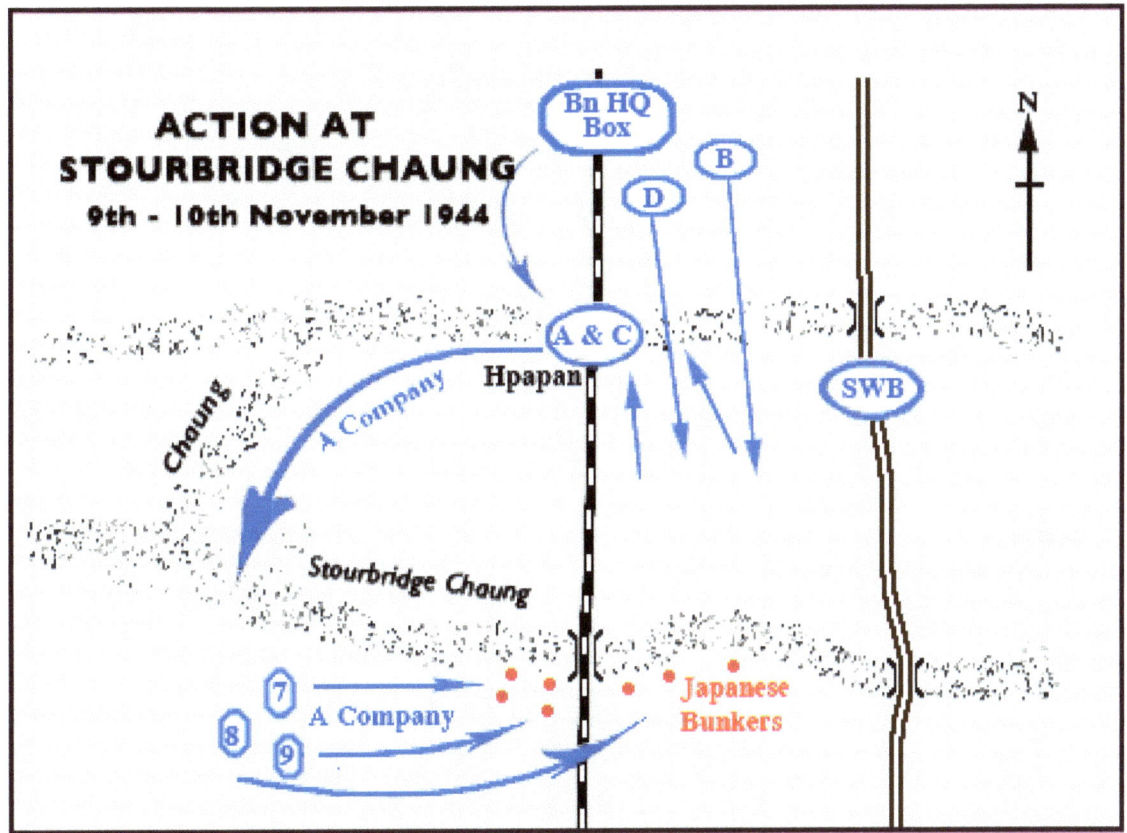

before, but it was also withdrawn temporarily. After an artillery concentration and heavy supporting fire from the Manchester Regiment, A Company carried out a model right flanking attack on *Stourbridge Chaung*, an enemy position which contained a high proportion of machine-guns and mortars, and destroyed both the main position, and other remaining pockets of resistance.

Leading the Company, Major Dickson put in a most determined attack from the flank, rolling up the enemy position, bunker by bunker, and finally causing the enemy to flee in disorder. During the attack, a strongly defended bunker held up one of the platoons and Private Govier, on his own initiative, seized a Bren-gun and, firing from the hip, charged at the bunker and killed the enemy inside it, thus allowing his platoon to overrun the position. Similarly, in one of the other platoons, Private Harris dashed forward with his Bren-gun and killed three Japanese in another strongly held bunker, thereby enabling the momentum of the platoon's attack to be restored. Both Govier and Harris were subsequently awarded the Military Medal, as was Private Powell, a stretcher-bearer who went forward under fire on more than one occasion, often placing his body between the wounded and the enemy fire, while he administered first aid and then recovered the casualties. For his conspicuous skill and gallantry under fire, and his personal example of courage, both during this *Stourbridge* attack and another attack on the following day, Major J.J. Dickson was awarded the Military Cross.

On 11th November, C Company continued to advance unopposed down the axis of the railway track, reaching a point one mile from Pinwe railway station, where it was stopped by heavy mortar and machine-gun fire. Battalion Headquarters and the main body of the Battalion were following C Company, and on meeting the opposition, the Commanding Officer set up a Battalion Box astride the railway line. The general layout was that A Company had formed a perimeter half way between C Company's more advanced

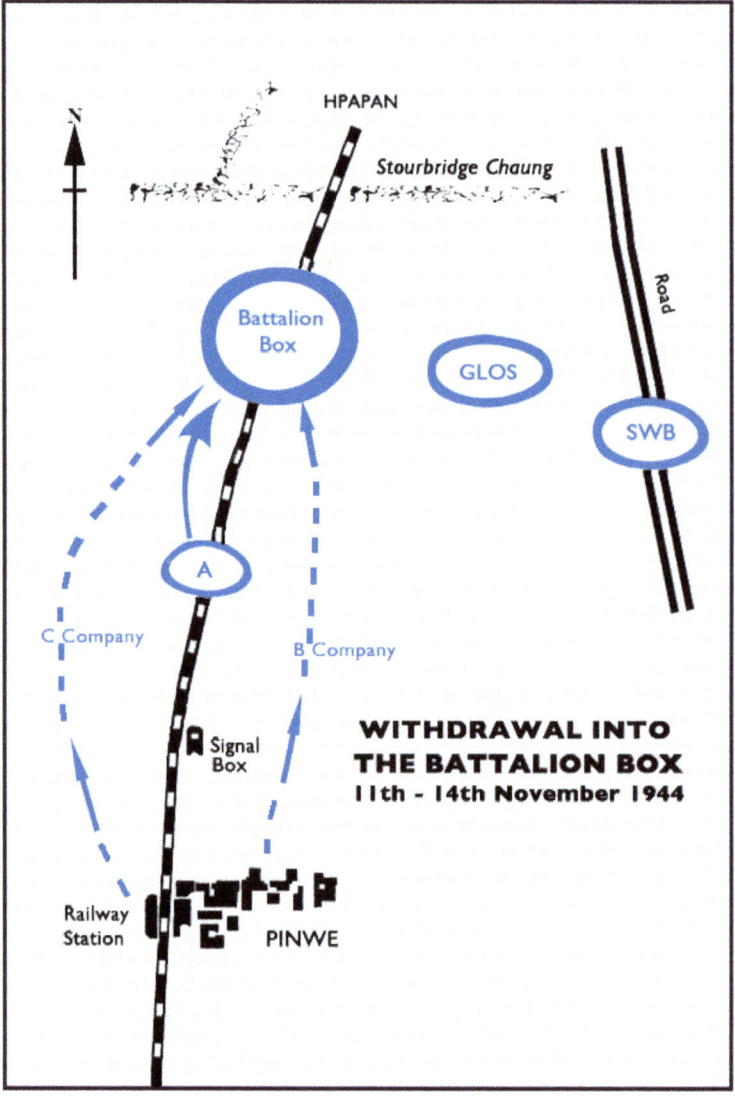

WITHDRAWAL INTO THE BATTALION BOX
11th - 14th November 1944

position and the Battalion Box. C Company, with B Company on its left flank, then made two frontal attacks on the enemy position at the railway station, but they were beaten back and dug in 500 yards north of the signal box. Here they suffered intense mortar fire and thus withdrew through the position held by A Company, with four men wounded. The A Company position was then pounded with extremely accurate mortar and 70mm fire, and within minutes suffered fifteen casualties, including CSM Butler, resulting in A, B and C

Companies being withdrawn into the safety of the Battalion Box. Although the Box was subjected to periodic enemy shelling, the next twenty-four hours or so were spent in active patrolling, with particular emphasis on counter-patrols, with losses incurred on both sides. The operational situation had reached a state of almost stalemate, with each side considering who would take the initiative, and who would make the first mistake? In the event, it was the Japanese who did both. At 7.10 am on the 14th of November, in the middle of the Commanding Officer's 'O' Group for an attack, the Battalion Box was attacked by the largest force of Japanese seen so far; the presence of a whole British battalion being concentrated in one place appears to have been too much of a prize, and the Japanese set out to annihilate it. If so, the Japanese commander must have forgotten Arakan, but perhaps through being stationed in the north he had probably never heard of it. Colonel Oliver had not forgotten, and the Box was a very tight one indeed; there were Bren-guns about every five yards, and one platoon of A Company were defending a perimeter segment of only ten paces long. It should be stressed that a Box, whether of Division or battalion strength, is not purely defensive. Inside are mobile fighting patrols ready to deal with any enemy who get through the perimeter and this was a decisive factor. The other decisive contribution to the defence of the Box was the part played by the company Bren-gun teams. Private V. Conetta fired his Bren-gun to great effect with coolness and determination, although he was being mortared and constantly under the fire of an enemy MMG[79] and LMG[80], at almost point-blank range. When taking part in a wavering counter-attack, he crawled forward with his Bren-gun and proceeded systematically to wipe out all the members of the MMG crew and their escort, killing ten Japanese in all. Similarly, Private J.W. Cox, the No. 2 of a Bren-gun, took over the gun when the No. 1 was wounded, despite the fact that he was also wounded himself, and fired it with great coolness, ignoring the continuous heavy fire directed at him. It was not long before he sustained a second wound, but undaunted, he carried on and continued to hold off the strenuous attempts of the enemy to close in on his post, and was wounded a third time. It was not until he received his fourth wound, in the throat, that he was compelled to relinquish his gun, but by that time he had succeeded in bringing the enemy attack on his post to a standstill. Privates Conetta and Cox were both subsequently awarded the Military Medal for their conspicuous bravery and determination.

During the Japanese attack, the recovery of the wounded under such close battle conditions presented great difficulties, as any movement brought forth bursts of automatic fire. While some stretcher-bearers wavered, Private Colesby, ignoring the enemy fire and with complete disregard for his own safety, not only carried reserve ammunition forward but also attended to five wounded men. Inspired by his example, other men then made their way forward and assisted him in getting the wounded to the rear. For his exceptional courage

---

[79] Medium Machine-Gun
[80] Light Machine-Gun

and initiative in the performance of his duties as a stretcher-bearer, Private C.A. Colesby was also awarded the Military Medal.

The attack, and the mopping up inside the perimeter, lasted five hours, at the end of which sixty dead Japanese were counted. The 9th Battalion's casualties were three killed, fifteen wounded and one missing. Unfortunately, slit trenches cannot easily be dug for mules, and forty of them were killed. During the battle, the Battalion received news that The Regiment had been awarded the Freedom of Brighton.

A written account of the battle by Captain Roy McKelvie, Public Relations Officer of South East Asia Command said the following:

> *"A day or two after the news had reached The Royal Sussex Regiment in North Burma that they had been given the Freedom of Brighton, the Japanese launched a suicide attack. As a matter of fact, the Sussex were just preparing to attack the Japs but were beaten to it by a few minutes. There is nothing the British soldier who fights in the jungle likes more than to catch the Jap in the open. It is, possibly, the only time he really sees the enemy. More often than not, the Japanese dig into the ground and have to be found and killed one by one – a long, nerve-straining, dangerous task. But, on this cold, misty morning, the Japanese crawled out of their foxholes, and with the full blast of war-cries charged the Sussex. The result, once the fog of confusion had cleared away, was that at least sixty Japanese dead were counted for the loss of only four Sussex. What better celebration and tonic to these jungle-seasoned warriors could there have been?"*

There is also an account of Brigadier Aslett's visit during the battle, and of his being greeted with a hail of Japanese small-arms fire – '*at which the Brigadier looked enquiringly at the Colonel, who returned the remark that this was absolutely nothing compared to what we'd had earlier on!*' The Commanding Officer's calmness and sense of humour on this occasion have been described elsewhere as, *"a tonic to us all."* Lieutenant Colonel D.H. Oliver was subsequently awarded the Distinguished Service Order for this and other previous engagements, where he showed himself to be an exceptional leader of men, unmoved by danger to himself, while his clear-headed orders under adverse conditions, gave his men the greatest confidence.

There might have been some grounds for thinking that the battle for Pinwe was all but over but anyone thinking that would have been mistaken; it was to be another fortnight before the Japanese decided that they had had enough. The South Wales Borderers were the first to run into trouble when they found a roadblock between themselves and the rest of the Brigade. On the 17th of November, D Company of the 9th Royal Sussex attacked the roadblock unsuccessfully, with Captain Evans, Lieutenant Nolan and two others being wounded. During this attack, the leading platoon, led by Lieutenant Nolan, came upon a strongly held enemy position, which was held by both MMGs and LMGs on the bank of a small river. Private Stonham crossed the river to the enemy's side alone with his Platoon Commander and they immediately came under automatic fire from a range of 20 yards. Lieutenant Nolan was severely wounded and unable to move, and both of them had now become isolated from the remainder of the platoon, which was unable to cross the river. Stonham managed to drag Nolan back across the river, and even though they were in an exposed position, he attended to his wounds. Camouflaging Nolan with leaves and undergrowth, Stonham then crawled back to hasten the stretcher-bearers forward and helped them to get his officer to the rear. For his gallantry and devotion to duty, and for further actions later that day, Private F.C.G. Stonham was subsequently awarded the Military Medal.

The 9th Battalion, as a whole, then moved up behind the 6th South Wales Borderers, with the roadblock at *Sussex Chaung* between them. As part of this, Lieutenant McArthur had taken a patrol, with thirty-nine laden mules, through thick jungle to help resupply the South Wales Borderers. At the same time, a convoy escorted by 9 Platoon, was driven hell-for-leather down the road to try and break through, and such was its momentum that it overshot the South Wales Borderers perimeter, passed *Gyobin Chaung* and ended up at *Bridge Chaung* some 300 yards behind the enemy positions. The truck crashed, injuring Private Wood, but Sergeant Herman and Corporal O'Neill got the small force safely back without loss, killing two Japanese on the way. Meanwhile, the 10th Glosters attempted an unsuccessful left hook on Pinwe itself but were forced back with heavy officer casualties – they then turned north and attacked *Gyobin Chaung*. This time they were successful although they suffered many more casualties. The 6th South Wales Borderers then moved forward to join the Glosters at Gyobin.

On the morning of 24th November, the 9th Battalion prepared to attack *Bridge Chaung*, with B and D Companies advancing each side of the road. In the event, D Company was held up almost at the start line but B Company, under Major J.M. Cash MC, supported by a heavy artillery barrage, fought right through a series of Japanese bunker positions and gained its objective, although the Company Commander was severely wounded, and his second-in-command, Captain J. Moon, had to take over. However, B Company then found itself in deep trouble as the enemy had somehow managed to re-establish themselves in their bunkers between them and C Company, the supporting company, which had been following up behind them. In spite of manful efforts by A and C Companies to extricate it, B Company was pinned down in its isolated position for forty-eight hours, without food or blankets and with only limited supplies of ammunition. On the second night, the Company crawled right through the Japanese bunkers, moving a foot at a time, while A Company fired the *Victory 'V'* on a Bren-gun to guide them home. Captain Moon succeeded in getting the whole company back in three hours, killing five Japanese on the way, but he was wounded himself during the last phase of this ordeal. The following extract is taken from a personal account of B Company's withdrawal written by Lieutenant R. Lysons for his local paper:

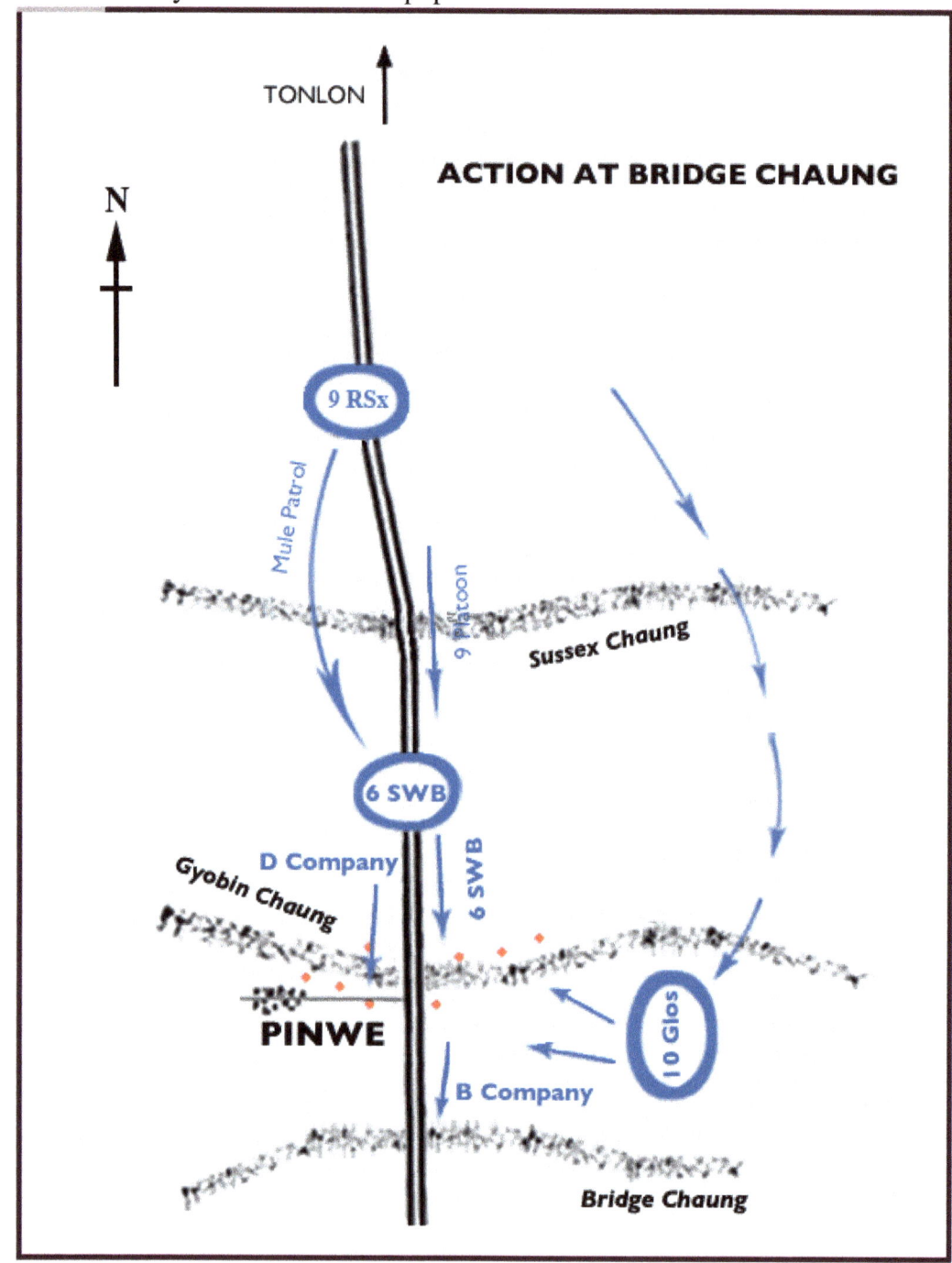

"..... *In the morning when the moon was down, we set out, using a compass bearing, with strict orders not to fire. We moved forward, slowly, hoping that the sound of the heavy dew dripping from the trees would cover our noise. The spirit of the men was magnificent. We brought our casualties with us. One of them, 'Chunky' Maynard, of East Garston, refused to be treated as a casualty and insisted on staying with his platoon.*

> *We passed enemy bunkers and could hear the Japanese snoring two yards away. Then there was the sound of a bolt being pulled back. The leading party reached our own trenches, but the centre and rear were caught with grenade and machine-gun fire. All the men eventually crawled into the perimeter. We had only seven casualties. It took an hour to cover 150 yards and the last man came in at 4.20 am. Even then we were not safe, but at 6 o'clock, with no more firing, we managed to withdraw a hundred yards to 'Sussex' stream where we were rewarded with the whole of the Battalion's breakfast."*

At 9 am on the 28th, B and C Companies left A Company's perimeter and rejoined the Battalion, followed afterwards by A Company itself, which withdrew through the Royal Scots Fusiliers position at Gyobin, who had earlier relieved the Glosters. After twenty days of ferocious fighting, the 72nd Brigade had still not set foot in Pinwe. On the 29th November, the 29th Brigade, without a shot being fired, was able to march into a deserted Pinwe with the pipers of the Royal Scots Fusiliers playing them in. Brigadier Stockwell was the first to acknowledge that the victory belonged to the 72nd Brigade, though at a cost of severe losses to the 10th Glosters in their attack on *Gyobin Chaung*.

The 9th Royal Sussex went back to Tonlon after the most nerve-wracking fortnight of their lives but with a grudging respect for the tough little men who had been responsible for it. Murray Gillings clearly describes this in his book:[81]

> "The tradition of the Samurai is as old as the European tradition of mounted knights in armour and just as inappropriate in modern warfare. Yet the spirit of Bushido, which motivates them and leads them into acts of rash and incomprehensible bravery even when there is little chance of success, and keeps them going when their leaders have been killed and their supplies have run out. The victory had been costly, but less so for the Royal Sussex than the South Wales Borderers and the Glosters, who had both suffered heavier losses. After Pinwe, the Glosters, who by their gallant action had lost such a high proportion of their officers, were never quite the same force again."

The 9th Battalion moved forward behind the 29th Brigade, and on entering Auktaw found it empty; it then received news that Katha, on the Irrawaddy, was also unoccupied. Elements of Headquarters Company and the whole of A Company, under the overall command of Major Dangerfield, embussed at Pinwe and drove directly into Katha on 11th December. The 29th Brigade had now passed the railway junction at Naba and branched southwest for Indaw; the railway corridor was cleared and the original allotted task completed.

---

[81] *The Shiny Ninth*, Murray Gillings, The Pinwe Club, 1986.

Katha was a delightful spot to reach just before Christmas. It was almost deserted when the 9th Battalion arrived, but gradually the inhabitants began to filter back. As an official communiqué described it:

> "As announced officially today, substantial forces of the British 36th Division are across the Irrawaddy. It is the most southerly crossing in force yet made in this campaign. Farther north, of course, the river has been crossed both by Americans and Chinese troops. The Irrawaddy at the point where the crossing took place is a magnificent stream, some 500 yards broad, shallow and slow moving at this time of year. Gilded Burmese dagobas[82], their bells tinkling in the breeze, stand on the bank, and in the distance are the mountain ranges, which cup the Irrawaddy plain. The weather just now is superb. All day long, once the morning mists are dispelled the sun beats down out of a clear, light-blue sky and the air is warm, fresh, and invigorating.
>
> The first crossing was made on the morning of 14th December in sampans by a small party of The Royal Sussex Regiment. On the next day the rest of the battalion began to cross. The leading company commander[83] hauled up a Union Flag. A three day patrol penetrated far to the southeast and established contact with the bearded Americans of the so-called Mars Force."

The Glosters then passed through to positions beyond the river, and the Royal Sussex gave themselves up to a celebration worthy of their past deeds.

On Christmas Day, Church Parade was duly held, with a whole-hearted singing of carols. Thereafter, the congregation received ample beer to counteract hoarseness. Bacon, ducks, chickens and geese were supplemented by fish 'blown' out of the Irrawaddy; a somewhat unusual catch (estimated at eight feet in length and past its prime) being deposited as a gift at Brigade Headquarters, much to the annoyance of the Brigade Major! A football match followed the Christmas Lunch, and Burmese dancers and musicians provided additional entertainment, but the day ended with the time-honoured touch of a campfire and a Sussex chorus round the blaze.

On Boxing Day 1944, the 9th Battalion pushed forward from the Irrawaddy. Moving from Katha to Kunchaung, the Battalion picked up the River Shweli and its line of march followed the east bank of the river to Yanbo, where a light aircraft strip was constructed in two days. From there it moved by march route to Kota, where A Company were ordered to cross the river while the remainder of the Battalion carried on towards Mahlainggon. While A Company had had a number of minor contacts on its side of the river, with the enemy generally melting away into the jungle, C Company ran into an ambush just north of

---

[82] Buddhist shrines.
[83] D Company.

Mahlainggon. Artillery fire and ground-attack aircraft were unleashed on the village, causing the Japanese defenders to move north to escape the barrage, only to run into B and D Companies, who pushed them back again, and then they themselves finally entered Mahlainggon on the 21st of January 1945. Although A Company had pushed on to Thitson, it re-crossed the Shweli and rejoined the Battalion on the Mahlainggon-Lawa road where, apart from routine patrols, the whole Battalion rested for ten days.

The Battle of the Shweli River

General Kimura, the Japanese Commander, had planned to make a stand somewhere in Central Burma, and to the east of the Irrawaddy. It seemed that the area north of Mandalay, centred on Mong Mit, would be the most likely battleground. This area was not only very strongly defended but the terrain of the Northern Shan States was also more difficult for advancing troops. Kimura realised that to strike first, before the 14th Army and the NCAC formations had joined up, might well upset General Slim's carefully laid plans, and would have the added advantage of allowing Kimura to extricate the remains of the Japanese forces retreating eastwards from the Chindwin. From subsequent information, it was later realised that General Kimura believed that his plans would be more ably achieved if he could destroy the British 36th Division.

At this stage of the campaign, Major-General Festing, the Commander of the 36th Division, decided to bring the 26th Indian Brigade forward so that fresh troops could be used for the attempt on Myitson, as his other two Brigades were both showing signs of strain after their hard and protracted operations. Its arrival would more than double the fighting strength on the eastern side of the Irrawaddy; the 29th Brigade was already detached and operating on the western side of the river. Nevertheless, the relief felt in the 9th Royal Sussex at the thought of an additional formation being available for the operation was mixed with a feeling of guilt, for the 26th Indian Brigade was so inexperienced while their own 72nd Brigade was so battle-tried. The 26th Indian Brigade, commanded by Brigadier Jennings, was a four-battalion Brigade, consisting of the 2nd Buffs, the 1st/1st Gurkha Rifles, the 1st Hyderabad Regiment, and the 2nd/8th Punjabis, all of them honoured names in British-India annals. General Kimura's new force arrived just in time to meet them.

On the 2nd of February, a company of the Buffs embarked in boats at mid-day against what had been reported as empty bunkers on the Myitson side of the Shweli River, but the Japanese had crept back overnight and their MMGs, LMGs and mortars opened up when the Buffs were in mid-stream. Against all the odds, a small bridgehead was established and held. The remainder of the 2nd Buffs now attempted to cross but fire was so heavy that only five boats out of forty remained and it had to be called off. When their ammunition ran out on the 3rd, the bridgehead had to be abandoned, and it was accomplished under smoke and artillery fire, and without the loss of heavy equipment and mortars. But of the 130 men who had held the bridgehead, only sixteen fit-for-duty men came back; twenty-eight were killed, fifty-five wounded and thirty-one missing, though some of the missing returned later.

A diversionary operation was mounted to make the Japanese think that the next attack would be against the island, while the 26th Brigade's main attack was made across the river to the north of Myitson, using two crossing points to avoid over-concentration. Although the crossings were successful, surprise was lost, but the Indian troops were able to fight their way into Myitson and consolidate. Their positions were heavily and continuously shelled, mortared and attacked by fanatical Japanese infantry on the 10th, 11th and 12th of February. In the meantime, the 26th Brigade's Headquarters had become separated from its forward troops by the establishment of a Japanese roadblock astride its main axis.

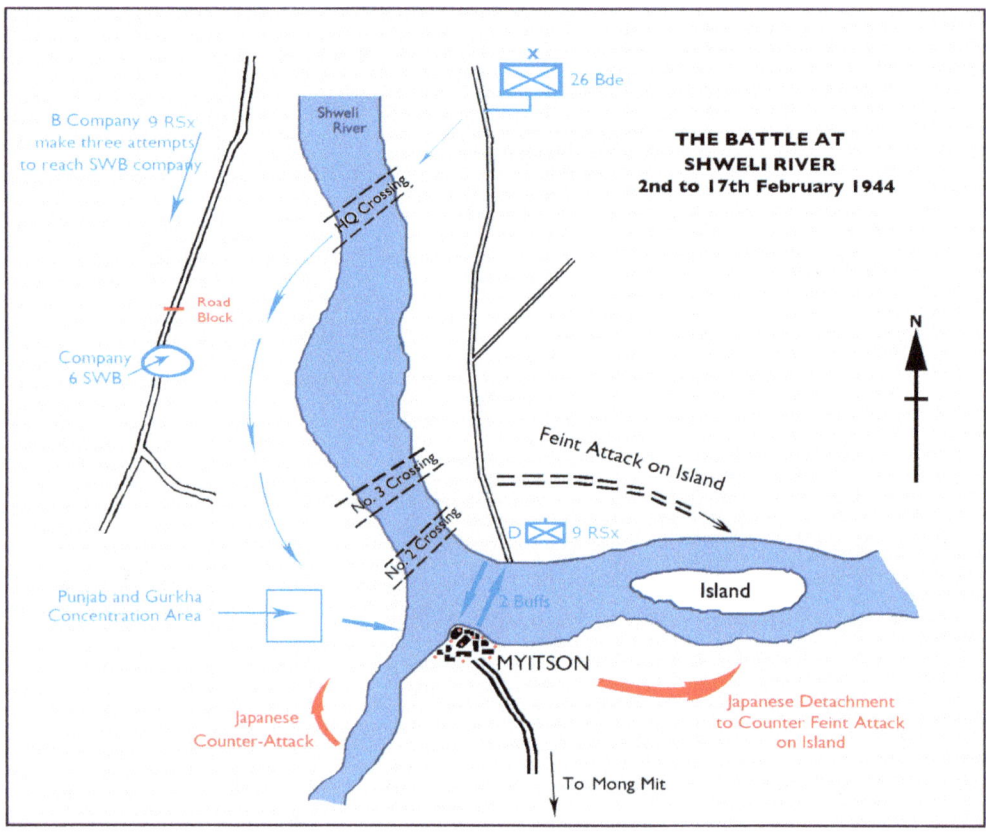

The troops in the town had to be supplied via the No. 1 crossing point and the casualties evacuated the same way. It was a dangerous business as the crossing was continually under fire by both day and night. The fighting continued until 17th February when the Japanese threw in everything they had, including flame-throwers. The Punjabis bore the brunt of that unexpected and deadly weapon and many were burnt in the slit trenches were they stood unyielding, and which, for many, became their graves. By the end of that day, the battle had been decided; the enemy in Myitson lost 350 killed and the beaten survivors withdrew. Kimura's plan for the destruction of the 36th Division had failed and the Japanese forces on that front were in a state of disorganisation.

It was a battle of vital importance to the 36th Division, and to the 14th Army as well. It was the one action in North Burma, which could be classified as a major battle; the battles at Thaikwagon and Pinwe could not compare in scale. Six hundred Japanese were killed altogether and the total of their wounded and missing has never been computed.

The casualties in the 26th Indian Brigade were also heavy and in Geoffrey Foster's words, *"Seldom can the blooding of a new formation have been so severe."*

The 9th Royal Sussex added its own rider, *"Seldom has a new formation proved its mettle so decisively."*

For the duration of the Shweli battle, the 9th Battalion had been fairly widely dispersed in various locations, some anxiously watching the progress of the battle, while others were out of sight of the action and awaiting news. A Company had moved from Bahe where it had been guarding the artillery, to a swampy water point near No. 2 crossing, surrounded by tall elephant grass; the elephants were still using it and were not particular as to where they trod! D Company was relatively close to A Company and was dug in near the No. 1 crossing, while C Company was actively patrolling in various locations.

Only B Company, under Major Hunt, played a more active part in the battle. The Company had crossed the Shweli on 14th February and established a bridgehead, with the intention of breaking a roadblock between themselves and a forward company of the 6th South Wales Borderers. B Company held a large perimeter with one platoon of another battalion under command and the bridgehead was subjected to considerable shelling, and under continual fire from grenades, LMGs and mortars. Between 14th and 18th February, the Company made three unsuccessful attempts to shift the roadblock although they accounted for between twenty-five and thirty Japanese, losing two killed, one wounded and one missing. During the entire battle, Major Hunt showed outstanding leadership and initiative and with complete disregard to his own safety, he moved continuously from platoon to platoon, encouraging and inspiring confidence in his men at a critical stage in the battle. At the close of the battle, he carried through his plan in the face of considerable fire and extricated the Company from a difficult position. Holding part of the Company's perimeter was Corporal Glover's section and for three days, his section was heavily attacked. On one occasion, when his section had been depleted in numbers, the enemy tried to rush his position, but Corporal Glover immediately seized a Bren-gun and drove off the attack, and then went forward alone and pursued the enemy with grenades, killing and wounding several of them. His coolness and courage in action under considerable fire was an inspiration to all ranks, and in no small way contributed to the successful withdrawal of the Company from the bridgehead.

On 19th February, B Company crossed back over the river again, passing through their old bridgehead perimeter and counted fourteen dead within fifty yards of it. They recovered much of the equipment that they had left behind as well as a Japanese LMG and documents. For their gallantry, determination and inspiration in the bridgehead battle, Major C. Hunt was subsequently awarded the Military Cross and Corporal P.L. Glover received the Military Medal.

By the 25th of February, the time had come to move forward again, and the 72nd Brigade led the way with the 9th Royal Sussex leading the advance through Myitson. The town was a complete shambles and not a tree or a house appeared to remain standing, and the smell of death and burnt cordite hung in the air.

The Road to Mandalay

As the Battalion moved forward, C Company had the first encounter, capturing a small pimple-like feature and killing four Japanese. D Company also met resistance and had a far from easy time making progress. A Company was therefore sent on a right hook through the jungle, avoiding the main road to Mong Mit and the track, which followed the Nameik *chaung,* both held by the enemy. In the event, there was not much room to manoeuvre between the track and the *chaung* and thus A Company was brought back onto the track to deal with a large hill feature about 500 yards long; code-named *Hill 800,* it overlooked the track and threatened to hold up the main advance of the whole Brigade.

A reconnaissance had established that the hill was occupied and following a thirty-minute artillery concentration, Major Dickson MC led A Company on to the objective with such vigour and speed that most never had the opportunity of worrying about success or failure. He had scored tactical surprise by attacking up a precipitous face, through dense jungle and avoiding the easier slopes, which offered the more obvious line of approach. Such was the fine-tuning of the artillery that the Company were literally moving up among the falling shells, causing some men to waver but Major Dickson personally led the way, while many of the Japanese ran back to get out of range. Lance Corporal Albert Pickard was the No. 1 of the Bren-gun in the left-hand leading platoon and some of the men in his section were somewhat hesitant because of the close-falling artillery. He at once cheered his men on and led them into the assault through tangled creepers and up bare rocks. On reaching the crest they encountered an enemy LMG, but Picard charged on alone, firing his Bren from the hip, and knocked it out and killed the crew. Further LMGs were holding up the advance and, again, Lance Corporal Picard went forward and destroyed them and, although wounded, he kept the gun in action until another member of his section worked his way forward to relieve him. Through such exploits, the Company was able to gain possession of the main part of the objective within half an hour. The rest of the objective, however, took longer to clear as numbers of the enemy had held on and were sniping from the trees and trenches with LMG and rifle fire. The Company Commander, rapidly grasping the situation, called for additional artillery fire and committing the reserve platoon to a left flanking attack, led them with such skill and determination that the enemy fled, leaving one officer and five Japanese soldiers on the field. During this assault, Sergeant Harry Herman, whose Platoon Commander had earlier become a casualty, had also led his platoon through the close-falling shells, and then took them forward on to the first objective with considerable dash and initiative. Having secured it, he then led them to the centre of the enemy's position, with the attack being pressed home with such skill and determination that the enemy did not wait for the final assault but broke and fled. Sergeant Herman charged forward alone and pursued the enemy down the further slope of the hill, inflicting further casualties with bayonet and grenades. It was clearly indicated from the number of the enemy's packs and weapons and other equipment left behind, that the position had been occupied by at least one company.

The Company then dug in as best it could and awaited the expected counter-attack, but after a night of false alarms, it never materialised. The following morning, General Festing came up onto the position and thanked and congratulated A Company, since it had opened the way to Mong Mit, capital of the Shan State of that name, and an important communications centre. That afternoon, Divisional Headquarters informed the Company that some of the documents they had captured contained plans for an immediate counter-attack by four platoons should *Hill 800* fall. That night they stood-to again, and were relieved at dawn when the 6th South Wales Borderers took over the position.

For his outstanding courage, initiative and superb leadership, combined with tactical skill of a very high order, which enabled the feature to be captured with the loss of very few casualties, Major J.J. Dickson MC was awarded a Bar to his Military Cross; the Military Cross he had been awarded only three months earlier. Sergeant H.E. Herman and Lance Corporal A.J. Pickard were both awarded the Military Medal for their outstanding courage and leadership in the face of considerable opposition.

The advance was resumed southwest moving through Letpangya and Myethin, where D Company encountered some unexpected opposition and had to pull back to Letpangya, with five men wounded. On 5th March, C Company established a roadblock on the track so that B Company could attack from the south, while A Company pushed on towards Thabyetha, which proved to be as pretty as it sounded. After eight days of jungle trekking it was bliss to settle down in a banana plantation, even though the bananas were not ripe. On reaching Thabyetha, information from the locals indicated that there were large parties of Japanese in the villages ahead but as the Battalion advanced, with the rest of the Brigade following, any resistance seemed to be melting away in front of them. Pushing on to Mong Mit, which had just been captured by the Gurkhas and Punjabis, the 9th Battalion motored or marched at a leisurely pace up into the Shan Hills where they rested and life became almost idyllic. The weather was lovely, the scenery beautiful, and the food and mail arrived daily.

All around were hundreds of square miles of the world's best hardwood, vast forest reserves inhabited by parakeets and golden pheasant; a form of paradise which allowed the harsh memories of the Shweli to fade away.

The advance continued, with the 26th Brigade pushing on towards Kyaukme on the Burma Road, where they would link up with units of the Chinese 6th Army. The 29th Brigade was following up with the 72nd Brigade behind them, when suddenly the 72nd came under orders to fly in to Mandalay. Earlier, in February 1945, General Slim had asked for the 36th Division to be passed back to the 14th Army but the request was turned down because it might bring operations in the NCAC area to a halt. However, by March, all units on the NCAC front had reached that stage anyway, and the agreed boundary line between the two theatres had been reached at Kyaukme. On 1st April, the request was granted and the 36th Division had to say goodbye to their American friends and allies. There is not the slightest doubt that the Division had carried out its military tasks with distinction but it had also achieved its secondary objective of improving understanding between the two nations. In General Slim's words:

> *"Festing and his division, besides a good fighting job, had done a great deal to dispel the cloud of uninformed criticism that at one time threatened to darken Anglo-American relations. Instead of only hearing second hand and often malicious stories, the soldiers of both nations had now seen one another fighting the enemy. The result was mutual respect."*

The Division was given a great send-off by its American friends, and they left with genuine regret, as it had been a rewarding relationship. As the 36th Division turned southwest towards Maymyo to join the 14th Army, General Slim ordered General Festing to fly one of his Brigades immediately into Mandalay. He was to concentrate his Division as quickly as possible in order to both relieve the 19th Division, which had captured Mandalay two days earlier, and to take over the responsibility of clearing up operations in the Mandalay-Maymyo area.

On 2nd April, Battalion Headquarters, with A and B Companies flew from the Mong Long airstrip and were soon encamped at the foot of Mandalay Hill. C and D Companies arrived the following day, and then Battalion Headquarters, with C Company and half of Headquarters Company, moved by MT to Maymyo, which is to Burma what Simla is to India. It was infinitely preferable to Mandalay, which still smelt of death and corruption, and where cholera had broken out. There appears to have been no doubt that The Royal Sussex was not attracted to the old royal capital as the following note indicates:

> *"Mandalay! 'Flattened' would be an understatement in describing this key city of Burma. Add to this a temperature of 103 in the shade and the aroma of Japs dead ten days, and one gets a true picture of this 'jewel of the East' as it is today, in rude contrast to the*

> *Kiplingesque picture of popular imagination. Fort Dufferin – big enough to accommodate the whole division – and Mandalay Hill are easily recognisable from the air. The Fort is in the middle of the city and is surrounded by a moat, and still looks an impressive sight, although the Royal Palace inside is now a mere black smudge on the ground. In the city itself, most of the big buildings are total wrecks, but small shops have opened up again in some places, making a pathetic bid to return to normal."*

Soon, the 9th Battalion was on the march again, the vanguard of a new brigade advance to the south towards Kalaw although they did not relish the prospect of further action; they were jaded, over-tired and over-used and had been continually on operations for 9 months. When it reached Pyinyaung, ahead of which was a massive escarpment several hundred feet high, straddling the road and well defended, it seemed the Brigade was about to embark on another 'Twin Tunnel-type' attack, or worse, in partnership with the 29th Brigade. Some battalions did actually go into action but not the 9th Battalion. The 72nd Brigade was split up and the Battalion moved by motor transport back to Meiktila between the 2nd and 5th of May. The Royal Sussex took no further part in the war in Burma but, of course, their comrades in the 14th Army achieved their objective of capturing Rangoon before the rains came, even though they came a fortnight early. Pressing on without let up, the 4th Corps and the 33rd Corps advanced along the parallel axes of the Irrawaddy and the Sittang rivers, but both were narrowly beaten by the 15th Corps, who landed south of the capital in a series of island hopping amphibious moves, and occupied Rangoon on the 3rd of May. They had got their amphibious craft at last!

On 7th May, the Battalion flew out to Imphal and the long haul from Myitkyina to Meiktila was over. It arrived in Poona on 17th May and had joined the 25th Indian Division in India, in preparation for an assault on Malaya. It was with great sadness that with this change of formation, Lieutenant Colonel D.H. Oliver also handed over command of the 9th Battalion to Lieutenant Colonel G.R. Stevens of the Royal Fusiliers.

Apart from a few weeks in Shillong, the 9th Royal Sussex, alongside their compatriots from Gloucestershire and Wales, had been in action for nearly fifteen months. They had collected no less than thirty-two awards for gallantry and as many had been Mentioned-in-Despatches. Many more had been recommended but as is often the case, did not gain the necessary higher approval. Nevertheless, it is right and proper that honour should be given to the hundreds who sweated it out with no reward except their campaign medals and the satisfaction of overcoming a ferocious enemy, the rigours of climate and disease, and their own fear. Many had not returned from Burma and, unlike the other theatres in which The Regiment fought, most of them lie in graves now lost without trace along the railway corridor from Pahok to Pinwe, or east of the Irrawaddy. Let their epitaph be the lines written by one of their own comrades:

"By the road and the hills lie the scattered seed
A bamboo cross on each lonely grave
Shimmering silence and jungle weed
Enfold and touch lightly – here sleep the brave.

Not yet the fruit of your dying be tasted
The sun and the rain no harvest unfold
But rest, we shall see that the seed was not wasted
The living remember, the tale shall be told."

(Sgt. C. Grimes, 9th Bn. Royal Sussex)

The general impression given by the 9th Battalion The Royal Sussex Regiment was one of an eminently happy battalion. That their morale was of a high order scarcely needs stressing after what has been written here; while they proved themselves such redoubtable warriors during that ordeal in the jungle, there was an extraordinary light-heartedness about the way in which they faced all its horrors. They referred to 'the Nips' as though they considered them sub-human creatures, and their general bearing recalls the spirit of that old, defiant company of the 9th Battalion in the Great War, jeering at the advancing enemy and daring them to come on.

At the conclusion of the Burma campaign, The Regiment was awarded the Battle Honours of North Arakan, Pinwe, Shweli and **Burma 1943-45,** with the latter Honour being emblazoned on the Colours.

Gallantry Awards for Burma in 1944-45

Distinguished Service Order:

Lieutenant Colonel D.H. Oliver	9th Battalion

Bar to the Military Cross:

Major J.J. Dickson	9th Battalion

Military Cross:

Major J.J. Dickson	9th Battalion
Major K.L. Callender	9th Battalion
Major F.W. Stanbrook	9th Battalion
Major C. Hunt	9th Battalion
Major J.M. Cash	9th Battalion

Military Medal:

Sergeant R Cadwallader	9th Battalion

Sergeant C. Davis	9th Battalion
Sergeant H.F. Felix	9th Battalion
Sergeant R. Hollingdale	9th Battalion
Sergeant N.E Sampson	9th Battalion
Sergeant G. F. Taylor	9th Battalion
Sergeant H. Herman	9th Battalion
Sergeant W.G. Leech	9th Battalion
Lance Sergeant R.L. Smith	9th Battalion
Corporal R. Owen	9th Battalion
Corporal P.L. Glover	9th Battalion
Corporal A. Harris	9th Battalion
Corporal J. Govier	9th Battalion
Lance Corporal V. Conetta	9th Battalion
Lance Corporal A. Picard	9th Battalion
Private D. Clark	9th Battalion
Private C.A. Colesby	9th Battalion
Private J.L. Cox	9th Battalion
Private A. Gentle	9th Battalion
Private S. Powell	9th Battalion
Private A.W. Rogers	9th Battalion
Private W. G. Rogers	9th Battalion
Private F.C. Stonham	9th Battalion
Private L.E. Selbourne	9th Battalion
Private A.W. White	9th Battalion

US Silver Star:

Major G.C. Cockell   9th Battalion

US Bronze Star

Lieutenant & Quartermaster H.N. Brockless   9th Battalion

Mentioned-in-Despatches:

Thirty-seven officers and forty-three men of the 9th Battalion were Mentioned-in-Despatches, and one man received a Certificate of Gallantry.

Royal Sussex Officers and Men attached to other Units in Burma in 1943-45

Distinguished Service Order

Colonel V. H. Jacques OBE MC   Special Operations

Military Cross:

Major R.B.S. Hogben   4th Bombay Grenadiers

Captain M.A.J. Budd   'V' Force
Captain H.A.C. Edelsten   4/14th Punjabis
Lieutenant G.H. Borrow   13th Kings

Mentioned-in-Despatches:

Seven officers and one Warrant Officer were Mentioned-in-Despatches.

NORTH-WESTERN EUROPE

General Service

No battalion of the Royal Sussex took part in the Normandy landings of June 1944 and, in sharp contrast with the end of the Great War, the Roussillon plume was not seen among the formations that broke the German power in the final assault on the Western Front. Yet, when this has been said, it should be recognised that many officers and men of the Regiment were fighting in North-West Europe, both before and after D-Day, serving with other regiments and corps, and their actions exercised a significant influence on events quite out of proportion to their numbers as these following examples demonstrate:

> Corporal G.R. Wheeler, serving with No. 2 Commando, took part in combined operations against St Nazaire on 27th March 1942. When it became clear that re-embarkation was impossible, he and a Lance-Corporal Simms were instructed to fight their way into the new town in the hope of getting into the country. Assisted by a number of French civilians they were given food, clothes and money, and after many adventures and escapades eventually found their way to Toulouse, where arrangements were made for their return to England. Corporal Wheeler was subsequently awarded the Military Medal for his determination.

> Taking part in the same St Nazaire operation with No. 2 Commando, Lance-Sergeant A.C. Searson was taken prisoner on 28th March and sent to a prisoner-of-war camp in Germany. He made several escape attempts, often at large for sometime but was recaptured each time. His final attempt with two other men was successful and they crossed into Switzerland on 25th October 1943. He was subsequently awarded the Military Medal.

> Private F.H. Trigg, also serving with No. 2 Commando, took part in the successful operation to destroy the important electric power plant at Glomfiord in Norway on 20th October 1942. Having to make their own escape, Private Trigg spent twelve days in enemy-occupied territory and in spite of great exhaustion and hardship, made his way out through Sweden. He was awarded the Military Medal for his skill and resolution.

> In June 1944, Lieutenant P.W.B. Thomson was awarded the Military Cross for his bravery and leadership while commanding a Company of the 9th Battalion The Durham Light Infantry in France. His father, Lieutenant Colonel A.L. Thomson had been awarded the Distinguished Service Order when he commanded the 7th Royal Sussex during the Great War.

In July 1944, Lieutenant A.R. Chittenden was awarded the Military Cross for his skilful leadership and bravery at Maitot in France while serving with the 5th Battalion The Wiltshire Regiment.

Also in July 1944 at Cloppenburg, Lieutenant R.A. Daniels was awarded the Military Cross for his dash, leadership and great courage while serving with the 7th Battalion The Hampshire Regiment.

In September 1944, for his great gallantry and complete disregard for enemy fire while directing and carrying out vigorous and aggressive close patrolling against the enemy defences at Le Havre, while serving with the 49th Reconnaissance Regiment Royal Armoured Corps, Major P.H. Rubie was awarded a Bar to the Military Cross; the Military Cross which he had been awarded for gallant conduct under fire as the 2nd Battalion's Carrier Platoon Commander in France in 1940.

In November 1944 at Tripsrath, Captain G.D. Hodgson was awarded the Military Cross for his courage and devotion to duty while serving with The Dorset Regiment.

In January 1945, during an attack in the Ardennes, Major H.J. Jourdain, while commanding A Company of the 2nd Battalion The Monmouthshire Regiment, was awarded the Military Cross for displaying the finest possible fighting spirit, a great tactical skill and cool personal courage, which inspired his Company under extremely trying conditions.

In March 1945 at Wesel, Sergeant F.A. Worthington, while serving with No. 6 Commando, was awarded the Military Medal for his initiative, gallantry and immediate action in destroying an enemy patrol, despite being wounded himself.

In April 1945, during an attack on Ibberuren, Lieutenant R.M. Williams, while serving with the 4th Battalion The Royal Welch Fusiliers, was awarded the Military Cross for leading attack after attack against a fanatical and determined enemy, and despite being wounded, his leadership and courage being quite outstanding.

Airborne Contingent

It will be recalled that, after the Royal Sussex Brigade went back to the Canal Zone in 1942, following the El Alamein campaign, the 10th Parachute Battalion was formed from Royal Sussex volunteers, and returned to England for special training.

Lieutenant Colonel Smyth was their Commanding Officer, but we hear nothing more of them until March 1944, when they were inspected in turn by General Montgomery and the King. Montgomery gave one of his informal talks, everyone breaking ranks to hear his summary of military events and the part that the Battalion was destined to play in them. A dress-rehearsal for what was called *'Secret Day'* then took place on Oakham football field, after which all ranks went – in true Montgomery style – for a cross-county run.

In June, while the Normandy landings were in preparation, the 10th Battalion of the Parachute Regiment stood by, ready to move at two hours notice, but their *'Secret Day'* did not dawn until September.

The Arnhem attack, launched from Somersby, is generally considered to have been a partial success, which might have provided a decisive victory. General Eisenhower, however, thought more highly of it than that.

> *"There has been,"* he wrote, *"no single performance by any unit that has more greatly inspired my admiration than the nine-day action of your Division between September 17 and 26."*

He considered that this great battle *"contributed effectively to the success of the operations to the southward of the battleground,"* and went on to say, *"your officers and men were magnificent."*

Among the officers referred to, Lionel Queripel of The Royal Sussex Regiment will always be remembered. A regular officer of the last term to pass out of The Royal Military Academy Sandhurst at the beginning of the Second World War, he was with the 2nd Battalion in the desert, and, after El Alamein, he volunteered for the 10th Parachute Battalion. *"Determined – rather dour, but with a quiet wit which soon endeared him to all of us,"* says a brother officer, *"there was no stopping him once he had decided to 'do something'."* It was this determined spirit, which characterised his great exploit at the battle of Arnhem, where he won the Victoria Cross; the only Victoria Cross awarded to a member of The Royal Sussex Regiment in the Second World War. During the whole of a period of nine hours of confused and bitter fighting, Captain Queripel displayed the highest standard of gallantry under the most difficult and trying circumstances. His courage, leadership and devotion to duty was magnificent and an inspiration to all. The citation for his award reads as follows:

> *"In Holland on the 19th September 1944, Captain Queripel was acting as Company Commander of a composite company composed of three parachute battalions. At 14.00 hours on that day, his Company was advancing along a main road which ran on to an embankment towards Arnhem. The advance was conducted under continuous medium machine-gun fire, which at one period, became so heavy that the Company became split on either side of the road and suffered considerable losses. Captain Queripel at once proceeded to reorganise his force, crossing and recrossing the road whilst doing so, under*

extremely heavy and accurate fire. During this period he carried a wounded Sergeant to the Regimental Aid Post under fire and was himself wounded in the face. Having reorganised his force, Captain Queripel personally led a party of men against the strong point holding up the advance. This strong point consisted of a captured British anti-tank gun and two machine-guns. Despite the extremely heavy fire directed at him, Captain Queripel succeeded in killing the crews of the machine-guns and recapturing the anti-tank gun. As a result of this, the advance was able to continue.

Later in the same day, Captain Queripel found himself cut off with a small party of men and took up a position in a ditch. By this time he had received further wounds in both arms. Regardless of his wounds and of the very heavy mortar and Spandau fire, he continued to inspire his men to resist with hand grenades, pistols, and the few remaining rifles.

As however, the enemy pressure increased, Captain Queripel decided that it was impossible to hold the position any longer and ordered his men to withdraw. Despite their protests, he insisted on remaining behind to cover their withdrawal with his automatic pistol and a few remaining hand grenades. This was the last occasion on which he was seen."

Captain Lionel Queripel died where he fell. After the battle the Dutch Red Cross collected his and a number of other bodies and buried them locally. After the war, their remains were reinterred in the Arnhem Oosterbeek Commonwealth War Graves Cemetery in the Netherlands.

Again at Arnhem, on the afternoon of the same day, Captain B.B. Clegg, another Royal Sussex officer, had taken over command of B Company 10th Parachute Battalion and by that stage, only one subaltern officer was left in his Company. Almost immediately Captain Clegg had to conduct a very difficult disengaging manoeuvre across a very exposed piece of ground, which was covered by machine-gun and mortar fire. By his personal example and leadership, and with complete disregard of all personal danger, Captain Clegg withdrew his Company in good order and with a minimum of casualties.

At dusk the same day, the enemy launched a very strong attack against the Battalion's new position, and before it had time to dig in properly. It was largely due to Captain Clegg's example, in moving hither and yon, encouraging his men to even greater efforts, that the enemy was unable to break through. Again, in the late morning of the 20th, he led his Company in a most spirited bayonet attack in the final stages of which he personally attacked and destroyed a German machine-gun post.

In the late afternoon, the Battalion now sorely depleted in strength, was ordered to attack and capture a crossroads held by the enemy on the Divisional perimeter at Osterbeck. To secure the crossroads it was necessary to clear eight houses and their gardens, and Captain Clegg personally led the assault and cleared three of these houses against bitter opposition from the enemy. In the third house he was seriously wounded in the jaw by machine-gun fire, but insisted on carrying on until all the enemy were exterminated, and the houses organised in a state of defence.

During this time he was losing a great deal of blood and was in great pain, and eventually collapsed, and the Company's senior Sergeant took over. Captain Clegg, in this period of very bitter and confused fighting carried out his duties in an exemplary manner, his leadership was outstanding and his personal courage and complete disregard of danger was an inspiration and example to all his men. Captain B.B. Clegg was subsequently awarded a Bar to the Military Cross, which he had been awarded at El Alamein.

Also at Osterbeck that day, another member of the Royal Sussex had already shown conspicuous bravery in hand-to-hand fighting since he had dropped on 18th September. Sergeant T.C. Bentley was in charge of a detachment of soldiers, using the top floor of a house as an observation post in the hard-pressed corner of the Divisional perimeter. The position was held by the remnants of the 10th Parachute Battalion, about fifty strong, continually under fire and frequently being attacked. From this post he not only directed killing fire on the enemy, but also received information vital to the defences, which he carried to his Commanding Officer, under fire from the enemy on each occasion. When the side of the house was blown in, he fell from the top floor to the basement, but crawled out and carried on from outside. He was shot at more than once that day but soon after another attack overran the Battalion Headquarters house, and the Commanding Officer was wounded and the few men there were captured.

Although the mortars had been lost, Sergeant Bentley led a patrol that night into the enemy occupied area and brought the mortars out, operating them from then on, often under heavy fire, under the personal direction of the Brigade Commander, for whom they were the last two in the Brigade. His citation says that it was difficult to praise too highly his courage, coolness, endurance and confidence and to underestimate his contribution, both material and morale in difficult situations. Sergeant Bentley was subsequently awarded the Distinguished Conduct Medal.

During two days of heavy and enforced fighting on the 18th and 19th of September, in the woods west of Arnhem, Company Sergeant-Major R.E. Grainger of the Royal Sussex, and serving with the 10th Parachute Battalion was continually in the forefront of the battle and later, when wounded, he attempted, under heavy fire and across completely open ground, to rescue the company clerk who had been wounded. He was later taken to a hospital in enemy hands and showed great initiative in escaping and evading captivity for over four weeks. CSM Grainger was subsequently awarded the US Bronze Star for his skill and determination.

Another officer of the Royal Sussex serving with the 10th Parachute Battalion was Lieutenant A.E. Baker. Having been wounded at Arnhem on 15th September, he was later put on a hospital train for transfer to Germany. His boots had been removed but, by a trick, he persuaded the guard to return them. Later, when the guards were sleepy, he smashed the window and threw himself out and, using his parachute training techniques, he 'landed' without serious injury. Whilst receiving shelter from civilians, he gave instructions to the 'Underground' in the use of explosives, and took part himself in a number of their operations. He met up with advancing Allied forces on 4th April 1945 and was subsequently awarded the Military Cross.

Company-Quartermaster-Sergeant L.E. Graham, originally in the 2nd Royal Sussex, was serving in the 9th Parachute Battalion in France in June 1944. While holding a vital piece of high ground, his Battalion was attacked in strength, and although knocked into a ditch by enemy fire, Graham crawled back to his machine-gun and continued to fire despite being wounded a second time. A short time later he was wounded yet a third time and collapsed while attempting to reach the gun again. He was subsequently awarded the Military Medal for his determination and complete disregard for his own wounds, and for the example he set to his own men that was worthy of the very best traditions of The Royal Sussex Regiment.

Higher Command

Meanwhile, the most distinguished of modern Royal Sussex officers was leading the way in the assault on Hitler's Fortress, and we learn something of his exploits from the author Norman Scarfe, who served in the 3rd Division, and in his *Assault Division*[84], brings us one more portrait of Major-General L.G. (*Bolo*) Whistler CB DSO.[85] It is interesting to note the semi-official bracketing!

> *"Major-General Rennie had been wounded, and on June 22nd, 1944, the famous 'fighting Brigadier' arrived to take command of the 3rd Division. His jeep was quickly recognised, and so was the cheery grin or wave that answered a salute."*

Scarfe also compares the effect of his presence with that of the British Commander before Agincourt, who visited his men 'with cheerful semblance':

> *"That every wretch, pining and pale before,*

---

[84] *Assault Division: A History of the 3rd Division from the Invasion of Normandy to the Surrender of Germany*. Norman Scarfe, 1947. Reprinted by Spellmount Publishers in September 2004.
[85] Later General Sir Lashmer Whistler GCB KBE CB DSO DL and Colonel of The Royal Sussex Regiment 1953-63.

Beholding him, plucks comfort from his looks."

Major-General Whistler's leadership of the 3rd Division, added to his already considerable reputation. With it there went always an ironic sense of humour, which was familiar to his old Regimental friends. It is a pity that we cannot publish his description of the Reichswald, which is said to have been *'appropriate but unprintable'*.

He had taken command of the Division before the capture of Caen, and he led the Division from Normandy to Bremen. It was the only British division to fight through all three of the decisive battles, which led to Germany's defeat.

This was an appropriate return for the man who had brought the 4th Battalion home from Dunkirk, led the Royal Sussex Brigade at the battle of Alam el Halfa, and fought through with the 131st Brigade to the capture of Tunis and the invasion of Italy, and being awarded three Distinguished Service Orders.

Later, after other commands in the Middle East and Palestine, he went to India for the withdrawal of the British troops, and was the last officer to pass through the 'Gateway of India' at Bombay.

Mentioned-in-Despatches

Nineteen officers and eighteen men of the Regiment were Mentioned-in-Despatches while serving in North-Western Europe, including a number of the 7th Battalion who became gunners after their withdrawal from France in 1940.

CONCLUDING STAGES OF THE SECOND WORLD WAR

1st Battalion

The 1st Royal Sussex (flying for the first time in its history as a Battalion) left Salonika, Greece, in a fleet of Dakotas[86] and flew direct to Klagenfurt in Austria on 10th July 1945, where it became part of the 6th Armoured Division (afterwards restyled the 1st Armoured Division). The Sector allocated to the Battalion was south of the Wortersee, up to the Yugoslav Border, and from where Tito's forces had recently withdrawn. Battalion Headquarters was situated at Victrine, with companies at Ferlac, Ebenthal, Keutschach and the Unter Loibl Pass.

Austria was something of a sinecure after the stresses and strains of Italy and Greece, with Platoons often on detachments beside picturesque lakes, and billeted in chalet-type, fully equipped and staffed hotels. However, it was not all play as the Battalion's main duty was patrolling passes into Yugoslavia, trying, yet again, to stop armed communists from entering Austria. But as Major Castle was to comment:

> *"Luck was in, having been sent to Austria, but like the fairyland that Austria seemed to be, it was all too good to be true as after seven weeks, the Battalion returned to Italy."*

The Battalion left this Sector on 4th September 1945 and it was then moved to Verona in Italy, where the living conditions were far from ideal. After a little persuasion, General Murray, the commander of the 6th Armoured Division, authorised the Battalion's move from Verona to Gardone on the shores of Lake Garda, where it arrived in February 1946. Here the companies were housed in the various large hotels round the lake, as was Battalion Headquarters. The Officers', Sergeants', and Corporals' Messes *etc* and Canteens were organised as in peacetime conditions. Some of the families even came out from England and what with boating trips on the lake, Casinos, Bars and every entertainment for the Troops, including ski-ing at Madonna di Campiglio, life was good for all of them. The only cloud on the horizon was the large numbers leaving on demobilisation, which caused quite a few headaches at Battalion Headquarters. Nevertheless, most things were gradually getting back to normal, even to the extent of having weekly Mess Dinner Nights in the Officers' Mess, and reviving old customs, which had lapsed over the war years.

---

[86] The Douglas DC-3, which entered service in 1935, is an American fixed-wing, twin-engine, propeller-driven aircraft, the speed and range of which revolutionized air transport in the 1930s and 1940s. Its lasting impact on the airline industry and the Second World War makes it one of the most significant transport aircraft ever made. Many civilian DC-3s were drafted for the war effort and just over 10,000 military versions were built. The armed forces of many countries used the military variant of the DC-3 for the transport of troops, cargo and wounded. The British variant was called the Dakota.

This idyllic state of affairs was brought to a sudden end after 6 months by orders from Brigade requiring the whole Battalion to move to Gradisca, where Lieutenant Colonel G.A. Phelps DSO handed over command of the 1st Royal Sussex to Lieutenant Colonel J.B. Ashworth DSO in August 1946.

The Battalion then moved to Trieste and was initially housed in a tented camp on the outskirts of the port, although later it was transferred to Banne Barracks above Trieste. The Battalion's main duty was to keep the peace, particularly as Tito was putting pressure on the Allies for Trieste to become part of Yugoslavia, and the Companies were often deployed in ensuring that opposing factions were unable to unduly damage each other. They were employed also in escorting by train 'repatriated' Yugoslavs who had fought with the Germans – a most traumatic and heart-rending duty.

In due course, the 1st and 2nd Battalions would amalgamate in 1948.

2nd Battalion

The 2nd Battalion remained with PAIFORCE throughout the remaining period of the war and eventually handed over Baghdad to the 8th Royal Fusiliers on 18th September 1945. The Battalion were then moved to Suez and were complete by 16th October and formed part of Canal (South) District.

On 11th November, Lieutenant Colonel C.F. Nix TD handed over command to Lieutenant Colonel A.J. Odling-Smee OBE, having been commanding the 2nd Royal Sussex for almost three years.

During its period at Suez, the Battalion was occupied with guards and duties but with a continuous turnover as personnel departed on the various release categories, with new drafts arriving to replace them.

In June 1946 the 2nd Battalion moved to Pola in Italy where it absorbed the 4th/5th (Cinque Ports) Battalion The Royal Sussex Regiment.

4th/5th (Cinque Ports) Battalion

Similarly, the 4th/5th (Cinque Ports) Battalion stayed with PAIFORCE until October 1945, following which it was moved to Haifa in Palestine on 26th October, and came under command of the 3rd Infantry Brigade. The Battalion, now under command of Lieutenant Colonel J.B. Ashworth DSO, remained there until the end of the year, spending most of the time on guards and patrolling.

Early in January 1946, the 4th/5th Royal Sussex moved from Palestine to Egypt, and then to Pola in Italy, where it manned road posts on the Morgan Line. When the Battalion arrived in Italy, demobilisation releases had reduced its strength to a weak numerical state, although efficiency was maintained at a high level. There were also plenty of opportunities for sport and other forms of recreation, with many additional activities to keep the mind and body occupied.

Just before the end of May, rumours began to circulate that the 4th/5th Battalion was to be absorbed by the Regiment's 2nd Battalion. As events proved, the 2nd Royal Sussex arrived in Pola on the 2nd of June 1946, and overnight, the 4th/5th Battalion was no more.

It was the hope of all those who had been members of the 4th Battalion and the 5th (Cinque Ports) Battalion, that each of their Battalions would start a new life when the Territorial Army was eventually reformed[87].

9th Battalion

On its return from Burma to India, the 9th Royal Sussex joined the 74th Indian Brigade, part of the 25th Indian Division. It was also a very sad time for the Battalion as Lieutenant Colonel D.H. Oliver DSO had to give up command[88] in May 1945. He had assumed command of the 9th Battalion on 25th September 1942, shortly after it had been re-converted to the infantry rôle, and had commanded it gallantly, wisely and with compassion, during almost two and a half years of intense and virtually continuous operational service. A quote in *The Shiny Ninth* clearly indicates the feeling within the Battalion on his departure:

> *"The 9th Royal Sussex was never its old self again."*

To make matters worse, the 9th Battalion had lost nearly all its senior officers and NCOs through repatriation or posting.

Two months later, on 20th July 1945, the Battalion moved to Coimbatore in Kerala State for further training. It was immediately plunged into a Combined Operations exercise, and soon after was briefed on a forthcoming operation; the most important and potentially the most dangerous British operation in the Far East, the re-conquest of Singapore and Malaya. It looked to be a major undertaking and even if it were to be crowned with ultimate success, there also seemed to be no early end to the war.

During the period in India, the operational-readiness situation had not been helped as about a third of the Battalion's strength had already been returned to England as part of the demobilisation programme, and the officers and NCOs endeavoured to instil some sense of preparedness and discipline into the men

---

[87] The 5th (Cinque Ports) Battalion (TA) was reformed on 1st May 1947. On Quebec Day 1948, it would resume its post-El Alamein amalgamated title of 4th/5th (Cinque Ports) Battalion The Royal Sussex Regiment (TA).
[88] Lieutenant Colonel D.H. Oliver DSO subsequently commanded the 1st Battalion The Royal Sussex Regiment from 1948 to 1950.

that had replaced them and were newly arrived from England. It was not an easy task, for the men had been sent to India at a time when they were looking forward to some of the sweets of victory – what little there were in post-war England – and no sooner had they celebrated the peace in Europe, when they were put on a boat to India and found themselves preparing for war. They could hardly be blamed for a lack of enthusiasm, although most of them became reasonably proficient. In addition, for the period prior to the Malayan operation, the 9th Battalion had lost most of its senior officers and NCOs, and had been without a commanding officer for several months, and thus there was an absence of direction and authority from the top; a critical situation with the potential for a likely catastrophe in the forthcoming operation. Fortunately, a week before embarkation, Lieutenant Colonel G.R. Stevens of The Royal Fusiliers assumed command of the Battalion and took firm control.

On 6th August, the new weapon was used for the first time at Hiroshima, followed two days later with the second bomb on Nagasaki. There was silence for a time and then reports began to filter through that the Japanese were willing to surrender. They did so on the 15th of August 1945, although General McArthur decreed that no landings should take place anywhere on Japanese-held territory until he had personally received the surrender of the Nippon Empire. This finally took place on 2nd September, while the forces of Southeast Asia Command marked time. However, the fact that the Japanese had now officially surrendered did not necessarily mean that all Japanese land forces would accept the decision.

Plans for the invasion of the Malaya peninsula had already been prepared and two beaches had been selected; one was at Morib near Port Swettenham and the other to the south of Port Dickson. Once beachheads had been established, the forces would advance on Johore and Singapore. The plan was code-named *Operation ZIPPER*. Whether the Japanese forces would oppose the operation was not known and thus the landings would be carried out tactically with nothing left to chance.

The 9th Battalion was embarked on the troop carrier *HMT Ranchi*, part of a vast armada of warships and landing craft, and were subsequently landed on schedule on the west coast of Malaya on 9th September. The Battalion duly went ashore to seize Morib airfield. It had been an unopposed landing and no Japanese were encountered in the Battalion's sector. The suspense was over at last – the Battalion's war had come to an end, not with a bang but with a resounding anti-climax!

Two days later the Battalion was seaborne again, bound for Butterworth where it was to act as an independent battalion and take over virtually all the northwest part of Malaya from Butterworth to the Thai border, until such time as the Civil Affairs people were able to relieve them. Within hours of the landings, a strange and hitherto unknown army began to emerge from the jungle; the Malayan Peoples' Anti-Japanese Army. Their ranks were composed entirely of

Chinese Communists, commanded by British Officers of Force 136[89].

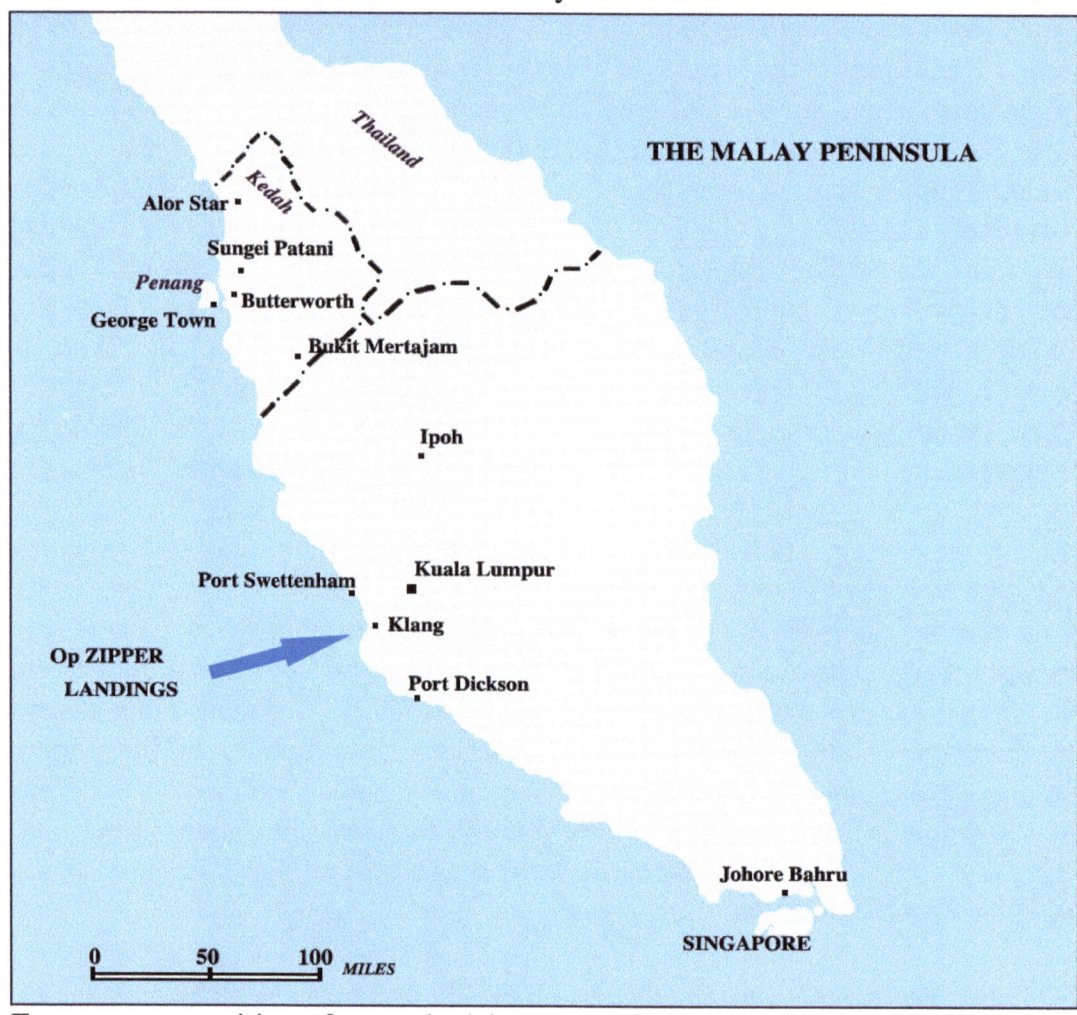

Enormous quantities of arms had been dropped to them, although they were now beginning to show signs of truculence towards their British officers. In the event, the Communists bided their time, cached their weapons in jungle hideouts, and awaited a more favourable opportunity before embarking on a process of murder, political subversion and intimidation, which grew into the Malayan Emergency; an emergency that would finally be countered six years later by Gerald Templar, the officer who had reformed the 9th Royal Sussex in June 1940.

In accordance with the guerilla situation, the 9th Battalion was dispersed to various localities and, thereafter, the Companies did not see much of each other; A Company went to Alor Star, B Company to Bukit Mertajam, C Company to Sungei Patani and D Company to Prai (*Perai*), just to the south of Butterworth. With the threat from the Chinese Communists over for the time being, the main job of the Companies was to assume responsibility for the Japanese prisoners of war. Gradually these were concentrated on the airfield at

---

[89] Force 136 was a British-led underground resistance group that operated in Malaya during the Second World War. There were about 50 members in the group, which performed acts of sabotage and espionage against the Japanese.

Sungei Patani where the great Surrender Parade was held on the 6th and 7th of October. Once these two main tasks were completed, there was nothing much left for the Battalion to do except support the civilian police, if needed, and to guard a few assorted dumps and stores depôts. The real problem was to avoid boredom and restlessness now that all training had ceased and the men were impatiently waiting for their demobilisation papers to come through.

Japanese Surrender in Malaya in 1945
9th Royal Sussex 'En Garde'

On the 1st of December, Lord Mountbatten issued his Order of the Day, disbanding the 9th Battalion and others, and congratulating them on their great victories. It was to be a process of gradual dismemberment, by repatriation without replacement, which the Army referred to as *'Waste-Out'*, which made it sound like a lingering disease. No date had been given for the final disbandment and it was assumed that one day the Battalion would simply cease to exist and the remaining men would be posted to other units. By January 1946, the Battalion strength was down to about 300 but it was not until 1st March that the 9th Battalion The Royal Sussex Regiment was officially disbanded.

The 9th Battalion's significant contribution to the war in the Far East is ably summed up in the following message from Lieutenant-General Sir Frank Messervy KBE CB DSO, General-Officer-Commanding Malaya Command, on the Battalion's disbandment:

"To Lt. Col. G.R. Stevens and all ranks 9th the Royal Sussex Regt.

Now that the 9Bn. The Royal Sussex Regiment is being disbanded, I would like to send a word of personal thanks to you all for the good work you have done in Malaya.

I have always taken a great interest in your Bn., it made itself into a highly efficient and trained Tank Regiment under my command in India in 1943. The same year the vagaries of war saw it retransformed into an Infantry Bn., which fought splendidly in the Arakan in 1944 alongside the 7th Indian Division, which I was then commanding.

After some tough and continuous successful fighting in North Burma, the Battalion eventually found its way to Malaya where I was delighted again to make its acquaintance, and to find it upholding its fine record of high morale, good discipline, and efficiency.

Thank you for all you have done and the best of luck to you all in the future."

28 March 1946

Remembrance

Those officers and men of The Royal Sussex Regiment who fell in the Second World War numbered 1,024.

In the Memorial Book in The Regimental Chapel, their Battalions are not specified, as is the case with the Memorial Panels for the Great War.

Annex A

National Archives – Battalion War Diaries

Serial	Battalion	Reference No.	Remarks
France and Belgium 1940			
1	2nd	WO167/833	
2	4th	WO167/834	
3	5th	WO167/835	
Home-Based 1940-1942			
4	2nd	WO166/4596	1939-1941
5	2nd	WO166/8902	Jan-May 1942
6	4th	WO166/4597	1939-1941
7	4th	WO166/8903	Jan-May 1942
8	5th	WO166/4598	1939-1941
9	5th	WO166/8904	Jan-May 1942
10	9th	WO166/4602	
11	9th	WO166/8906	Conversion
North Africa			
12	1st	WO169/365	
13	1st	WO169/1748	
14	1st	WO169/5073	
15	1st	WO169/10303	
16	1st	WO169/2830	
17	2nd	WO169/5067	
18	2nd	WO169/10304	Re-org Phase
19	2nd	WO169/16324	1944
20	2nd	WO169/20094	1945
21	4th	WO169/5068	
22	5th	WO169/5069	
23	4th/5th	WO169/10305	Re-org Phase
24	4th/5th	WO169/16325	1944
25	4th/5th	WO169/20095	1945
Italy and Greece			
26	1st	WO170/1478	
27	1st	WO170/8035	
28	1st	WO170/5072	Greece
Burma and Malaya			
29	9th	WO166/8906	
29	9th	WO172/2550	
Home-Based 1945-1947			
31	1st	WO264/11	
32	1st	WO264/12	

Annex B

A German Perspective of Cassino

The Account of Feldwebel Wilhelm Weier – German 1st Fallschirmjägerdivision

We are fortunate in having been given access to the personal recollections of a German ex-Parachute Sergeant (Feldwebel) named Wilhelm Weier, who took part, amongst other campaigns, in the defence of Point 593, the principal objective of 1st Royal Sussex, and who also witnessed the death of Captain Bernard Gain. Following detailed research, Feldwebel Weier was located and interviewed in Germany by ex-Sergeant Leslie Deacon, who, like his father before him, served in The Royal Sussex Regiment.

At the age of 17, Weier joined the Paratroopers during the Second World War and, following the German invasion of Crete, he was promoted to Sergeant in the 3rd Battalion of the 3rd Regiment, in the 1st Fallschirmjägerdivision[90]. His Battalion (III 3 FSJ) was known as the 'Green Devils'. He fought first in Russia, where the German 12th Parachute Division was decimated at Smolensk in 1942, and then on many fronts, including the battles for Crete, Sicily, Cassino, Rome, and later in Normandy, the Ardennes, Rhine and Northern Germany. Of the original 2,400 paratroopers in his unit, only a few dozen survived the War.

Feldwebel Weier and his unit were some of the last to be withdrawn from Sicily, and after a short break in Calabria, were sent to Cassino from Anzio in early 1944. After the bombing of the monastery, only remnants of the two Parachute Battalions were left. They were organised in small mixed groups, who mostly fought independently, but alongside the 15th Panzer Grenadiers based in Cassino Town.

Feldwebel Weier's position on Pt. 593 was isolated; the nearest German troops were entrenched 250 yards away, at a lower altitude and further towards Castle Hill, while the rest were around the area of the fort at the tip of Pt. 593. The group was based in a cave, and consisted of a young Lieutenant named Otto Fritsch (who was later killed in action), Weier and ten other paratroopers. They were static for most of the time, the cave being carefully camouflaged with tarpaulins and thus not readily prone to mortar or air attack. The group rarely vacated their position, except to get water or to take evasive action. In front of the cave, a small defensive wall had been built from rocks. The cave

---

[90] The German 1st Parachute Division was an elite military parachute landing Division. It was originally raised as the 7th Flieger-Division, or Air Division, before being renamed and reorganised as the 1st Fallschirmjägerdivision in 1943. Although not brought up to full strength before 1941, elements of the division had played significant roles in the Wehrmacht operations of 1940.

was in the lower forward rock-face of Pt. 593, near where its plateau flattens out of the crags, onto the continuation of Snakes Head Ridge. They had rigged up a rope and could gain access to the plateau at night, after a short climb.

From this cave position the group could carry out flanking attacks on any troops advancing up the sloping plateau from the north and east, as well as able to get up towards the summit by scaling the short climb with their personal weapons, which were mostly MP40s[91], plus their MG34[92] light machine-guns. The Germans would initially hinder the frontal assaults, and then would wait until the forward assault elements had passed through, after which they would climb into their flanking position. These tactics were used on all of the four allied attempts to storm the plateau.

The Germans were well supplied with close-quarter weapons, most of which were automatic. They also received significant supplies of grenades, mainly the 'Egg'[93], 'Stick'[94] and satchel varieties. The supply routes were 'up the back' from the Albaneta Farm direction or the Mule route from the Town (until Castle Hill was taken). In addition to their personal weapons, the group had one Mauser 98K[95] sniper rifle, two MG34 light machine-guns, one MMG 42[96] (*Spandau*), one 50mm Mortar, ten P08[97] Lugers, one Bren Gun (taken from one of the night attacks), and a Thompson-Gun from a Punjab MFC[98] team, whom they surprised when they strayed into the scrub on the plateau. They also had two 98K rifles with drilled out barrels for grenade launching.[99] They made their own cartridges with

Feldwebel Wilhelm Weier on Point 593 in 1944
Lieutenant Fritsch is on the left

---

[91] MP40 (Maschinenpistole 40) – 32x9mm Parabellum
[92] Mauser MG34 (Maschinengewehr Modell 34) General Purpose Machine Gun – 7.92x57mm
[93] Modell 39 Eihandgranate
[94] Modell 24 Stielhandgranate
[95] Mauser Karabiner Kar 98K Rifle – 7.92x57mm with telescopic sight
[96] Mauser MG42 (Maschinengewehr Modell 42) General Purpose Machine Gun – 7.92x57mm
(Generally referred to as the' Spandau' Machine Gun)
[97] Mauser Luger P08 (Pistole Parabellum 1908) – 9x9mm Parabellum
[98] MFC – Mortar Fire Controller
[99] Schiessbecher Rifle Grenade Launcher

double loads and could fire double grenades with an increased charge out to 40-50 yards. The only thing they lacked was fresh water.

Feldwebel Weier judged the distance to the first allied scrapes as being about 70 yards, but maybe less, due to the rising ground. The nearest were Punjab or Ghurkha, but he could also see all of the Royal Sussex positions, even the Battalion Headquarters in the 'Doctors House' (*the small ruined cottage*). From the cave wall, and often armed only with their pistols, his group would launch large quantities of grenades, generally throwing and propelling them 'blind' into the shrubs, reacting always to noise or 'bobbing British helmets'.

In Feldwebel Weier's view the Royal Sussex had little firepower at their disposal, with no air support and only unreliable artillery support (their own positions were much too near the enemy most of the time, both in the attack and defence, and the terrain restricted the trajectory of the guns. His other very pertinent comment was that the frontal attacks by infantry, on a single objective, with normally heavy losses, were repeated over and over again - from the US Regiments to the Polish Regiment - fifteen times altogether – such a waste.

Weier said the German strength in the fort, at the summit of the Pt. 593 escarpment was never more than platoon strength, but small groups were entrenched in dotted positions around the plateau and eastward to the Farm. He said, contrary to the history books, that there were ALWAYS Germans in the Monastery, even before the bombing, and consisting of a small Headquarters and Signals unit, MFCs and AFCs[100], a Medium Mortar Platoon and a small echelon unit with mules.

After the final Polish attack, which eventually captured the Monastery, Feldwebel Weier and his group withdrew from the Cassino area, and around the 25th of May, they quietly left the Gustav Line. The group slipped over Piedmont Hill and then heading north passed over Route 6, and back to the Gothic Line. Feldwebel Weier and his group had been in continuous close-quarter battles for nearly six months, and considered that they had held the line throughout. Perhaps another pertinent comment is that made by Field Marshall Alexander:

> *"No other troops in the world but German paratroops could have stood up to such an ordeal and then gone on fighting with such ferocity."*

Finally, Feldwebel Weier recalled what happened the night when Captain Bernard Gain was killed:

> *"During the Battalion attack at around midnight of the 16th-17th*

---

[100] AFC – Artillery Fire Controller

February 1944, the group in the cave proceeded to defend the approach to the plateau with heavy automatic fire. As it developed into hand-to-hand combat, they must have thrown many grenades at the dark shapes emerging from the shrub.

Suddenly, towards the end of the battle, figures emerged only feet from the parapet. Captain Gain was hit by one of the Lugers; the round struck him under the nose and killed him instantly. His sergeant lay next to him, hit by an 'Egg' grenade, which had exploded at his feet, just in front of the wall. They both fell, only feet from Weier.

After the failed assault, his group removed the bodies to the plateau, which was littered with many of the fallen. He had not seen that many except in Russia.

At the time, Feldwebel Weier removed Captain Gain's personal papers and belongings and took them back with him to Germany, where they were passed on to an Intelligence Corporal in the British Occupation Forces Office in Hamburg, who stated that he knew Captain Gain and his family. The Corporal promised to get the items back to them but the outcome of this has yet to be confirmed.